Oriental Influence in the Aegean and Eastern Mediterranean Helmet Traditions in the 9th–7th Centuries B.C.: The Patterns of Orientalization

Tamás Dezsö

BAR International Series 691
1998

Published in 2019 by
BAR Publishing, Oxford

BAR International Series 691

Oriental Influence in the Aegean and Eastern Mediterranean Helmet Traditions in the 9th-7th Centuries B.C.: The Patterns of Orientalization

© Tamás Dezsö and the Publisher 1998

The author's moral rights under the 1988 UK Copyright,
Designs and Patents Act are hereby expressly asserted.

All rights reserved. No part of this work may be copied, reproduced, stored,
sold, distributed, scanned, saved in any form of digital format or transmitted
in any form digitally, without the written permission of the Publisher.

ISBN 9780860549291 paperback
ISBN 9781407350042 e-book
DOI https://doi.org/10.30861/9780860549291
A catalogue record for this book is available from the British Library

BAR Publishing is the trading name of British Archaeological Reports (Oxford) Ltd.
British Archaeological Reports was first incorporated in 1974 to publish the BAR
Series, International and British. In 1992 Hadrian Books Ltd became part of the BAR
group. This volume was originally published by John and Erica Hedges in conjunction
with British Archaeological Reports (Oxford) Ltd / Hadrian Books Ltd, the Series
principal publisher, in 1998. This present volume is published by BAR Publishing,
2019.

PUBLISHING

BAR titles are available from:

          BAR Publishing
          122 Banbury Rd, Oxford, OX2 7BP, UK
EMAIL info@barpublishing.com
PHONE +44 (0)1865 310431
FAX   +44 (0)1865 316916
          www.barpublishing.com

CONTENTS

PREFACE	iii
CHAPTER 1: INTRODUCTION	1
The role of Assyria	4
Historical	4
Military	6
The Aegean	7
CHAPTER 2: LEVELS OF INFLUENCE IN AEGEAN HELMETS	11
Level 1: Direct import	11
Level 2: Copying and formal reinterpretation of Oriental patterns	12
Level 3: Copying and iconographical reinterpretation of Oriental patterns	13
Level 4: Cypriote and Greek helmets inspired by Oriental	
(Syro-Assyrian) helmet types	15
Cyprus	16
Crete	22
Greek Mainland	30
I. Geometric pointed helmets with earflaps and made of five pieces	32
II. Geometric pointed helmets with a high, crescent shaped crest	35
III.A. Geometric hemispherical helmet with a high crest curving forward	37
III.B. Geometric pointed helmet with a separately added small crest	
curving forward	39
III.C. Geometric pointed helmet with a high cap curving forward	39
APPENDICES	41
APPENDIX I	
Fragments of Greek Geometric helmets	42
APPENDIX II	
Anatolian composite bronze and iron helmets	44
APPENDIX III	
The development of early Corinthian helmets	47
APPENDIX IV	
Catalogue of Near Eastern and Eastern Mediterranean helmet representations	50
BIBLIOGRAPHY	71
ILLUSTRATIONS	85

Please note that additional material is available to download from www.barpublishing.com/additional-downloads.html.
The original foldout has been reduced in size to match the A4 format of this book, the image is therefore not as clear as the original foldout. Please refer to the original foldout via the download for the original content.

PREFACE

This monograph is a contribution to the study of the material evidence for contacts between the mainland Near East and the east Mediterranean World between 900-600 B.C. An orientalizing phase in the cultural development of archaic Greece has long been recognized and consequently much studied, not least through objects of Oriental manufacture and copies of them found in the Greek World. This research has not until now included a systematic study of the evidence provided by copper alloy and iron helmets.

This is perhaps not surprising as there is at the present no such study of the Near Eastern evidence to provide the basis for sound comparison between both the actual helmets and the representations of them found in east and west. In 1993 I completed a dissertation on the Near Eastern helmets of the Iron Age, to be published in the *Prähistorische Bronzefunde* series. This provides the frame of reference for the following catalogue and commentary, which assemble all the evidence known to me outside the mainland Near East for the presence and possible cultural and military significance of Oriental helmets in the Greek World, including Cyprus.

With this examination of orientalizing helmets of the Aegean and Eastern Mediterranean I hope I can add something to the general picture of the period. As Muscarella wrote: "*The 8th century BC was truly one of the major periods in the history of the western world. During this century, primarily in its second half, the Greeks, fully emerged from Dark Age, commenced active trade and multi-level cultural exchange with the Near East, the Orient. The evidence for these activities is primarily the creation of the Greek alphabet, and also the presence of manifold oriental objects and motifs recovered in Greek soil.*" (Muscarella 1992, p. 16). It is my intention to provide a framework here for the study not only of helmets, but also of other material indicators of eastern contacts with Greece at this time. To this end I have at the beginning of this monograph defined four distinct levels of orientalization, which thereafter form the basis of my analysis. It is my hope that having demonstrated the use of these categories, they might serve as a general system for investigation of this and other comparable multi-level cultural contacts.

This paper is the result of my Mellon Research Fellowship at the American School of Classical Studies at Athens, 1993. I am very much indebted to the School and to Dr. William Coulson, director of ASCSA, for their help and to the Mellon Foundation, sponsor of my research.

I am most grateful to Dr. P.R.S. Moorey, Dr. J.E. Curtis and Prof. C.H. Greenewalt, Jr. for a careful reading and comment of the manuscript. For the final version I am wholly responsible.

CHAPTER 1

INTRODUCTION

Earlier studies of Near Eastern and Aegean/Eastern Mediterranean contacts in the Geometric and Early Archaic Periods were based mainly on investigation of oriental or orientalizing objects which were found in Greek sanctuaries (e.g. Olympia, Delphi and Samos)[1]. The examination of votive objects raised the question *"to distinguish between objects imported from the Near East and those produced locally but deriving their inspiration from the Near East (Oriental versus Orientalizing)"*[2]. The purpose of this approach is to identify if an object was oriental, which part of the Near East it came from[3].

Winter in her detailed study of North Syria as a bronzeworking centre in the early first millennium B.C.[4] proposed the following system of diffusion or spread of objects outside their area of origin: *"Objects found outside their area of origin can be understood as 1. result of the movement of individuals, households or large numbers of people from one territory to another; 2. the accumulation of booty or tribute by a conquest state; 3. the product of gift-giving; 4. evidence for organized commercial relations (trade) between centers."*[5]

These four possibilities gave us a complete system, and three of them explain the presence of oriental objects in Greek sanctuaries, or at least show us alternative ways in which these objects might have reached Samos, Delphi or Olympia.

The first possibility, the migration of oriental groups or craftsmen to the Aegean is a well discussed question[6]. The reason for migration and/or settlement of oriental people in different parts of the Aegean (e.g. Athens, Crete) would be either political or commercial. Winter argued, that as Assyria between the 9th and mid-7th centuries B.C. successively incorporated the North Syrian states into the Assyrian Empire, *"luxury production decreased as the viable, independent economy of the region was subsumed into the central polity, occasioning a "migration of demands (and of craftsmen) to places where no retarding development has taken place"."*[7] The theory of the retarding effect of the Assyrian conquest is the best known example for migration of oriental craftsmen to the Aegean inspired by political reasons. The presence or settlement of oriental people (first of all Phoenician traders) on Aegean islands inspired by commercial reasons can be reconstructed not only from the appearance of oriental objects in Greek sanctuaries, but from the presence of oriental sanctuaries in Greece as well. One of the best examples is the recently excavated and probably Phoenician "tripillar shrine" at Kommos (Southern Crete)[8] which was in use in the 8th century B.C. As will be discussed later, the westward expansion of Phoenicians in the 9th-7th centuries B.C. was not a reaction to the Assyrian conquest and definitely not an escape from the Assyrian weapons. The Phoenician commercial expansion in the Mediterranean was "a function of the Neo-Assyrian imperialism"[9] and was supported, or at least not obstructed, by the Assyrians. At this point the role of Assyria looks controversial (see later).

The second possibility, the accumulation of booty or tribute by a conquering state is not relevant in the connections of the Orient and the Aegean/East Mediterranean. It happened in the Near East (e.g. Assyria) or in the Aegean with different ideological background (e.g. votive offerings after different wars in Olympia).

The third case is a possibility, which emerged recently in its developed form in some pub-

---

1 Most recently: **Guralnick 1988**, pp. 151-176; **Guralnick 1992**, pp. 327-340; **Muscarella 1992**, pp. 16-45; **Curtis 1994**, pp. 1-25; see furthermore the detailed statistical study of foreign objects in Greek sanctuaries: **Kilian-Dirlmeyer 1985a**, pp. 215-254.
2 **Curtis 1994**, p. 1.
3 For the problems of identification see **Curtis 1994**, pp. 1-25.
4 **Winter 1988**, pp. 193-225.
5 **Winter 1988**, p. 208.
6 **Dunbabin 1957**, pp. 41, 49; **Boardman 1970**, pp. 18-19; **Coldstream 1977**, pp. 56, 70, 100, 103, 187-188, 358; **Coldstream 1982**, pp. 266-268, 271; **Boardman 1980**, pp. 57-59.
7 **Winter 1988**, p. 214.
8 **Shaw 1980**, pp. 229-237, 245-248; **Shaw 1989**, pp. 165-183.
9 **Frankenstein 1979**, pp. 263-294.

lications[10]. Winter proposed royal gift-giving as a form of political connection between Carchemish and Phrygia[11]. Muscarella extended the idea for Phrygian and Greek contacts[12]. He argued that North Syrian objects could reach Greece via North Syrian harbours (e.g. Al Mina), or on land routes via Cilicia and Phrygia (with the main relay point probably in Gordion)[13]. As North Syrian objects (for example from Carchemish) reached Phrygia[14] probably as diplomatic gift-giving to Midas (Mita of Mushki) for an anti-Assyrian coalition, Phrygian and (North Syrian) objects could reach Greece in the same way as well. He argued that the Phrygians knew, for example, the Delphic oracle probably from Cilician cities and offered a wide variety of definitely votive objects to the Greek sanctuaries in the form of royal or diplomatic gift-giving. He mentioned the best known example: how Midas, king of Phrygia offered his throne to the Delphic oracle[15]. Furthermore Muscarella proposed that: *"Correct understanding of the Midas dedication as a gift exchange generates a model that might explain how other material as well may have reached Greece."*[16]

The fourth possibility (trade) is I think the most probable way on which almost all the oriental material reached Greece. The role of the Phoenician traders is certain[17]. Between the 9th and 7th centuries B.C. the Phoenician westward expansion covered almost all the Mediterranean. Phoenician expansion as has been mentioned not only flourished under Assyrian domination and from the middle of the 8th century B.C. under the Assyrian rule[18], but was also a function of Assyrian imperialism. *"They played a specialist function which was rather symbiotic than 'parasitical'"*[19]. And indeed, as Kopcke argued: *"...archaeology does not show a downturn for Phoenician cities under Assyrian domination, if anything the opposite. Now specialists like Irene Winter, Susan Frankenstein and Guy Kestemont have argued that landbound Assyrian power and seaborne Phoenician might - not of all, but of some cities - in effect entered into a compact, aiding one another. According to that theory, the Assyrians' needs and guarantee of safety made of Phoenicians more than ever before providers. As Susan Frankenstein has phased it: 'Phoenician western expansion was a function of Assyrian imperialism.'"*[20]

But whether this trade was an organized commercial relation between two centers or not, is unknown. As Muscarella proposed to extend the gift exchange model[21] to other oriental material found in Greek sanctuaries (see above), Curtis in his recent article examining the "Mesopotamian" objects from the Samian Heraion emphasized his doubts: *"... Further, the handful of Mesopotamian objects that we have from Greek sites does not have the homogeneous appearance of items that were deliberately brought from Mesopotamia to be dedicated. Nor is there any indication that they were necessarily dedicated by people even of Near Eastern, let alone Mesopotamian, origin. It is more likely, it seems to me, that these objects came into the hands of Greeks or others and were prized as "objects d'art" or curios. Because some value was attached to them, they would then have been deemed worthy of dedication to Hera or other deities."*[22].

I think this is the right conclusion which can be drawn from the examination of oriental or orientalizing objects found in Greek sanctuaries. These objects can be discussed as works of art, they can be examined metallurgically[23] and can be more or less identified with a given part of the Near East,

---

10 For earlier proposals see: **Jantzen 1962**, pp. 39-43; **Kilian-Dirlmeyer 1985a**, p. 242.

11 **Winter 1988**, pp. 208-212.

12 **Muscarella 1989**, pp. 333-334.

13 **Muscarella 1992**, pp. 41-42.

14 Gordion, Tumulus W: two cauldrons with bull attachements; Tumulus MM: two animal headed situlae; **Muscarella 1992**, pp. 41-42.

15 **Herodotus** I:14; **Muscarella 1992**, pp. 41-43.

16 **Muscarella 1992**, p. 42.

17 See most recently: **Schauer 1983**, pp. 175-194; **Röllig 1992**, pp. 93-102; **Kopcke 1992**, pp. 103-113; **Aubet 1993**.

18 For the history of Phoenicia in that period see: **Oded 1974**, pp. 38-49; **Tadmor 1975**, pp. 36-48; **Frankenstein 1979**, pp. 263-294; **Garelli 1983**, pp. 61-66; **Kestemont 1983**, pp. 53-78; **Elayi 1983**, pp. 45-58; **Elayi 1985a**, pp. 19-26; **Elayi 1985b**, pp. 393-397; **Briquel-Chatonnet 1992**, esp. pp. 141-226; **Aubet 1993**.

19 **Falsone 1988**, pp. 227-228.

20 **Kopcke 1992**, pp. 106-107; On the role of the Phoenicians in the transfer of culture and certain objects, see: **Röllig 1992**.

21 For the gift exchange see **Coldstream 1983**, pp. 201-206.

22 **Curtis 1994**, p. 23.

23 **Magou - Pernot - Rolley 1991**, pp. 561-577 (with further references).

but the value of the explanations of the different types of contact or influence built simply on this material is very limited. Without an understanding of the cultural setting of these objects in Greek life no serious conclusion can be drawn. These are actual pieces of artwork and they have a limited value as the indicators of influence. Even Muscarella has argued that it is a *"question whether the oriental cauldrons arrived in Greece with hammered griffin protomes and sirens as an ensemble, or whether the protomes were added to the siren cauldrons in Greece to satisfy (unknown) local needs."*[24]

The fact that for example, 78.8 % of the dedicated material found in the Samian Heraion can be identified as oriental (with Cyprus and Egypt)[25] or orientalizing gives us useful information, but it probably reflects only the geographical position of Samos (next to the Anatolian coast, near or on a major maritime trade route) and it may reflect the extended commercial networks, the flourishing trade (Phoenician, Greek, Phrygian, etc.) which was at that period one of the most impressive signs of the beginning a new age in the Mediterranean. The examination of the Perachora Hera sanctuaries (the area of another important trade center) revealed the same picture: the Phoenician material was 74 % of the total number of objects dedicated there[26]. But the inland sanctuaries of Greece (far from trade routes or the interest of traders) yielded much smaller percentages of oriental objects: Olympia 12.76 %[27], while at the Artemision at Pherai (Thessaly) only 2 % of the votive objects was foreign, and only 11.6 % of the foreign objects came from the Near East[28].

For a more useful approach we should not think in terms of official journeys, special dedicatory trips of oriental people to Greek sanctuaries or "organized orientalization". We should simply discover the mechanisms of this cultural influence.

We have to identify at first the terms of "contact" and "influence". We could use the right distinction of Muscarella between them: *"The correctly defined import yields evidence of a "contact" of some form and degree between Greece and the Orient; its presence in a sanctuary informs us that some local entity accepted the object. The copy or adaptation indicates "influence", a heightened and more complex consumption of the original import, an absorption into the local culture."*[29]. Contact and influence make the distinction between oriental and orientalizing. But "influence" is a too general term to be used in the study of orientalizing objects or in the study of the mechanism of cultural diffusion. Sometimes not an actual object makes the influence but simply the fact, that there are objects which have a special value (for example the iron and bronze conical helmets of the Assyrians, the most famous and victorious standing army of the period or the known world of that time for almost three centuries, which were tested in hundreds of battles). In the case of helmets, different levels of contact can be revealed from the direct import to "inspiration". The last level of influence ("inspiration") can be termed much better as "stimulus diffusion" (a term borrowed from ethnoarchaeology and prehistory): *"In stimulus diffusion, it is not the details of the full complexity and elaboration of a new product or a new process which is transmitted, but rather the idea, the realization that such a process is possible, and some understanding of how to bring it about."*[30]. At the last level of influence not simply an object or object type inspired similar objects but the idea of their usefulness for example the helmets in battle or the fame of the Assyrians. As the result of stimulus diffusion only the general shape of the Greek helmets was similar to the (pointed and crested) shape of the oriental helmets, but their details and process of execution were quite different. For example they used pointed and crested helmets (Late Geometric, see below) riveted together from five pieces (which technique is unknown at the moment from the Near East), but they did not use iron helmets as the Assyrians did in the second half of the 8th century B.C. The early Aegean crested helmets (8th century B.C.) probably did not use the colour or decoration of the crest to identify different units of their army as the Assyrians did. They probably used the crest only for apotropaic reasons.

---

24 **Muscarella 1992**, pp. 35-36.
25 **Kilian-Dirlmeyer 1985a**, pp. 235-243, fig. 18.
26 **Kilian-Dirlmeyer 1985a**, pp. 225-230, fig. 8.
27 **Kilian-Dirlmeyer 1985a**, pp. 230-235, fig. 13.
28 **Kilian-Dirlmeyer 1985a**, pp. 216-224, fig. 1.
29 **Muscarella 1992**, p. 38.
30 **Renfrew 1983**, p. 122.

THE ROLE OF ASSYRIA

HISTORICAL

In the Neo-Assyrian period (911-614/612 B.C.) Assyria was the leading power of the Near East and consequently the Eastern Mediterranean. The power of Assyria was based first of all on its powerful army, which was reformed in the Middle Assyrian period to become one of the most modern armies of the contemporary world, which - at least in its *élite* troops (chariotry, cavalry, different classes of heavy infantry) - consisted of Assyrian professionals. The Assyrian army became one of the most important (if not the most important) source of the state's income (booty, tribute). In the early 9th century B.C. after conquering the territories of North-Mesopotamia, Southeast-Anatolia (Upper Euphrates) rich in iron ore, and the early ironworking centres of the region[31] the Assyrians started to equip their army not simply with iron weapons (which were used much earlier), but iron armour as well. There is a wall-painting fragment from Ashur[32] showing an Assyrian soldier wearing the characteristic conical helmet painted yellow, carrying an Assyrian spiked shield painted yellow. The helmet and the shield date the fragment exclusively to the 9th century B.C. The yellow paint means that the helmet and the shield was made of bronze. However, the scale armour attached to the rim of the helmet, covering the shoulders of the soldier (under which the body armour was situated) was painted light blue - the colour of shining iron. Huge amount of iron scale armour plates were discovered in the Neo-Assyrian capitals. After the Assyrian army was equipped with iron scale armour[33], in the early 8th century B.C. the first iron helmets appeared in the Assyrian army. The first written evidence for iron helmets is in two cuneiform letters mentioning iron helmets (*gurpisi parzilli*)[34] from Tell Halaf dated to the same period. The first representations undoubtedly depicting iron helmets are the Til-Barsip wall-paintings, possibly from the reign of Tiglath-Pileser III (745-727 B.C.). On the Til-Barsip wall-paintings[35] there are helmets coloured light blue (shining iron) as are the iron blades of the swords, certainly depicting iron helmets. The yellow decoration on two of them might indicate the same bronze inlay decoration as on the well known Zinçirli iron helmet fragments[36], Nimrud conical[37] and crested iron helmet fragments[38]. The Til-Barsip helmet representations are the earliest evidence both for the Near Eastern iron helmets and iron helmets decorated with bronze inlay. By the end of the 8th century B.C. there can be no doubt that iron was a common material and widely used[39]. Place mentioned in his work[40] the discovery of a hoard of very well preserved ironwork: grappling irons and chains, ploughshares, hammers, pick-axes and several hundred iron ingots, the total weight of which was estimated by Place in the region of 160,000.00 kg. The *élite* troops of the Assyrian army were equipped with iron helmets at least in the second half of the 8th century (see below). This army clad in iron and using the best war tactics conquered North Syria and the Levant in the second half of the 8th century B.C.

---

31 **Maxwell-Hyslop 1974**, pp. 139-154

32 Ass.10756, **Andrae 1925**, pl. 9e.

33 At least by the end of the 9th century B.C., soldiers of the main heavy troops of the Assyrian army were covered probably with iron scale armour.

34 **Friedrich et al. 1940**, nos. 49:1, 52:10.

35 **Thureau-Dangin - Dunand 1936**, pls. XLXI-LI; **Dezsö 1993**, Chart 2, nos. 165-167.

36 Zincirli, North Palace, Inv. no.: S.3964; **von Luschan - Andrae 1943**, pp. 76-79, 163, fig. 88, pl. 41; **Barnett 1953**, p. 102; **Borchhardt 1972**, p. 100, Kat. 22 B I 3; **Overlaet 1979**, p. 54, note 7, p. 55; **Curtis 1979**, vol. I, pp. 182-183; **Özgen 1982**, pp. 20, 52 note 5; **Dezsö - Curtis 1991**, pp. 124-125, fig. 22; **Dezsö 1993**, Cat. no. 28, Group no. NS.1, pp. 34-35, pls. 41-42.

37 Nimrud, North-West Palace, London, British Museum, BM 22496; **Barnett 1953**, pp. 101-102, pls. 31-32; **Calmeyer 1969**, p. 90, note 295; **Borchhardt 1972**, p. 99, Cat. no. 22 A I; **Pleiner - Bjorkman 1974**, p. 291, fig. 5; **Calmeyer 1975**, p. 316; **Ligabue - Salvatori 1977**, p. 8; **Gamber 1978**, fig. 196; **Overlaet 1979**, p. 54, note 6; **Curtis 1979**, vol. I, pp. 178-181, vol. II, p. 32, pl. 27; **Curtis et al. 1979**, p. 385, fig. 34; **Horn - Rüger 1979**, p. 313, fig. 187; **Özgen 1982**, pp. 20, 51, note 3; **Gröschel 1986**, p. 73, note 225; **Dezsö - Curtis 1991**, pp. 122-126, fig. 21, pl. 19; **Dezsö 1993**, Cat. no. 6, Group no. A.2.1, pp. 12-17, fig. 2, pls. 9-11.

38 London, British Museum, 48-11-4, 113-115; **Dezsö - Curtis 1991**, pp. 105-126, pls. 15-20; **Dezsö 1993**, Cat. nos. 12-27, Group nos. A.4.1-A.4.16, pp. 25-33, pls. 22-40.

39 **Curtis et al. 1979**, p. 382

40 **Place 1867-1870**, vol. I, pp. 84-88.

With the reign of Tiglath-Pileser III (745-727 B.C.) a new age began in the history of the Near East. After several administrative reforms Tiglath-Pileser III (a former general) reformed the Assyrian army as well. From the archaeological point of view it meant the beginning of the standardization of army equipment, which was undertaken finally in the last quarter of the 8th century B.C. This change can be detected most prominently in the use of crested helmets in the Assyrian army: as is shown on Assyrian sculptures, crested helmets are always worn by spearmen carrying round wooden shields and wearing breastplates (*kardio phylakes*). Not only the Assyrian light infantry, or troops said to be North Syrian allies or associated with Anatolian[41] or Phrygian[42] auxiliaries of the Assyrian army, but also their enemies, recruited when defeated as auxiliary units, wore crested helmets[43]. But, while at the end of the 9th century B.C. - first half of 8th century B.C. the crested helmet indicated the nationality of its wearer (Syrian, Anatolian or Phrygian troops), later, from the reign and army reform of Tiglath-Pileser III it simply indicated the membership of a special service, the light infantry of the Assyrian imperial army. The Assyrian horsemen, charioteers and chariot warriors, and even the heavy infantry always wore conical/pointed helmets. From that time soldiers of any nationality could be recruited to the light infantry, the auxiliary units of the Assyrian army. Thus, the crested helmet finally lost its national (North Syrian, Anatolian) character in the Assyrian imperial army. The result of the reform was the 8th century B.C.[44] "new model Assyrian imperial army" which consisted of the following arms:

chariotry	round bronze shield	iron scale armour[45]	conical helmet
cavalry	-	iron scale armour	conical helmet
heavy infantry	round bronze shield	iron scale armour	conical helmet
armoured archers	-	iron scale armour	conical helmet
armoured slingers	-	iron scale armour	conical helmet
light infantry	round wooden shield	*kardio phylakes*	crested helmet

auxiliaries (mainly foreign archers)

From 738 B.C. this new model army controlled the Levant. The Assyrians became neighbours of the Greek world. This close proximity resulted in a series of effects, which played a primary role in the transmission of oriental influence. One of these effects was the new Assyrian Phoenicia-policy which resulted in the emphasized western expansion of the Phoenicians discussed above. The Assyrians controlled part of the Phoenician fleet (probably a given contingent of the warships). On a Til-Barsip wall-painting fragment[46] there are Assyrian soldiers (wearing pointed bronze helmets) on board a Phoenician warship fighting a naval battle with an unfortunately unidentified enemy. There are representations of Phoenician ships on the palace-reliefs of Sennacherib (704-681 B.C.)[47] as well. Furthermore we know from the famous Cyprus stele of Sargon II now in Berlin[48] that in the last years of his reign (probably around 707 B.C.) Sargon controlled in some way "Ia' a district of Iatnana (Cyprus)", which was "situated a seven day's journey in the sea of the setting sun"[49]. Sargon's governor of the

---

41 **Barnett - Falkner 1962**, p. xix, pls. XXXVI, XXXVIII, p. xxiii, pl. LI.

42 **Barnett - Falkner 1962**, p. xxiii, pl. LII.

43 **Barnett - Falkner 1962**, pp. xix-xx, fig. 2:1, pl. XLI (Eastern campaign of Tiglath-Pileser III, 2nd and 9th palu); pp. xx-xxiv, fig. 2:2, pl. LI (Anatolian [Phrygian?] campaign of Tiglath-Pileser III, 3rd palu); pp. xxii-xxiv, fig, 2:13, pl. LXV (Urartian warrior?), (Urartian campaign of Tiglath-Pileser III, 3rd palu) and pl. LXI.

44 In the 7th century B.C. the standardization of the army equipment went on (**Dezső 1993**, pp. 20-21: changes in the form of crested helmets; see also below), and new army organization developed under the reigns of Sennacherib (704-681 B.C.), Asarhaddon (680-669 B.C.) and Ashurbanipal (668-627 B.C.).

45 The using of iron scale armour can be detected not only from the actual finds of iron armour plates, but from the 8th century B.C. representations of scale armours on Assyrian palace-reliefs, where the patterns of the armour attachement makes it clear, that iron scale armour did not need overlapping surfaces as the bronze scale armour needed. **Curtis 1979**.

46 Aleppo Museum; **Amiet 1980**, pl. 105.

47 Nineveh, S-W. Palace; London, British Museum, WA 124772.

48 Probably from Kition. English translation of its inscription: **Luckenbill 1927**, vol. 2, pp. 100-103.

province Que (Cilicia) attacked the land of Mita (Midas) of Mushki (Phrygia), and destroyed three provinces of Mushki. In consequence of the Assyrian campaigns, Mita sent tribute to Sargon (around 708 B.C.). Sennacherib (704-681 B.C.), son of Sargon II, consolidated Assyrian rule in the occupied territories of the Eastern Mediterranean from Cilicia to Juda and the Egyptian border (701 B.C.). His son and successor on the Assyrian throne, Esarhaddon (680-669 B.C.) conquered Lower-Egypt in 672-671 B.C., and his son, Assurbanipal (668-627 B.C.) reached Thebes, the capital of Upper-Egypt. The Assyrians held Egypt for nearly twenty years. In the course of the 7th century B.C. Assyria controlled the Near East and was a close neighbour of the Greek world[50].

So it can be concluded that in the second half of the 8th century B.C. the high standard of the organization of the Assyrian imperial standing army was the standard which might be the historical base of the influence or "stimulus diffusion" exerted by oriental, let alone Assyrian helmet types on the Aegean/Eastern Mediterranean helmet tradition.

MILITARY

The evolution of Near Eastern conical helmets probably took place in Assyria[51] in three phases (the earliest known representation of a Neo-Assyrian conical helmet is on the White Obelisk[52], and later on the palace-reliefs of Ashurnasirpal II [883-859 B.C.]). From the second half of the 9th century B.C. this type of helmet became widespread on the periphery of the Assyrian Empire as well: the first known Urartian examples can be dated to the reign of Ishpuini (830-810 B.C.)[53], the first known North-West Iranian examples were found in Hasanlu and can be dated to around 800 B.C.[54].

There are no actual conical helmets known from North Syria before the Assyrian conquest. All the North Syrian conical helmets can be dated to the second half of the 8th century B.C., when North Syria was already under Assyrian control. Consequently these helmets cannot unreservedly be considered as North Syrian helmets. Much rather they should be regarded as the products of Neo-Assyrian imperial art and metalworking, which gradually assimilated the culture and crafts of the nations of the empire creating a *koine* at least in the case of warfare, arms and armour. There are three helmets excavated in the North Palace at Zincirli. These three helmets are from the destruction level which can be connected with the siege of the city by Sargon II in 720 B.C. There is no evidence to indicate whether these helmets were worn by local soldiers[55] or Assyrians or North Syrian soldiers of the Assyrian army (from cities already under Assyrian rule). So the problem of the North Syrian helmets as a separate group can not be understood without the fact, that the bronze and iron industry of North Syria at that time worked probably for the Assyrian army. North Syria might produce weapons and let us say helmets for Assyrian customers, but within the general Assyrian shape (conical/pointed) they could use local, North Syrian elements in the decoration (for example the winged sun-disk)[56]. From the Til-Barsip wall paintings depicting Assyrian soldiers it is quite obvious that troops of the Assyrian army garrisoned in North Syria could wear local, regional or provincial versions of the Assyrian equipment: for example garment and helmet decoration. That is the main reason why I beleive that the North Syrian conical helmets can be regarded as part of the Neo-Assyrian imperial art and metalworking (Assyrian helmet decorated with North Syrian motifs for members of the imperial army). It had to be

---

49 **Luckenbill 1927**, vol. 2, p. 36: display inscription from the Palace at Khorsabad.

50 It is known that Assyrian troops even met Greek (Ionian and Carian) mercenaries in Egypt and probably in Anatolia as well.

51 **Dezső 1993**, pp. 1-7.

52 British Museum, WA 118807, from Nineveh, probably reign of Ashurnasirpal I (1050-1032 B.C.); **Börker-Klähn 1982**, pp. 179-180, no. 132, pls. 132a-d.

53 For a detailed study of Urartian helmets: **Dezső 1993**, Cat. nos. 53-103, pp. 52-68, 134-163, pls. 77-136 (with further references).

54 For a detailed study of North-West Iranian helmets see: **Dezső 1993**, Cat. nos. 35-44, pp. 41-44, 124-129, pls. 52-61; for Hasanlu helmets see: **Dezső 1993**, Cat. nos. 45-52, pp. 45-51, 129-134, pls. 62-76 (with further references).

55 **Winter 1988**, p. 194.

56 The winged sun-disk is one of the evidences on which the identification of two other helmets of the group was based: there are three helmets in the group decorated with this motif at the front (Zincirli, S.3695; Palaepaphos, see below; London, BM 134611); **Dezső 1993**, pp. 34-37.

discussed to understand the mechanism of the influence of Assyrian helmet types from the middle of the 8th century B.C. via the North Syrian and Phoenician allies and provinces of the Assyrian Empire. So the more accurate name of the North Syrian group of helmets would be Syro-Assyrian group of helmets. The Assyrian iron industry in the second half of the 8th century B.C. developed the techniques of ironworking to previously unknown heights, particularly the iron weapons, armours and helmets - as the most important and mass-produced[57] objects. Furthermore the Assyrian weapon industry with its continuous and enormous orders of iron weapons, armours and tools was the base, on which the Assyrian (and North Syrian) iron industry reached the highest standard in the ancient world. The best example for this is the high pointed Assyrian iron helmet[58] hammered out from one piece of iron and decorated with bronze inlay. Both hammering out a (pointed) helmet from one piece of iron and inlaying the iron with bronze are unknown from other territories of the ancient Near East and emphasize the overall technical skill of the Assyrian blacksmiths and the highest standard of the Assyrian iron (and consequently the Assyrian weapon) industry. In fact, these are the earliest known iron helmets of the world. Similar helmets were not to be produced for hundreds of years elsewhere after the fall of Assyria. On the contemporary peripheries of the Assyrian Empire (Urartu[59], "North-West Iran"[60]) - maybe for lack of the necessary technical skill - the pointed iron helmets were made from two similar halves which were riveted together with the help of iron bands inside the helmet, this cheaper technique was of course used in Assyria as well[61]. In the second half of the 8th century B.C. the high standard of the weaponry of the Assyrian army was the standard which might be the archaeological base of the influence or "stimulus diffusion" exerted by Assyrian helmet types on the Aegean/Eastern Mediterranean helmet tradition.

THE AEGEAN

At this point I have to emphasize that the process of spread of a new weapon or armour type is usually quite different from the spread of other types of objects. New useful weapon types usually spread more quickly than other types of objects (as can be traced in the history of modern times and nowadays as well)[62]. The process of influence of a given weapon type or let us say the oriental helmet types is even quicker, if there is an "open area", which can be the "receiver". And this was exactly the situation in Dark Age Greece.

There was a hiatus in the development of Aegean/Mediterranean helmets in the 10th-8th

---

57 The Assyrian army needed probably thousands of iron weapons, armours (scale-armours), helmets and tools in every year for several hundreds of years (9th-7th centuries B.C., especially from the middle of the 8th century B.C. to 614 B.C.).

58 Nimrud, North-West Palace, London, British Museum, BM 22496; **Barnett 1953**, pp. 101-102, pls. 31-32; **Calmeyer 1969**, p. 90, note 295; **Borchhardt 1972**, p. 99, Cat. no. 22 A I; **Pleiner - Bjorkman 1974**, p. 291, fig. 5; **Calmeyer 1975**, p. 316; **Ligabue - Salvatori 1977**, p. 8; **Gamber 1978**, fig. 196; **Overlaet 1979**, p. 54, note 6; **Curtis 1979**, vol. I, pp. 178-181, vol. II, p. 32, pl. 27; **Curtis et al. 1979**, p. 385, fig. 34; **Horn - Rüger 1979**, p. 313, fig. 187; **Özgen 1982**, pp. 20, 51, note 3; **Gröschel 1986**, p. 73, note 225; **Dezsö - Curtis 1991**, pp. 122-126, fig. 21, pl. 19; **Dezsö 1993**, Cat. no. 6, Group no. A.2.1, pp. 12-17, fig. 2, pls. 9-11.

59 From Urartu: Munich, Prähistorische Staatssammlung, Inv. no. 1971/2022; **Kellner 1976**, p. 78, Cat. no. 137a; **Kellner 1979**, p. 152, fig. B; **Vanden Berghe - De Meyer 1982**, p. 133, no. 25 (fig.); **Yesaian 1986**, p. 33, pl. 13:10; **Wartke 1991**, p. 330, fig. 4; **Dezsö - Curtis 1991**, pp. 125-126; **Dezsö 1993**, Cat. no. 97, Group no. U.7.3, pp. 16-17, 66-67, 159, pls. 130-131; Munich, Prähistorische Staatssammlung, Inv. no. 1971/1997; **Kellner 1976**, p. 78, Cat. no. 137; **Fuchs - Kellner 1978**, p. 386, pl. 2; **Kellner 1979**, p. 152, fig. 1; **Vanden Berghe - De Meyer 1982**, p. 133, no. 26 (fig.); **Yesaian 1986**, p. 33, pl. 13:11; **Calmeyer 1991a**, no. 19 (pl.); **Dezsö - Curtis 1991**, pp. 125-126; **Dezsö 1993**, Cat. no. 96, Group no. U.7.2, pp. 16-17, 66-67, 158-159, pls. 128-129; Adana, Regional Museum; **Kellner 1979**, p. 156, note 6; **Overlaet 1979**, p. 54, note 9; **Dezsö - Curtis 1991**, pp. 125-126; **Dezsö 1993**, Cat.no. 98, Group no. U.7.4, pp. 16-17, 66-67, 160.

60 Bruxelles, Musées Royaux d'Art et d'Histoire, Inv. no. IR 1241; "Amlash"; **van Pée 1965**, pp. 196-198, pl. on p. 196; **Vanden Berghe 1967**, p. 22; **Overlaet 1979**, pp. 53-55, fig. 1, pls. 1-2; **Dezsö - Curtis 1991**, pp. 125-126; **Dezsö 1993**, Cat. no. 35, Group no. NWI.1, pp. 16-17, 43, 124, pls. 52-53.

61 Munich, Prähistorische Staatssammlung, PS. 1980/6227-6228, "Eastern Turkey (Urartu)"; **Kellner 1993**, pp. 325-331; **Dezsö 1993**, Cat. no. 7, Group no. A.2.2, pp. 14-17, pls. 12-14; For the general discussion of Near Eastern iron helmets see: **Dezsö - Curtis 1991**, pp. 105-126, pls. 15-20; **Dezsö 1993**, pp. 12-17, 25-33.

62 For example in the case of hitech weapons.

centuries B.C. As A.M. Snodgrass has pointed out: *"It is striking that, of the Bronze Age examples so far published, no two can be shown to be of the same type, although the Ialysos cheek-piece could equally well have been attached to the cap of any of the others. Nor is any one of them close enough in form to the specimens found from the Late Geometric period onwards for us to conclude that there was any continuity of use through the dark period between the eleventh and eight centuries in Greece."*[63]. This tendency was observed by other scholars as well[64]. The Bronze Age Aegean helmet tradition ended in the 11th century B.C. probably with the submycenaean helmet from Tiryns[65] and the new Mediterranean helmet tradition from the 8th century B.C. developed under the influence of the 9th-8th centuries B.C. Syro-Assyrian helmet tradition.

The political and economic structure of the two regions, the Near East (Assyrian Empire) and the Eastern Mediterranean (Aegean) was characteristically different. This difference determined the difference of their military power and military structure as well. The military structure of the Near Eastern kingdoms from the 3rd millennium B.C. onwards was characterized by a standing army which was supported by the state. Besides hundreds of handworkers employed by the state and the army, all the craftsmen, bronzeworkers and blacksmiths were obliged to work for the state as well within the framework of "communal works" (Akkadian *ilku*) filling part of their working time. This system was the base of the state supported war machines of the Near Eastern kingdoms and empires. As a consequence of this mass-production system, the standing army of the Assyrian Empire consisting of professional soldiers was characterized by the high level standardization of weaponry of the different arms (especially in the case of the 8th-7th century B.C. "new model army"). The heavy weaponry of the Assyrian army was a weaponry invented definitely for huge masses of professional soldiers fighting in close order. The heavy weaponry was not individual weaponry[66] but a weaponry of a heavy unit fighting in close order.

The Greek or Aegean political and military system was quite different. It was characterized by smaller states and armies based mainly on the military power of the social *élite*. Consequently the Greek world borrowed and used the weaponry of the Assyrian army (invented for a standing army units fighting in close battle formations) out of context, and in the beginning did not use the idea of the "Assyrian hoplitism" which was orginally attached to the heavy weaponry of the Assyrian heavy infantry ("Assyrian hoplites"). This difference (the use of the Assyrian style heavy weaponry as a weaponry of the individual soldiers or heroes) is manifested by Homer's *Iliad* as well. In this probably 8th century B.C. epic the Greek and Trojan heroes used the oriental weaponry out of its original context. Wearing their heavy weaponry they went to the battlefield in their chariots, but fought single combats mainly on foot. In its Near Eastern context the chariot for example was not a definitely individual arm. The Mittannian *maryannu* (professional *élite* chariot fighters) for example were supported by chariot troops recruited by the state from the common people, and we know a supplementary *militia* system as well: ordinary citizens were equipped from the state arsenals with chariots, horses etc. in case of danger[67]. Consequently, the Near Eastern armies (for example the Hittites in the Battle of Qadesh, 1295 B.C., and the Assyrians) deployed thousands of chariots fighting in (close) order and not individually. We know a few cuneiform sources (Hittite and Middle Assyrian texts) dealing with the problem of training chariot horses, drivers etc[68]. In the Greek world the heavy weaponry (and the chariotry of the 8th century B.C.) for a long time was the weaponry of the social and military *élite*[69] and was used in a dif-

---

63 **Snodgrass 1964**, p. 4

64 **Schauer 1988**, fig. 9

65 Tiryns, Tomb XXVIII; H.: 17 cm, W.: 22.5 cm; **Daux 1958**, p. 706, fig. 26; **Verdelis 1963**, pp. 17-19, fig. 9, pls. 6-7; **Borchhardt 1972**, pp. 43-44, pl. 8:4-5.

66 The hoplite heavy weaponry was useful only in close order. When the lines of the phalanx broke the weaponry of the individual hoplite was too heavy to fight with one or more peltastes and hindered him in the escape.

67 For example in Nuzi, a vassal town of the Mittannian Kingdom (16th-mid 14th century B.C.). See **Kendall 1975**.

68 The training of chariot horses and drivers took two or three years. To avoid the confusion and a possible disaster, the chariot units - consisting of hundreds or thousands of chariots - had to perform the troop movements in the battle totally accustomed.

69 The same difference can be detected in case of the Eastern Mediterranean and Near Eastern siege warfare as well. The Near Eastern techniques arrived in the Mediterranean much later. See for example the total lack of siege scenes form the Iliad!

ferent way, in single combats. On the earliest fighting scenes of the Geometric vases we can see only single combats and never representations of fighting military formations[70]. The first representations of Greek soldiers fighting like the later hoplites in close order can be dated to the middle of the 7th century B.C.[71], when the Greek *polis* was strong enough to have an army which consisted of its citizens, who equipped themselves with hoplite weaponry. In the Greek world the state-supported standing armies appeared much later.

These basic differences (the use of oriental weaponry out of its original context) resulted in contrasting tendencies in the development of the helmet traditions of the two regions as well. These two contrasting tendencies are noticeable in the helmet representations of the two regions (*Ills. 4-5*). While in the Near East (in the Assyrian Empire of the 9th-7th centuries) the tendency was a high level of standardization of military equipment, particularly the helmet forms and decorations (*Ill. 4, O.1.1-O.1.89; Ill. 5, O.2.1-O.2.51*), the Eastern Mediterranean (Cypriote and Aegean) tendency from the middle of the 8th century till the last quarter of the 7th century was just the opposite. The Aegean tendency was characterized not by standardization[72] but almost by free combination, let us say permutation of the different elements of the basic Near Eastern helmet types and local inventions: conical/pointed *versus* hemispherical shape, open face (Oriental) helmets *versus* covered face (Eastern Mediterranean, Greek) helmets, the appearance of different types of crests on the same type of helmet, the appearance of different types of profiled cheek pieces and face masks on the same type of helmet, etc. Even the early history of Corinthian helmets shows the parallel development of different early helmet traditions, which resulted in the different versions of the early Corinthian helmets (*Ill. 3*) as well.

These statements are valid first of all for the fourth level of oriental influence ("Cypriote and Greek helmets inspired by oriental (Syro-Assyrian) helmet types", *see* below). The first three levels of oriental influence can be defined much more exactly (1. import, 2. copying and formal reinterpretation, 3. copying and iconographical reinterpretation).

It is impossible to determine a given route for this oriental influence. Nevertheless there are centres, which must have played an important, mediatory role in the process of the spread of oriental helmet types. *Cyprus* - as significant centre of the Eastern Mediterranean maritime trade - was inevitably an important relay point in the process. Three of the four levels (levels 1, 2, 4) of oriental influence can be detected with actual helmet finds on the island. *Crete* played a similarly important role: This is the only place in the Aegean, where the two distinct chronological phases of orientalization can be separated from the helmet representations (late 9th-early and mid 8th century B.C.; second half of 8th-7th centuries B.C.). On the Greek mainland the Peloponnese, and first of all *Argos* must have played an important role in the process of orientalization. Two levels of oriental (helmet) influence is attested here in the second half of the 8th century B.C. (levels 3 and 4). Furthermore in the historical tradition the big round bronze shield, the *hoplon* (which has the same oriental history, development and origin as the helmets[73]) bore the name: Argive shield. The earliest known hoplite equipment (a last quarter of 8th century B.C. helmet made of five pieces and furnished with a crescent shape crest, a bell armour and a hoplite shield) was found in Argos[74]. The only example of level 3 helmets came from Argos as well. Its appearance indicates some direct oriental influence, but from this single piece no further conclusions (like migration of oriental craftsmen, etc.) can be drawn. However the fact that in Argos reinterpreted oriental helmets were worn indicates some special role for Argos in the process of

---

70 See **Ahlberg 1971** passim.

71 See for example the famous Chigi-vase now in Rome.

72 The standardization of Greek military equipment and helmet forms started in the second half of the 7th century B.C. with the spread of the Corinthian and Illyrian types of helmets. See the chapter on the early history and origins of Corinthian helmets. However, while the oriental standardization of military equipment was a government policy, the standardization of Greek weaponry (hoplite equipment) was the result of a spontaneous evolution.

73 The earliest "hoplite shields" are known from Assyria. In the British Museum there are two Assyrian round bronze shields (WA 22484 and WA 22486) from Nimrud (diameter of the complete piece is 82 cm) which can be dated to the 9th-early 8th century B.C. Similarly to the conical/pointed bronze and iron helmets the Assyrian round bronze shield was a standard element of the "Assyrian hoplite" equipment. This type of shield - as part of the standard equipment of an "Assyrian hoplite" described on p. 6 - spread probably the same way and together with the oriental helmets. For detailed study of the orientalizing Cretan shields see **Kunze 1931**. For the detailed study of Argive shields see **Bol 1989**.

74 Argos, Tomb 45. **Courbin 1957**, pp. 322ff., figs. 19, 39-45, pls. 1, 4.

orientalization.

Four different levels of influence from the 9th-8th century B.C. Assyrian helmet tradition can be reconstructed from actual helmet finds. They give us a better chronological basis of orientalization than the deposits in Greek sanctuaries:[75]

Level 1: **Direct import**
Level 2: **Copying and reinterpretation of the forms of oriental patterns**
Level 3: **Copying and iconographical reinterpretation of oriental patterns**
Level 4: **Cypriote and Greek helmets inspired by oriental (Syro-Assyrian) helmet types** ("stimulus diffusion")

---

[75] Dezső 1993, pp. 37-39.

CHAPTER 2

LEVELS OF INFLUENCE IN AEGEAN HELMETS

LEVEL 1:
DIRECT IMPORT

Palaepaphos, Kouklia, Mavrommatis Tomb [Tomb 7-8] (Cyprus, Nicosia, Cyprus Museum, Inv. no. 1965/XI-29/62; H.: 24.6 cm, Diam.: 21.4 cm; Cypro-Archaic I Period [750-650 B.C.])[76]. (*Ill. 6*)

It has a conical shape with pointed top. There is a series of holes around the rim for attachment of a lining. The helmet has been decorated with *repoussé* technique. There are two horizontal ribs around the base of the helmet which end on the front in one pair of arcs ("crooks") with rounded extremities (animal heads). There is a winged sun-disk between the arcs. Complete.

This helmet is probably an original North Syrian helmet imported from the Near East and found in Cyprus. P. Schauer suggested[77] that this helmet might have arrived in Cyprus with some troops of Sargon II (see the Kition stele of Sargon II above). The winged sun-disk is one trait identifying this helmet as Syro-Assyrian, manufactured probably in North Syria in the second half of the 8th century B.C. The identification of two other helmets as Syro-Assyrian was based on this motif[78]: there are three helmets in the group decorated with this motif at the front. One of them is the Palaepaphos helmet, the second is a bronze helmet from Zinçirli[79], and third is from unknown provenance but said to come from "Luristan" now in London[80]. Von Luschan and Andrae recognized[81] on the fragments of the Zinçirli iron helmet[82] the elements of a winged sun-disk, which is a characteristically North Syrian motif[83]. On 9th century B.C. Assyrian helmets the winged sun-disk is only a complementary motif above the tree-of-life. There is not a single Assyrian helmet known on which the winged sun-disk was an independent motif. So as has been mentioned we can assume that these helmets (which were made in the last third of the 8th century B.C., when almost the whole territory of North Syria was already under Assyrian rule) were made probably in North Syrian workshops for the Assyrian army, or for let us say North Syrian contingents of the Assyrian imperial army (which might contain Assyrian and North Syrian troops as well). The winged sun-disk as an independent motif for some unknown reason was connected with Urartian helmets[84]. After this explanation the Palaepaphos helmet (for the same unknown reason) became an "Urartian helmet"[85]. But from the middle of the 8th century there was no Urartian influence exerted on North Syria any more. Furthermore, I must say there is not a single

---

76 Karageorghis 1966, pp. 321-322, fig. 55; Karageorghis 1967, pp. 234-235, figs. 20, 24; Borchhardt 1972, p. 99, Kat. 22 A II; Overlaet 1979, p. 55, no. 1; Tatton-Brown 1979, p. 105, Kat. 327, fig. 327; Özgen 1982, pp. 20, 53 note 8; Schauer 1983, fig. 5a; Maier - Karageorghis 1984, p. 175, pl. 162; Pflug 1988b, 34-36, fig. 9; Dezsö 1993, Cat. no. 32, Group no. NS.2.4, p. 37, fig. 7, pl. 47.

77 Schauer 1983, pp. 186-187.

78 Dezsö 1993, pp. 34-37, fig. 7 (drawing of winged sun-disks from "North-Syrian" helmets).

79 Zinçirli, North Palace, Room K3, Inv. no.: S.3695; von Luschan - Andrae 1943, pp. 75-76, 162-163, figs. 84-85, pl. 40a;; Calmeyer 1969, p. 91, fig. 93; Borchhardt 1972, p. 100, Kat. 22 B I 2, pl. 34:6; Dezsö 1993, Cat. no. 29, Group no. NS.2.1, pp. 34-35, 120-121, fig. 7, pl. 43.

80 London, British Museum, Inv. no. WA 134611; Barnett 1967, p. 38, pl. 12a; Lloyd 1967, p. 116, fig. 123; Calmeyer 1969, p. 89, no. 44C, fig. 91; Borchhardt 1972, p. 108, Kat. 24 VIII 2, fig. 12; Barnett - Curtis 1973, pp. 133, 136, pl. 64b; Dezsö 1993, Cat. no. 34, Group no. NS.2.6, pp. 36-37, 123-124, fig. 7, pls. 50-51.

81 von Luschan - Andrae 1943, p. 78.

82 Zinçirli, North Palace, Inv. no.: S.3964; von Luschan - Andrae 1943, pp. 76-79, 163, fig. 88, pl. 41; Barnett 1953, p. 102; Borchhardt 1972, p. 100, Kat. 22 B I 3; Overlaet 1979, p. 54, note 7, p. 55; Curtis 1979, vol. I, pp. 182-183; Özgen 1982, pp. 20, 52 note 5; Dezsö - Curtis 1991, pp. 124-125, fig. 22; Dezsö 1993, Cat. no. 28, Group no. NS.1, pp. 34-35, pls. 41-42.

83 I. Winter phrased the winged sun-disk of the bronze Zincirli helmet (note 70) as a "good 'North-Syrian style' winged sundisk"; Winter 1988, p. 194.

84 Borchhardt 1972, pp. 100, 103-105; Pflug 1988b, p. 34.

85 Maier - Karageorghis 1984, p. 175, pl. 162.

Urartian helmet decorated with winged sun-disk, and there is not a single unprovenanced helmet decorated with winged sun-disk which has been or would be attributed to Urartu[86].

These helmets of course might not have reached different parts of the Mediterranean exclusively via military campaigns. They could reach territories outside their area of origin as booty, or with actual objects of trade. Schauer sited a bronze fragment from the point of a helmet from the Ría de Huelva weapon deposit as a fragment of an oriental helmet, which might have reached Spain with Phoenician traders.[87] Hencken however showed that the piece is from an Europaean type of crested helmet which was used from Spain to Germany and Italy[88].

There are altogether 7 Assyrian and 6 North Syrian pointed bronze and iron helmets and fragments known[89] and these are actual examples of the Syro-Assyrian and Assyrian pointed helmet tradition of the second half of the 8th century B.C. which exerted influence on the Aegean and Eastern-Mediterranean pointed helmet tradition of the 8th and 7th centuries B.C.

LEVEL 2:
COPYING AND FORMAL REINTERPRETATION OF ORIENTAL PATTERNS

Cyprus, Alassa, "Pano-Mandilaris", Tomb 16 (Cyprus, Nicosia, Cyprus Museum, Inv. no. T.16/1; H.: 18.5 cm, W.: 21.3 cm; Cypro-Archaic I Period [750-650 B.C.])[90]. *(Ills. 7-8)*

Fragment from the front of a conical helmet. There are two horizontal embossed ribs around the base of the helmet. The lower rib ends on the front, the upper rib continues in a widening out curve (arc). There is a series of holes (only four are extant on the fragment) around the base of the helmet at regular intervals of 65 mm. At the front of the helmet there was an eye or face cutout. The finished edge of the cutout is still visible on the fragment. There is a fifth hole for fastening the lining along the edge of the cutout at a regular interval of 28 mm. This cutout followed the contour of the curving arc on the front of the helmet and probably ended in a nose projection between the two curves. On the top part (at the point) of this fragmentary helmet a small section of the vertical rib running from the top to between the two curves exists.

There are six further fragments belonging to this helmet: **1** undecorated fragment from the side of the helmet (15.5 x 8.0 cm); **2** undecorated fragment from the side of the helmet (4.6 x 4.3 cm); **3** undecorated fragment from the side of the helmet (5.0 x 3.7 cm); **4** from the rim of the helmet with the lower rib and four holes (8.7 x 3.0 cm); **5** from the front of the helmet, the base of the antithetic curve of the front is visible on this fragment (6.2 x 2.3 cm); **6** from the front of the helmet, probably the right point of the eye/face cutout with an existing hole for the lining (2.9 x 2.5 cm).

The Syro-Assyrian inspiration of the structure of this helmet is unquestionnable (see for example the squat conical shape, the pair of ribs around the base, the curve and the vertical rib at the front). This helmet is a local, Cypriote product, and was made by copying the structure of a Syro-Assyrian helmet in the late 8th - early 7th century B.C.[91] But the widening out *repoussé* curve and the eye or face cutout at the front of the helmet are clear signs of local reinterpretation, especially in the shape. As will be discussed later, there was another, iconographical type of reinterpretation of Oriental patterns known from an Argos helmet.

The eye or face cutout is an entirely new feature appearing for the first time on this helmet[92].

---

86 For detailed study of the decorative systems of Urartian helmets see **Dezső 1993**, pp. 61-66.

87 **Schauer 1983**, pp. 185-186, fig. 5b.

88 **Hencken 1971**, pp. 72-74, fig. 48a-b.

89 For detailed study see: **Dezső - Curtis 1991**, pp. 105-126, pls. 15-20; for Assyrian conical bronze and iron helmets and fragments: **Dezső 1993**, Cat. nos. 1-7, Gruop nos. A.1.1-A.1.5, A.2.1-A.2.2, pp. 1-17, pls. 1-14; for North-Syrian bronze helmets and iron fragments: **Dezső 1993**, Cat. nos. 28-34, Group nos. NS.1, NS.2.1-NS.2.6, pp. 34-39, pls. 41-51.

90 **Karageorghis 1988**, p. 798, no. 1, fig. 6; **Dezső 1993**, Cat. no. 33, Group no. NS.2.5, pls. 48-49.

91 Both of the helmets (Palaepaphos and Alassa) were found in tombs which can be dated to the Cypro-Archaic I Period (750-650 B.C.).

92 Appears earlier only on the 12th-11th century B.C. Iranian helmets decorated with figures of deities on the front. **Dezső 1993**, Cat. nos. 109-113, pp. 71-76.

The origin of this eye cutout is clearly the reinterpretation (and/or misinterpretation) as eyebrows of the Oriental *repoussé* curves on the front of the helmet in a foreign cultural background. This helmet is probably the forerunner of the later Anatolian and Cypriote tradition (late 7th - early 6th century B.C.) of composite iron and bronze helmets of radial type furnished with similar eye cutouts[93]. This eye cutout, or the reinterpretation of the oriental curves appear on contemporary Scythian helmets of Kuban type, which probably had a connection with the Anatolian radial type of composite iron and bronze helmets (see later). This helmet type is part of the Mediterranean "covered face" helmet tradition, which is one of the best known differences between the Near Eastern "open face"[94] and the Mediterranean "covered face" traditions. The Alassa helmet might be a transitional form between the two traditions and the two regions as well. It shows the first sign of the deepening of the sides of the helmet for better protection, which culminated in the Tamassos and "Geryon" types of helmets in Cyprus, and in the Corinthian and its attached types of helmets in the Greek mainland[95]. Furthermore it shows us that the Mediterranean covered face helmet tradition may be traced back to the Oriental helmet tradition.

This helmet therefore - together with the Tamassos type helmets - is one of the best pieces of evidence for the innovative role of Cyprus in the new Eastern Mediterranean helmet tradition of the 8th and 7th centuries B.C., and the intermediatory role of the island in the connection of the Near East and the Mediterranean.

LEVEL 3:
COPYING AND ICONOGRAPHICAL REINTERPRETATION OF ORIENTAL PATTERNS

Argos, Odos Perseous 41, warrior grave of Geometric Age (Argos, Archaeological Museum; third quarter of 8th century B.C.)[96] (*Ill. 9*)

Greek version of an oriental conical helmet. The oriental features are shown very well on the helmet: (squat) conical shape, the vertical rib on the front, a pair of curves bending inward; but the original oriental curves were not understood and were (re)interpreted as eyebrows so two apotropaic eyes were incised under them.

The problem may be similar to the *"question whether the oriental cauldrons arrived in Greece with hammered griffin protomes and sirens as an ensemble, or whether the protomes were added to the siren cauldrons in Greece to satisfy (unknown) local needs."*[97] In our case even the helmet was made in Greece (probably in Argos), and the apotropaic eyes were added to the original (and now meaningless, or at least reinterpreted) oriental features to satisfy (in this case known) local needs[98].

The history of the original oriental motif, which is the most characteristic feature of oriental conical helmets is well known[99] (*Ill. 1, nos. 1-4*). The first appearance of the typical decoration of Assyrian conical helmets which characterized the 9th-7th century B.C. Near Eastern helmet tradition is on the palace reliefs of Ashurnasirpal II (883-859 B.C.): 1-3 pairs of *repoussé* curves bending towards the middle ("*Krummstab*") with a vertical rib running from the point of the helmet between them (*Ill. 1*). These horizontal and vertical ribs and curves undoubtedly represent the *repoussé* ribs strengthening the bronze sheet of the actual conical helmets. This decorative system can be exclusively connected to the early 9th century B.C. Assyrian conical helmets, and could not have appeared in another context. A

---

93 From Sardis, and probably from Old-Smyrna, Idalion and Lindos as well. See later.

94 As have been mentioned the 9th century B.C. (and occasionally in the 8th century B.C.) Assyrian helmets were furnished with a scale armour (mostly iron! - see the Assur fresco fragment mentioned above) faceguard, which was attached to the rim of the helmet. This, scale armour type of face protection was virtually unknown in the Mediterranean.

95 For the early evolution of the Corinthian and its attached types of Greek helmets see fig. X.

96 **Protonotariou-Deilaki 1973**, pp. 97-99, pl. 95e; **Gröschel 1986**, pp. 71-72, fig. 4; **Dezső 1993**, p. 39.

97 **Muscarella 1992**, pp. 35-36.

98 For the reinterpreted Oriental motifs or Oriental motifs used by local metalsmiths out of their original context to satisfy local needs see **Curtis 1994**, p. 1 (bronze disk in the Iraklion Museum) and a bronze sheet (Olympia, B 5085a, Chart 1, no. M.5.23) discussed later (p. 30).

99 For detailed discussion of the evolution of Near Eastern conical helmets and the evolution of their decorative systems in three phases, see **Dezső 1993**, pp. 1-7.

9th century B.C. Assyrian conical bronze helmet and two fragments which are the earliest actual examples of this decorative system[100]:

1. **Venice, Maria & Giancarlo Ligabue Collection, "Luristan"** (H.: 29 cm, Diam.: 22.5 cm)[101] (*Ills. 10-11*)
"Conical helmet with *repoussé* and traced decoration. There are three embossed ribs around the base of the helmet. There are three pairs of arcs curving towards the centre and a vertical rib between them on the front of the helmet. The two outer arcs and the vertical rib end in rams' heads. Just behind the heads the fleece is depicted. The innermost pair of curves has rounded extremities. There are rows of traced rosettes between the curves. A fourth horizontal rib is interrupted by the curves. Between the arcs there is a symmetrical scene of a tree-of-life under a winged sun-disk, and on either side of the tree there is the adoring king (worship of the tree) with his attendant armed with a sword behind him. On the sides of the helmet - between the two upper ribs (d.: 2.2 cm) - there is a traced frieze of 17[102] attendants in procession. Complete."[103]

2. **Venice, private collection, "Luristan"** (H.: 12 cm, W.: 18 cm)[104] (*Ill. 12*)
"Fragment from the frontal part (right half) and border of a conical helmet with *repoussé* and traced decoration. The figural decoration of the fragment is similar to the Ligabue helmet discussed above. The only difference is that there were two attendants behind the king on either side of the tree-of-life (surmounted by a winged sun-disk) instead of one. Only one of the innermost curves ending in a ram's head[105] is preserved completely, the two outer are fragmentary. The border decoration consists of 3 + 2 horizontal embossed ribs. There is a 2.3 cm high strip between the 3rd and 4th ribs which is taken up by a frieze of six figures of dignitaries armed with long swords[106] proceeding to the left."[107]

3. **Teheran, private collection** (H.: 6.1 cm)[108] (*Ill. 13*)
"Small fragment from the front of a helmet with *repoussé* and traced decoration. The decoration of the fragment is similar to those mentioned above. Only the innermost arc ending in an animal's head (snake head?) is preserved on the fragment. Under the arc there is the figure of an adoring king with his attendant behind him."[109]

With their arcs curving towards the centre and with their traced figural decoration these three helmets undoubtedly represent the 9th century B.C. Assyrian helmet tradition, the first phase of the evolution of Assyrian helmets.[110] As this decorative system from the very end of the 9th century became widely used on the conical helmets of the Near East a number of explanations have been proposed for the origin of this device. Calmeyer[111] derived the motif from the Zagros region, whence he argued the Urartians adopted it in the early 8th century B.C.[112]. But the earliest known examples in

---

100 Dezsö 1993, pp. 7-12.
101 **Salvatori 1975**, pp. 255-264, figs. 1-2, pls. 36-38; **Ligabue - Salvatori 1977**, pp. 7-8; **Overlaet 1979**, p. 56; **Curtis 1979**, vol. I, p. 184; **Gröschel 1986**, p. 73, note 226; **Dezsö - Curtis 1991**, pp. 122-124; **Dezsö 1993**, Cat no. 1, Group no. A.1.1, pp. 7-9, 10-12, 106, pls. 1-3.
102 Salvatori 1975, fig. 2; 9 + 8 (the 9th is probably missing) figures processing towards the front of the helmet.
103 Dezsö 1993, p. 8 and p. 106.
104 **Ligabue - Salvatori 1977**, pp. 7-8, fig. 1; **Gröschel 1986**, p. 73, no. 3, note 227; **Dezsö - Curtis 1991**, pp. 122-124; **Dezsö 1993**, Cat. no. 2, Group no. A.1.2, pp. 8-9, 10-12, 106-107, pl. 4.
105 Ligabue - Salvatori 1977, pp. 7-8 writes: horse head.
106 The double projections on the scabbards are unique.
107 Dezsö 1993, p. 8.
108 **Calmeyer 1975**, p. 316, fig. 2; **Ligabue - Salvatori 1977**, p. 8; **Overlaet 1979**, p. 56, note 16; **Gröschel 1986**, p. 73, note 228; **Dezsö - Curtis 1991**, pp. 122-124; **Dezsö 1993**, Cat. no. 3, Group no. A.1.3, pp. 8-9, 10-12, 107, pl. 5.
109 Dezsö 1993, p. 8.
110 Dezsö 1993, pp. 1-7.
111 Calmeyer 1969, pp. 90-91.
112 On Urartian helmets with royal inscriptions: Argishti I (789-766 B.C.): Dezsö 1993, Cat. nos. 80-81; Sarduri II (765-733

Western Iran are on conical helmets[113] from Hasanlu IVB (Iron II Period), c. 800 B.C.[114], where there is considerable evidence for Assyrian influence. As this motif appears in Assyria by at least the reign of Ashur-nasir-pal II, it is perhaps more likely to be of Assyrian origin, although it is already shown in a developed form at this time. The first known Urartian examples of this decorative system are dated a hundred years later, to the early 8th century B.C., and are inscribed with the name of Argishti I (789-766 B.C.), king of Urartu[115].

There are at least two possibilities for the significance of the decoration (curves or crooks, interpreted often as "snakes") on the front of Iron Age Near Eastern helmets. They may have originated 1. in the use of animals (or animal headed snakes) in an unknown cultic tradition as apotropaic symbols, which would be very appropriate on the front of a helmet; 2. in frames for figural scenes on the front of helmets (an Assyrian king with attendants, see above, or winged sun-discs on the second half of 8th century B.C. North Syrian helmets, see above), as on the later Assyrian conical helmets (a new type of frame reminiscent of a stele, see *Ill. 1, nos. 6, 10, 11*). And there is an other possibility: 3. representation of eyebrows on the front of a helmet, which may also have been apotropaic, however this possibility is not documented on Near Eastern conical helmets at all. The only Near Eastern example of such a use is a hemispherical crested helmet from Hasanlu[116], the decorative system of which is a unique and interesting mixture of Transcaucasian - North-West Iranian (incised geometric and figurative) motifs and Near Eastern (let us say Assyrian) motifs out of their original context and tradition[117]. The decoration of this Hasanlu hemispherical crested helmet is probably a local misinterpretation of the original Assyrian motif.

LEVEL 4:
CYPRIOTE AND GREEK HELMETS INSPIRED BY ORIENTAL (SYRO-ASSYRIAN) HELMET TYPES

This level of influence may be characterized as the level of stimulus diffusion discussed above. In this case only the general shape of the Greek helmets was similar to the (pointed and crested) shape of the oriental helmets, but their details and process of execution was quite different. All the following helmet types were furnished with new, local elements, innovations which are unknown on oriental helmets.

There are three main regions from which this level of orientalizing helmet tradition can be reconstructed. These regions are **Cyprus, Crete** and the **Greek mainland** (furthermore Southern Italy, probably inspired from the Greek mainland). These regions undoubtedly present a hypothetical route of influence (or diffusion). Surprisingly there is no evidence at all that would imply any role for Anatolia (Phrygia, Lydia, Caria) in this evolution. Yet, Western Anatolia has yielded evidence (the Old-Smyrna and Sardis iron and bronze composite helmets, see below) for a quite different 6th century B.C. "Phrygo-Persian" helmet tradition. The early 1st millennium B.C. Anatolian helmet tradition belonged to the Near Eastern helmet tradition (Anatolian and North Syrian Neo-Hittite states transmitted the 2nd millennium B.C. Near Eastern crested helmet tradition to the early first millennium B.C. Near East). The 8th century B.C. Assyrian palace-reliefs show Anatolian and Phrygian crested helmets of general Near Eastern form, but we do not know much about the Anatolian helmets of the 7th century B.C. The only representations are three crested helmets on 7th century B.C. architectural terracottas from Gordion (*Ill. 5, O.2.49-51*). It is most likely that in the 7th and 6th centuries B.C. a Greek helmet tradition spread in Anatolia from the west (e.g. local versions of Ionian types of helmets,

---

B.C.): **Dezső 1993**, Cat. nos. 82-85.

113 **Dezső 1993**, Cat. nos. 45-47.

114 For the problem of the connection of an Urartian attack and the destruction level of Hasanlu IVB see recently: **Medvedskaya 1988**, pp. 1-15; **Dyson - Muscarella 1989**, pp. 1-27; **Medvedskaya 1991**, pp 149-161.

115 One complete and a fragmentary conical bronze helmet from Karmir Blur, now in the Historical Museum of Armenia, Yerevan. For detailed description and references see **Dezső 1993**, Cat. nos. 80, 81.

116 Teheran, Musée Iran Bastan, Inv. no.: HAS 60-528, Hasanlu, Burned Building II, northwest corner; **Barnett - Falkner 1962**, pp. xx, xxii, fig. 2:15; **van Loon 1966**, p. 119, note 195; **Borchhardt 1972**, p. 107, Kat. 24 IV 1, pl. 40:2; **Muscarella 1980**, p. 29, note 55; **Muscarella 1988**, p. 50; **de Schauensee 1988**, p. 55, pl. 55; **Dezső 1993**, Cat. no. 49, Group no. H.2.2, pp. 47-50, 132, pls. 70-71.

117 **Dezső 1993**, pp. 48-50.

which was inspired by the Corinthian and other types of Greek helmets of the mainland), but unfortunately there is not a single surviving example, which could argue for an earlier, genuine Anatolian helmet tradition. In view of this development the Sardis composite iron and bronze helmet may represent an oriental (probably Persian) influence (see later).

The three regions mentioned above do not imply any given route (e.g. Cyprus --> Crete --> Mainland Greece) for the transmission. However, Cyprus might be an important relay point - not only because of the actual Assyrian contacts (stele of Sargon II, Palaepaphos helmet and the Alassa helmet, the only example for the 2. level of influence, see above) - but because of its crucial location on the main maritime trade routes which connected the Near East with the Aegean. With this maritime trade all of the three regions might be connected with the Near East at the same time. The orientalizing helmets of these regions are parallel, and different results of the "stimulus diffusion". Different solutions for (probably) the same problem.

CYPRUS

Tamassos, Royal Tomb XI (Berlin, Antikenmuseum, Inv. Misc. 8142,620, H.: 42.3 cm)[118]
It has a conical shape with a feature which is a characteristic of the three "Tamassos-type" helmets: their tubular point bulging like a knob at the top. There are two pairs of horizontal ribs around the base and another bunch of ribs above them to strengthen the rim of the helmet. The helmet was furnished with detachable cheek-pieces attached to helmet by hinges along their upper edge and face-masks. There are fragments of the neck-guard and of two small earflaps belonging to the Berlin helmet.
Late 7th century B.C.[119]

Tamassos, Dromos of Royal Tomb IV (Nicosia, Cyprus Museum, Inv. no. 98/1971; H.: 31.3 cm, with cheek pieces: 42.3 cm; Diam.: max.: 27.4 cm, min.: 14 cm)[120] (*Ills. 14-15*)
It has a shape similar to the Berlin helmet, but there is only one rib around the base to strengthen the rim of the helmet. The cap of the helmet was hammered out from a single piece of bronze. This helmet was furnished with detachable earflaps different from the two piece earflaps of the Berlin helmet. While the Berlin helmet has its separate face-mask parts, the Nicosia helmet has a composite cheek-piece made of a single piece of bronze sheet and furnished with eye and mouth cut-outs. There are 8 holes along the rim on the front and 15 holes along the rim on the back of the helmet (diam.: 2 mm). The height of the earflaps/cheek-pieces is 13.0 cm, their width is 13.3 cm. The earflaps/cheek-pieces were fastened to the cap of the helmet by hinges.
Late 7th century B.C.

"Cyprus" (Istanbul, Archaeological Museum, Inv. no.: 16)[121]
It has a shape similar to the Berlin and Nicosia helmets, but the Istanbul helmet has lost its cheek-pieces and face-masks. Fragmentary.
Late 7th century B.C.

There are several representations of this "Tamassos-type" of pointed helmet known from Cypriote art. They are shown on two fragmentary terracotta heads from the Samian Heraion[122] and a third terracotta head from Idalion, Cyprus, now in the Antikenmuseum, Berlin[123].

---

118 **Buchholz 1978**, pp. 197-200, figs. 45a-e; **Pflug 1988b**, pp. 27-41; **Pflug 1989**, Cat. no. 1, pp. 17-18, 49, fig. 11, pl. on p. 49; Dezső 1993, p. 39.
119 Pflug 1988b, pp. 40-41.
120 **Buchholz 1972**, p. 185, pl. 32:2; **Buchholz 1973**, pp. 334, 388, figs. 36a-d; **Karageorghis 1973**, p. 665, fig. 101; **Borchhardt 1977**, pls. E V b-c; **Pflug 1988b**, pp. 29-31, fig. 2; Dezső 1993, p. 39.
121 Pflug 1988b, pp. 29-31, figs. 3-4; Dezső 1993, p. 39.
122 1. Samos, Heraion, terracotta head (Samos Museum, Inv. no. T.2637, H.: 9.1 cm); **Schmidt 1968**, pl. 44; **Borchhardt 1977**, pl. E V a; **Pflug 1988b**, figs. 5-6; 2. Samos, Heraion, terracotta head (Samos Museum, Inv. no. T.2741, H.: 7.5 cm); **Schmidt 1968**, pls. 44, 46.
123 Idalion, Cyprus, terracotta head (Berlin, Antikenmuseum, Inv. no. 499x); **Schmidt 1968**, pl. 44; Pflug 1988b, figs. 7-8.

This type of helmet is a characteristic example of the oriental inspiration or the stimulus diffusion of the oriental conical helmet types. This type of helmet, in spite of its later date may be traced back to the late 8th century B.C. conical helmets of the Near East, namely Assyria. Its shape with the long tubular point appears in Assyrian art in the middle of the 8th century B.C. On the Til-Barsip wall-paintings[124] there are Assyrian helmets with high, tubular points and, another new feature, a neckguard. The points of these helmets were sealed by a rectangular element, which might be added separately to these (iron) helmets. The tubular point bulging like a knob on the Tamassos helmets may be a late ancestor of this form. Earlier representations of conical helmets with a kind of bulging knob are visible on a Karatepe sculpture depicting an Assyrian horseman probably from the first half of the 8th century B.C.[125]. But this kind of tubular point bulging like a knob is clearly a local development on the Tamassos helmets. Only the shape is oriental, but further details, like the detachable earflap combined with a face-mask are local. The face-mask, or earflaps covering parts of the face on the early Corinthian helmets and their Cretan versions[126], became a characteristic Greek feature. This kind of face mask, as part of the defensive armour was never known in the Near East. The Assyrians in the 9th century B.C. used scale armour attached to the rim of their helmets to guard parts of their faces. These scale armour "face-masks" are characteristically 9th century B.C. Assyrian features and appear in the palace reliefs[127] of Ashurnasirpal II (883-859 B.C.), on the Balawat gates[128] of Shalmaneser III (858-824 B.C.), and on a wall-painting fragment discussed above[129]. The oriental "open faced helmet tradition" can be contrasted with the "covered face Aegean helmet tradition" which was introduced probably with the early Corinthian helmets at the end of the 8th century B.C. The face mask might have originated in the development of earflaps to cover larger parts not only of the ears but also face. The Lindos earflaps[130], one of which was considered by Pflug as parallel for an Olympian earflap[131], is from a helmet made of five parts. The Lindos type of earflaps (from an unknown type of probably Eastern Greek helmet[132]) with the eye and mouth cut-outs might be inspired by the mainland Greek "covered face tradition" appears in its developed form with the early Corinthian helmets, or might be a parallel development. These Lindos earflaps have a clear similarity to the earflaps of the terracotta representations of the Tamassos type of helmet[133]. One of the helmets of these terracotta heads is furnished with a detachable earflap - face-guard[134], while the other has a solid earflap - face-guard[135]. There is a row of rivet holes at the upper edge of one of the Lindos earflaps[136] which means that the construction of the helmet to which this earflap belonged to was similar to the Greek Geometric helmets[137] made of five separate parts (see below). So it is clear that in case of the Tamassos type of helmet there were a

---

124 Wall-paintings, Til-Barsip, Room XXIV, reign of Tiglath-pileser III (745-727 B.C.); **Thureau-Dangin - Dunand 1936**, pls. XLIX, upper register, LI; **Dezsö 1993**, nos. 165, 166.

125 Karatepe, "Obere Grabung", **Bossert et al. 1950**, pl. XIII, no. 64; **Orthmann 1971**, p. 494 (Sph III), pl. 18f; **Dezsö 1993**, no. 177.

126 **Hoffmann 1972**, passim.

127 **Budge 1914**, passim.

128 **King 1915**, passim.

129 Ass.10756, **Andrae 1925**, pl. 9e.

130 **Blinkenberg 1901**, pp. 189-190, nos. 571-576, pls. 22-23.

131 **Pflug 1988a**, p. 21.

132 **Pflug 1988a**, p. 21. However, the general form of this type is indicated by a miniature votive bronze crested helmet found on the Lindos Acropolis (**Blinkenberg 1931**, p. 391, no. 1564, pl. 63:1564). This votive miniature helmet was made of two parts - similarly to the Cretan miniature votive helmets: Gortyn (**Hoffmann 1972**, p. 2, pl. 41:4), Praisos (**Bosanquet 1901-1902**, p. 258, pl. 10; **Benton 1939-1940**, pl. 31:17) and Palaikastro (**Benton 1939-1940**, pl. 28:31). The two-piece construction of the actual helmets of this type was proved by the Hamburg Cretan crested helmet from Praisos (see below). The characteristic form of the Lindos earflaps is clearly visible on the Lindos miniature helmet.

133 Terracotta head (Berlin 499x), H.: 8.4 cm: **Schmidt 1968**, pl. 44 ("aus Samos"); **Pflug 1988b**, pp. 32-33, figs. 7-8 (note 31: "aus Idalion"); Terracotta head (Samos, Heraion, T.2637), H.: 9.1 cm: **Schmidt 1968**, pl. 44; **Pflug 1988b**, pp. 32-33, figs. 5-6; Terracotta head (Samos, Heraion, T.2741), H.: 7.5 cm: **Schmidt 1968**, pls. 44, 46.

134 Terracotta head (Samos, Heraion, T.2637), H.: 9.1 cm: **Schmidt 1968**, pl. 44; **Pflug 1988b**, pp. 32-33, figs. 5-6.

135 Terracotta head (Berlin 499x), H.: 8.4 cm: **Schmidt 1968**, pl. 44; **Pflug 1988b**, pp. 32-33, figs. 7-8.

136 **Blinkenberg 1901**, pp. 189-190, no. 571, pl. 22.

137 **Pflug 1988a**, p. 21; **Pflug 1988b**, p. 32.

few (local?) variants in use at the same time:

1. With solid earflap (cheek-piece) - face-mask: terracotta head (Berlin)[138]
2. With detachable cheek-piece - face-mask: Nicosia helmet and a terracotta head (Samos)[139]
3. With detachable cheek-piece and detachable face-mask: Berlin helmet
4. The helmet type of the Lindos earflaps[140] (only the earflap construction is similar to the 2nd group)

The relatively late date[141] of the Tamassos type of helmets makes it possible that the face-guard as idea came from the Corinthian helmets of earlier date, but one can argue for a parallel, East Greek development (see the Lindos earflaps) as well[142].

The history of (8th-) 7th-6th century B.C. genuine Cypriote helmets can be partly reconstructed from several representations (terracotta sculptures, bronze statuettes, etc.) of different types of headdress or helmet. But the identification of the headdresses is difficult. In several cases it is not possible to judge whether the headdress represented on a terracotta sculpture is a metal helmet or a leather helmet or a linen cap[143]. At this point we have to exclude all the headdresses and "helmets" made of soft, perishable materials (leather, linen) and concentrate only on the metal helmets. The identification of metal helmets needs some additional features (e.g. a crest, or definite earflaps). *"It should be noted, that simple conical headdresses, without such additional identifying features, appear on many terracottas of otherwise unarmed horseback riders. Here it must remain uncertain whether helmets or caps were intended."*[144] There are two major groups of terracotta and bronze statuettes representing helmets or different types of headdress which were interpreted in earlier studies as helmets:

1. "Civilians" or figures without additional indication of the warlike character of the representation.
2. Warriors with additional indication of their warlike character: warriors armed with a shield and/or a weapon; horsemen armed with shield and/or a weapon; chariot models with armed warriors.
3. A third group contains all the representations of known types of helmet (e.g. the terracotta representations of the Tamassos type of pointed helmet; representations of crested helmets; and the "Geryon"-type of Cypriote helmets (see below). And there are the representations of metal helmet forms with definite additional features, like profiled earflaps, which would be unnecessary or redundant on leather caps.

There is no definite coincidence between the representations of headresses on the first two groups: there are, for example, no crested helmets on the heads of the first group, and there are no profiled earflaps on the headdresses of this group. However, there are "earflaps" and plumes on the caps of this group, but certainly not made of metal. The shape of their headdresses, however, sometimes similar or the same as that of the metal helmets, but without any strict indication of their material they must be excluded from further study here. Furthermore it is well known that there were leather helmets in use in Cyprus at this period. There are several representations of leather helmets in the second group, the definite warlike character of which would otherwise exclude the use of leather or linen caps. However, there is a coincidence between these leather helmets and some of the representations of the first, "not warlike" group[145]. On the chariot groups for example there is an observable

---

138 Terracotta head (Berlin, Antikenmuseum, Inv. no. 499x), H.: 8.4 cm: **Schmidt 1968**, pl. 44; **Pflug 1988b**, pp. 32-33, figs. 7-8.
139 Terracotta head (Samos, Heraion, T.2637), H.: 9.1 cm: **Schmidt 1968**, pl. 44; **Pflug 1988b**, pp. 32-33, figs. 5-6
140 1. Lindos, Acropolis, (right side earflap); H.: 14.5 cm; W.: 11.6 cm; **Blinkenberg 1931**, pp. 189-190, no. 571, pl. 22; 2. Lindos, Acropolis (left side earflap); H.: 13.4 cm; W.: 10.9 cm; **Blinkenberg 1931**, p. 190, no. 572, pl. 22.4; 3. Lindos, Acropolis; H.: 13.3 cm; **Blinkenberg 1931**, p. 190, no. 573.
141 **Pflug 1988b**, pp. 40-41.
142 **Pflug 1988a**, p. 21.
143 For detailed study see **Törnkvist 1974**, pp. 21-32; **Tatton-Brown 1979**, pp. 281-284; moreover, **Pflug 1988b**, p. 36.
144 **Crouwel - Tatton-Brown 1988**, p. 81.
145 Compare for example the leather helmets of the crew of chariot no. 1781+798 (**Gjerstad et al. 1935**, pl. CCXXXV:3) with

tendency for the chariot warrior (or at least one member of the crew) to wear a helmet of metal shape, while others of the crew wear helmets of "leather shape"[146]. In a few cases all the two or three members of the crew wear headdresses which can probably be identified as leather helmets[147].

So the remaining helmet representations ("metal forms") provide a well known picture of the early oriental or orientalizing types of pointed helmets:

1. pointed helmet without earflaps[148] (*Ill. 4, no. M.2.1*)
2. pointed helmet with solid earflaps (without indication of hinges)[149] (*Ill. 4, no. M.2.2*)
3. pointed helmet with detachable earflaps[150] (*Ill. 4, no. M.2.3*)
4. pointed helmet with a tubular point bulging like a knob and with earflaps (probably an early example or predecessor of the Tamassos-type of pointed helmets)[151] (*Ill. 4, no. M.2.4*)

On the second level there are three interesting representations of warriors helmets which represent the intermediate phase in the evolution of Cypriote helmets between the early oriental or orientalizing and the developed Cypriote helmet types discussed later:

1. Tubular pointed helmet with earflaps with cut-outs for the eyes and mouth[152]. This helmet with its characteristic earflaps might be an early version of the later Tamassos-type of pointed helmets (*Ill. 4, no. M.2.7*).
2. Tubular pointed helmet with a point bulging like a knob and furnished with a nose-guard and long, curving earflaps[153]. This helmet with its nose guard and curving earflaps might be the predecessor of the later "Geryon-type" of Cypriote helmets (*Ill. 4, no. M.2.5*).
3. Tubular pointed helmet with a point bulging like a knob and furnished with long earflaps curving in a right angle to form a cheek-piece[154]. Similarly to the 2. representation, this helmet might be an intermediate stage between the original oriental form and its modified Cypriote version, the "Geryon-type" (*Ill. 4, no. M.2.6*).

On the third level there are the later (late 7th - early 6th century B.C.) Cypriote types, helmets which represent only the oriental inspiration combined with characteristic local or Aegean features (curving cheek-pieces and face-mask):

---

the leather cap (with long projection hanging at the back of the cap and "soft earflaps") of a terracotta sculpture of the first group (**Gjerstad et al. 1935**, pl. CCVII:1-2, no. 1509).

146 **Gjerstad et al. 1935**, pls. CCXXXIV:4 (no. 1715); CCXXXIV:5 (no. 2000); CCXXXIV:6 (no. 1046); CCXXXV:1 (no. 1125); CCXXXV:2 (no. 1124); CCXXXV:3 (no. 1781+798); CCXXXV:4 (no. 1170); CCXXXV:5 (no. 1998). Second half of Cypro-Archaic I, mid-7th century B.C.

147 **Gjerstad et al. 1935**, pl. CCXXXIV:2 (no. 1166); **Crouwel 1987**, pls. XXXVIII:1a-b, XXXVIII:3, XXXIX:2. Second half of Cypro-Archaic I, mid-7th century B.C.

148 Ayia Irini, terracotta chariot group, Nicosia, Cyprus Museum; **Gjerstad et al 1935**, pl. CCXXXIV:5 (no. 2000). Second half of Cypro-Archaic I, mid-7th century B.C.

149 1. Ayia Irini, terracotta chariot group, **Gjerstad et al. 1935**, pl. CCXXXIV:6 (no. 1046); 2. Ayia Irini, terracotta chariot group, **Gjerstad et al. 1935**, pl. CCXXXV:5 (no. 1998); 3. Ayia Irini, terracotta sculpture of a warrior with shield, **Gjerstad et al. 1935**, pl. CCXXXII:7 (no. 1032); 4. Ayia Irini, terracotta head, **Gjerstad et al. 1935**, pl. CCXXXII:15 (no. 2384); 5. "Cyprus", terracotta horseman, Edinburgh, Royal Scottish Museum 1921.354, **Crouwel - Tatton-Brown 1988**, pl. XXVI:4. Second half of Cypro-Archaic I, mid-7th century B.C.

150 1. Ayia Irini, terracotta chariot group, **Gjerstad et al. 1935**, pl. CCXXXIV:6 (no. 1046)?; 2. "Cyprus", terracotta horseman, London, British Museum, 1876.4.9.92, **Crouwel - Tatton-Brown 1988**, pl. XXVI:2. Second half of Cypro-Archaic I, mid-7th century B.C.

151 1. Ayia Irini, terracotta chariot group, Nicosia, Cyprus Museum, **Gjerstad et al. 1935**, CCXXXV:3 (no. 1781+798); 2. Ayia Irini, terracotta chariot group, Nicosia, Cyprus Museum, **Gjerstad et al. 1935**, pl. CCXXXV:4 (no. 1170). Second half of Cypro-Archaic I, mid-7th century B.C.

152 Ayia Irini, terracotta sculpture of a warrior armed with a spiked shield, **Gjerstad et al. 1935**, pp. 721-722, pl. CXCIV, no. 1385+1530.

153 "Cyprus", terracotta statuette of a warrior, **Heuzey 1880**, fig. F.

154 "Cyprus", terracotta statuette of a warrior, **Heuzey 1880**, fig. G.

1. Representations of the Tamassos-type of pointed helmets discussed above in detail.
2. Representations of the Cypriote "Geryon-type" of helmet[155].

The Geryon-type of helmet is a special Cypriote helmet type without actual finds named here by the present author after its connection with the traditional representations of Geryon (*Ill. 2*). The main feature of this type of helmet is not the shape (because I think it had a conical and a crested version as well), but the characteristic skull-piece of the helmet, which like the Corinthian type covered the head entirely, the nose-guard and the almost horizontal cheek-pieces. There are at least two possibilities for the origin of this type of helmet. The first possibility as has been mentioned is the evolution of the Cypriote pointed helmet with a tubular point bulging like a knob (see above and *Ill. 2*). The second possibility is that this type of helmet is the local version of the "covered face Greek helmets" (the Corinthian, its Cretan version[156] and the Ionian helmet). As the Geryon-type of helmet has a local development in Cyprus, the first suggestion seems more probable under the undoubted influence of the "covered face" Greek helmets. There were at least two phases in the evolution of the Geryon-type of helmet.

1. In the first phase the helmet consisted of a pointed skull-piece which entirely covered the head (and the ears as well). It had a prominent nose-guard, and a pair of almost horizontal cheek-pieces. On the terracotta representations of this phase there are some indications that the cheek-piece was detachable, or was made of other material (?). Unfortunately all the examples of this phase have a broken top, so we can only assume that they have a pointed top (as later changed probably for a crested one). This phase has its closest parallel or even predecessor in the terracotta representation of a warrior[157] wearing tubular pointed helmet with nose-guard and long curving earflaps forming a cheek-piece mentioned above (*Ill. 4, no. M.2.5*). In this phase there were additional elements which may be connected with the helmet: a wide (bronze) collar and a rectangular backplate which covered the neck of the warrior. There are three representations of the first phase of the Geryon-type of helmet so far known:

    1. Geryon terracotta, Pyrgia[158]
    2. Terracotta warrior, Tamassos[159]
    3. Terracotta chariot warrior, "Cyprus"[160]

2. In the second phase of evolution the skull-piece of the helmet covered the neck much more, the helmet consequently lost the collar and the neckplate as well. On representations of this phase it is quite clear that the horizontal cheek-pieces are now of solid construction, without any sign of "detachability". This might be the result of the much more likely influence of the Greek "covered face" helmets at this phase. Since almost all the representations of this phase are from Salamis, it might be a local version as well:

    1. Terracotta archer, Salamis[161]
    2. Terracotta archer, Salamis[162]
    3. Terracotta archer, Salamis[163]
    4. Terracotta horseman, Salamis[164]
    5. Terracotta warrior drawing a sword from its scabbard, "Cyprus"[165]

---

[155] The first detailed study of this type, see **Tatton-Brown 1979**; **Pflug 1988b**, pp. 37-39.
[156] For the relation between the Corinthian and Cretan helmet types see the detailed study of H. Hoffmann (**Hoffmann 1972**, esp. pp. 1-2, notes 5-7).
[157] **Heuzey 1880**, fig. F.
[158] British Museum, 1917.7-1.13, H.: 24 cm; **Tatton-Brown 1979**, pl. XXXII, 670/660-600 B.C.
[159] **Pflug 1988b**, fig. 13.
[160] **Heuzey 1880**, fig. H.
[161] Sal.6471 = Tc. 2112; **Monloup 1984**, pp. 182-183, no. 663 (fig.), pl. 33.
[162] Sal. 3535 = Tc. 1038; **Monloup 1984**, p. 184, no. 665 (fig.), pl. 33.
[163] Sal. 4992 = Tc. 1839; **Monloup 1984**, p. 184, no. 666, pl. 33.
[164] Sal. 5022 = Tc. 1909; **Monloup 1984**, p. 184, no. 668 (fig.).

There is a further representation of a helmet of this phase but in this case with a high crest, which is different from the known crest types of Corinthian or Ionian helmets:

6. Terracotta warrior, Salamis[166]

As the cheek-pieces are not profiled (there are no eye and mouth cut-outs on the cheek-pieces at all) this type of helmet can not be connected with other known types of helmets (e.g. Tamassos-type, or the helmet of the Lindos earflaps). However the traditional (and always archaizing or orientalizing?) representations of Geryon outside Cyprus show a different and probably unknown type of crested helmet[167], which was interpreted as being between the Corinthian and Ionian helmets, but there is a definite mouth cutout on the cheek-pieces, no nose-guard at all, and the front piece of the helmet shows a different structure as if the cheek-pieces and the entire front part were added separately to the body of the helmet. These features (separately added face-part) distinguish this unknown type of helmet from the known types of Corinthian and Ionian helmets. There are two further, and probably later representations of this type of helmet from Cyprus[168]. The difference between these two helmets and their probably earlier versions mentioned above is that the nose-guard is entirely missing.

As V. Tatton-Brown assumed: *"Our helmets belong to a Cypriote group of "hybrid" metal helmets which combine a well-established type of cap with sophisticated and more protective features like the "Corinthian" cheekpieces and noseguard. It is improbable that any are earlier than the first half of the sixth century when Cyprus came into contact with Greece, since it is likely that the concept of providing total protection, but not all the individual elements like the hinges, was the result of Greek influence."*[169].

Our point of view differs only in placing more emphasis on local evolution[170], and less emphasis on the Greek (Corinthian type of helmet) influence. From the late 7th - early 6th centuries B.C. the Greek world became a *koine* in case of helmet types, on the periphery of which (Ionia and Anatolia, Cyprus, Crete) different features of the helmets (shape, shape of cheek-pieces [with or without cutouts], detachable or solid cheek-pieces, crest shapes) might vary freely[171].

---

165 Cesnola Collection, New York (MMA); **Myres 1914**, p. 157, no. 1049.

166 Sal. 4923 = Tc. 1840; **Monloup 1984**, p. 184, no. 663 (fig.), pl. 33.

167 See for example the Geryon scene on a bronze horse's pectorale from Samos, Museum Vathy, Inv. B.2518; last quarter of 7th century B.C.; **Brize 1985**, pls. 15-17, 20:1; **Pflug 1988b**, fig. 12; further examples are quoted by Ph. Brize: Geryon scene on an ivory plaque, Samos, Museum Vathy, Inv. E.127; **Brize 1985**, pl. 22:2; Kaineus scene on a bronze sheet, Olympia, Inv. BE.11a, **Brize 1985**, pl. 24:2. Furthermore see the Bronze statuette of Geryon: **de Chanot 1880**, pl. 22.

168 1. Kourion, Sanctuary of Apollo Hylates, terracotta chariot group, T.1700 (Philadelphia, U.M.?), H.: 19.5 cm; **Young - Young 1955**, pp. 55-56, no. 1055, pl. 60, "close to the seventh century B.C."; 2. "Cyprus", terracotta warrior with a crest fitted centrally across the hemispherical cap of the helmet, Pierides Foundation Museum, H.: 15.3 cm, **Karageorghis 1985**, p. 204, no. 199 (pl.), "Cypro-Archaic Period".

169 **Tatton-Brown 1979**, p. 284.

170 See the two terracotta warriors with pointed helmets: "Cyprus", terracotta statuette of a warrior, **Heuzey 1880**, fig. F; "Cyprus", terracotta statuette of a warrior, **Heuzey 1880**, fig. G.

171 For mouth cut-outs on Corinthian helmets see **Dawkins 1929**, pl. XVI, where several types of early Corinthian (?) helmets worn by Spartan warriors can be observed: early Corinthian (?) helmet with eye and mouth cut-out and separate neck-guard with two types of crests. **Dawkins 1929**, pl. CVIII shows a Spartan hoplite wearing an orientalizing high crested helmet with a crescent-shaped crest and an earflap with eye and mouth cut-outs (similar to those found on the Lindos Acropolis). A bronze statuette of a hoplite from Olympia (**Furtwängler 1890**, pp. 17-18, no. 41, pl. 7:41) shows an interesting helmet: the cap of the helmet was made a single piece of bronze and was furnished with a high crest curving forward. The lower part of the helmet originally was probably riveted to the cap and has eye and mouth cut-outs on the solid cheek-pieces. The whole shape of the helmet is similra to the Corinthian helmets, but its construction (and the cut-outs on the cheek-pieces) separates this piece from the canonical Corinthian helmets. However, there are early Corinthian helmets made of separate parts (two halves, or even a skull-piece made of two halves and riveted to the lower part of the helmet! Helmet from Torre di Satriano, Tomb 11, **Pflug 1988c**, pp. 71-72, fig. 7). The helmet type of the Lindos earflaps is belonged probably to the same level of unknown early Greek helmet variants. For other 7th century B.C. variants based probably on the Corinthian type of helmet or representing parallel developments influenced by the same principles as the Corinthian helmet, see fig. XX. Cf. **Benton 1939-1940**, p. 81.

MISCELLANEA

There are a few miscellaneous "helmets" or helmet parts, which have to be mentioned to provide a total review[172] of genuine Cypriote helmet types of the (8th-) 7th-6th centuries B.C.

Gjerstad reported two fragmentary helmet mountings from Idalion. The first of them is said to be from the back of a leather helmet[173], but it seems more likely that the piece (if it comes from a helmet at all) covered the side of a leather helmet and the hinges hold the earflap. The second fragment, a tubular spike[174] is similarly curious. There is no doubt it could be mounted on a hemispherical leather helmet, but we do not know a single representation of such a "composite" (leather and bronze) helmet so far. Furthermore the protection which this type of helmet could offer must have been very limited. There are two other bronze objects from Enkomi, Tomb 10, of Mycenaean Age, which are most probably helmets. One of them is a 42.5 cm high bronze helmet tapering in a long tubular point[175] which is a very good second half of 8th century B.C. Near Eastern and Cypriote form, but in spite of the total lack of evidence and representations for this type of helmet from the Mycenaean Period, the grave context secures its date to the 14th-13th century B.C. The problem is the same in case of the other piece[176] from the same grave and burial group[177], but this piece - a hemispherical bronze cap and tubular point with solid circular base fastened to the cap by two rivets - is more likely to be a shield boss, as the riveted construction of the point is unique on helmets, but well known on shields, where the smaller or bigger bosses were usually riveted to the wooden body of the shield.

There were three earflaps found in Idalion, two of which[178] undoubtedly belong to Anatolian composite iron and bronze helmets of radial construction known from Sardis and Old-Smyrna, and will be discussed later. A third, bronze earflap from Idalion[179] shows a different shape. It has a rounded point with a hole for the chin-strap. There are remains of hinges along the upper edge of the earflap, which would determine the helmet type to which it was attached. However there is not a single similar earflap known so far, and unfortunately there is not a single helmet type with which it can be connected. The relatively late, 5th century B.C. date[180] excludes it from the oriental tradition (if not of Persian origin) and connects this earflap to a local version of a classical or even hellenistic type of helmet.

CRETE

Praisos (Hamburg, Museum für Kunst und Gewerbe, Inv. no.: 1970.26c; H.: 44.6 cm, H. of the crest: 10 cm; W. of the crest at front: ca. 1.5 cm, at the sides: ca. 3 cm; mid-7th century B.C.)[181]
"Openfaced helmet with high crest rising vertically from the crown for 10 cm. and then curving forward (slightly less than half of the original arc is preserved). Somewhat less than half the helmet -

---

172 The Cypriote crested helmets of the period as not characteristic local versions, but obvious results of the oriental influence will be discussed in the next chapter together with the Praisos crested helmet.

173 "Mounting to a cap-shaped leather helmet with hinged neck cover; pierced by holes along the edge for attachment to the leather." (**Gjerstad 1948**, p. 140); **Gjerstad et al. 1935**, pl. CLXXIX:2; **Gjerstad 1948**, p. 140, fig. 24.

174 "Mounting to a nearly hemispherical leather helmet with tubular spike; pierced by triangularly placed holes for attachment to the leather." (**Gjerstad 1948**, p. 140); **Gjerstad et al. 1935**, p. 535, no. 130; **Gjerstad 1948**, p. 140, fig. 24.

175 Enkomi, Tomb 10, Burial Group IV, no. 299A, H.: 42.5 cm, Diam.: 22 x 26 cm; **Dikaios 1969**, pp. 364-365, 381, pls. 148:3, 211:40; **Catling 1964**, pp. 137-138, pl. 17a-b.

176 Enkomi, Tomb 10, Burial Group IV, no. 299, H.: 30.5 cm, Diam.: 20 cm; **Dikaios 1969**, pp. 364-365, 380-381, pl. 211:41; **Catling 1964**, pp. 137-138, pl. 17c-d.

177 This is quite unique to have two helmets in the same grave and grave group together. I would prefer the first suggestions, that this "helmet" was a conical shield boss - which would be a more appropriate explanation for finding the two pieces together. But this context: a pointed helmet with a pointed shield boss is known again from the late 8th - early 7th century Cyprus (Tamassos, Royal Tomb XI, **Buchholz 1978**, pp. 193-195, figs. 44a-c; for similar shield boss see e.g. **Gjerstad et al 1935**, pl. CLXXV, and the famous Amathus shield boss now in the British Museum.)

178 **Gjerstad 1935**, pl. CLXXVIII:14 (no. 505), 15 (no. 1071); **Gjerstad 1948**, pp. 132-133, fig. 20:8.

179 Idalion, 80/929/F618, West Terrace, Area C Loc. 009, L.: 14.1 cm, W.: 9.5 cm; **Waldbaum 1989**, pp. 334-336, pl. 1:25. Cypro-Classical Period.

180 **Waldbaum 1989**, pp. 334-336.

181 **Hoffmann 1972**, pp. 5-6, 42, pl. 13; **Dezső 1993**, p. 40.

one side of the crown and most of the crest - is preserved. The crest is of a two-piece box construction throughout, each of the halves forged in one with a half of the helmet. The overlapping seams are crimped and riveted together at intervals of 2.6 cm. (only two rivets preserved). The crown is shallow. ... The ribs on the sides of the crest continue onto the crown of the helmet for ca. 5 cm., one pair in front, two pairs in back (in both cases flanking the seam). The ribs on the right side have split open due to excess torsion. Two pairs of deeply chased horizontal lines spaced 2 cm. apart go around the helmet at forehead level. Between them traces of finely incised decoration (turrets?) are visible. There are no loops or other apparent provision for the fastening of a plume or horse tail."[182]

This high crested helmet was undoubtedly inspired by oriental crested helmets. Its Assyrian archetypes can be dated to the middle, or third quarter of the 8th century B.C.[183].

The evolution of Near Eastern and Aegean/Eastern Mediterranean crested helmets[184]

The earliest known crested helmets of the Iron Age are those shown on the sculptures of Carchemish (*Ill. 5, nos. O.2.1-4*)[185]. The reliefs depicting crested helmets are from the reign of Katuwash (ca. 900-873 B.C.)[186], king of Carchemish, a contemporary of Ashur-nasir-pal II (883-859 B.C.). Their characteristics are the almost conical shape with a small crest at the top decorated with tassels dangling on the back, and three horizontal ribs around the base (*Ill. 5, nos. O.2.1-2*). There are no horizontal ribs on the third helmet, but on the front of it appears the small projection (a boss or knob - maybe a horn) characteristic of so many of the Carchemish helmets (*Ill. 5, no. O.2.3*). The fourth helmet (*Ill. 5, no. O.2.4*) shows the first signs of the later development of conical crested helmets with its point curving forward ("Phrygian shape"). The shape (almost conical) and construction of helmets (small crest at the top and tassels on the back) depicted on the sculptures follow the tradition of Late Bronze Age Hittite and North Syrian helmets known from the sculptures of the "King's Gate" at Bogazköy[187] and from Egyptian wall-paintings depicting Syrians, e.g. from the Tomb of Amenmose at Thebes[188]. This Late Bronze Age Hittite - North Syrian helmet tradition reached Mesopotamia through North Syrian Neo-Hittite states (e.g. Carchemish) in the second half of the 9th century B.C. The same "Carchemish-type" of crested helmet is shown on a similar orthostat slab from Kültepe(?) from the 9th century B.C. (*Ill. 5, no. O.2.5*)[189]. The difference between that piece and those on the Carchemish reliefs is that the Kültepe helmet has two projections (bosses) on the front, and its crest is on the back of the helmet. What may be variants of the "Carchemish-type" of crested helmet appear on the early 8th century B.C. Zinçirli orthostat reliefs (*Ill. 5, nos. O.2.6-7*).

This type of crested helmet would have been not only the predecessor of the Mesopotamian (Assyrian) crested helmets, but it was also widespread in late 9th - early 8th century B.C. Urartu, and from North Syria influenced the development of helmets in the East Mediterranean (apparently during the decline in the Dark Age), (e.g. Crete: bronze belts from Fortetsa: *Ill. 5, nos. M.3.1-2*[190]; Kavousi: *Ill. 5, no. M.3.5*[191]; Kato-Symi: *Ill. 5, no. M.3.3*[192]). However, there are four helmets illustrated on the

---

182 **Hoffmann 1972**, pp. 5-6.
183 Tiglath-Pileser III (745-727 B.C.): Chart 2, nos. O.2.17-18, 20 (**Dezsö 1993**, Chart 2, nos. 149, 150, 152); Sargon II (721-705 B.C.): Chart 2, nos. O.2.35-36 (**Dezsö 1993**, Chart 2, nos. 201-202).
184 This chapter is based on my previous studies on Iron Age helmets of the Near East (**Dezsö 1993**, pp. 17-34). The detailed study of the evolution of Near Eastern crested helmets is important for the understanding of the oriental influence exerted on the Aegean/Eastern Mediterranean crested helmet tradition in two phases: 1. North-Syrian crested helmets (9th - first half of 8th century B.C.); 2. Assyrian crested helmets (second half of 8th century - 7th century B.C.).
185 **Hogarth 1914**, pls. B.2a, B.2b; **Woolley 1921**, B.26c; **Woolley - Barnett 1952**, pls. B.44, B.45, B.46.
186 **Woolley - Barnett 1952**, p. 245; **Orthmann 1971**, pp. 29ff.; **Hawkins 1976-1980**, pp. 439-441.
187 **Akurgal 1962**, p. 98, pls. 64-65.
188 **de G. Davies 1933**, p. 29, pls. XXXIV-XXXV.
189 **Bittel 1976**, fig. 321.
190 Iraklion, Archaeological Museum, Inv. nos. 1568, 1569; **Brock 1957**, pls. 115-116; **Borchhardt 1972**, pl. 25:5.
191 **Boyd 1901**, pp. 147-148, figs. 10-11; **Kunze 1931**, p. 218, fig. 31, pl. 56e.
192 **Lempesi 1985**, pl. 57, G4.

two "belts" from Fortetsa. These four helmets represent three helmet types the joint appearance of which is anachronistic or at least difficult to explain. Namely, two of the four helmets represent the Carchemish-type of crested helmet mentioned above (reign of Katuwash, ca. 900-873 B.C.; *Ill. 5, nos. M.3.1-2*); the third helmet is an "Urartian-type" of hemispherical crested helmet known from the second half of the 9th century B.C. in Urartu and at Hasanlu. It disappeared in the early 8th century B.C. (Hasanlu)[193]; the fourth helmet however is a beautiful example of the developed North Syrian and Assyrian conical crested helmet (known from Urartu as well), (*Ill. 5, no. M.4.1*). This type of helmet appeared in the last quarter of the 9th century - early 8th century B.C.[194]. While the first and second types appear together only in the middle of the 9th century B.C., the second and third occur together only at the end of the 9th - beginning of the 8th centuries B.C. So the four helmets on the two belts (dated to the second half of the 8th century B.C.) represent more than a hundred years (from early 9th century B.C. to the early 8th century B.C.) of the evolution of North Syrian conical crested helmets and the hemispherical crested helmets. Consequently these three helmet-types mentioned above 1.) would have been depicted as a "wandering motif" from a set of stereotyped motifs; 2.) or in 8th century B.C. Crete (and Eastern Mediterranean) there were archaizing helmets in use; 3.) or we are forced to raise the date of the Fortetsa belts from the second half of the 8th century B.C. to the first half or early 8th century B.C. (of course without any effect on the dating of the tombs in which they were found)[195]. This problem appears on a smaller scale on the Kavousi bronze sheet, where an already developed version of a North Syrian and Assyrian conical crested helmet (*Ill. 5, no. M.4.2*)[196] appears together with a Carchemish type of crested helmet (*Ill. 5, no. M.3.5*)[197].

On contemporary early 9th century B.C. palace reliefs of Ashur-nasir-pal II (883-859 B.C.) there are no representations of crested helmets at all. The first appearance of crested helmets in Neo-Assyrian art is on the Balawat gates of Shalmaneser III (858-824 B.C.) worn by soldiers identified as Urartian troops and as the troops of Sangara of Carchemish[198]. However, this type of hemispherical crested helmet with its round (hemispherical) cap (with or without earflaps) and with a crest fitted centrally across the top differs from the conical type of crested helmet of the Carchemish tradition. This hemispherical type of crested helmet originated in 14th century B.C. Transcaucasia[199] and it was widespread in the territories north of Mesopotamia (North-West Iran, Transcaucasia, Urartu and for a short period North Syria as well). Several representations of this type of helmet are known (first of all from Urartu or from other territories showing Urartian warriors) from the second half of the 9th century B.C.[200]. There are at least five examples of this type excavated at Hasanlu (Level IVB, Iron II Period, ca. 800 B.C.[201] These helmets or rather the Zinçirli chariot relief (dated to the first half of the 8th century B.C.[202]) could have been the latest examples of the hemispherical type of crested helmets. But, as has already been mentioned, from the Balawat Gates of Shalmaneser III it is known that soldiers, said to be troops of Sangara, king of Carchemish (ca. 873-850 B.C.), sometimes wore this

---

193 Brock 1957, pl. 115; Borchhardt 1972, p. 70, Kat. 15 II 2; Dezsö 1993, Chart 2, no. 118.
194 Assyrian: Munich, Prähistorische Staatssammlung, PS 1979/1181; Dezsö 1993, Cat. no. 9, Group no. A.3.2, pp. 17, 21-22, 111, pls. 16-17; Karlsruhe, Badisches Landesmuseum, Inv. no. 89/12; Dezsö 1993, Cat. no. 10, Group no. A.3.3, pp. 17, 22-24, 111-112, pls. 18-20; Urartian: Mainz, Römisch-Germanisches Zentralmuseum, O 39702; Dezsö 1993, Cat. no. 53, Group no. U.1, pp. 17, 51-52, 134, pls. 77-78.
195 The tomb was continuously used from Late Protogeometric to Orientalizing Period (850-630 B.C.); Brock 1957, p. 101.
196 Boyd 1901, pp. 147-148, figs. 10-11; Kunze 1931, p. 218, fig. 31, pl. 56e.
197 Boyd 1901, pp. 147-148, figs. 10-11; Kunze 1931, p. 218, fig. 31, pl. 56e.
198 King 1915, pls. 3-4, 7, 9-12, 37-42; de Schauensee 1988, p. 55.
199 Ltshashen: Dezsö 1993, Chart 1, nos. 46-49; Lori-Berd: Dezsö 1993, Chart 1, nos. 50-51; Shirakavan: Dezsö 1993, Chart 1, no. 52.
200 On Nimrud ivories (Dezsö 1993, Chart 2, no. 109); Balawat gates (Dezsö 1993, Chart 2, nos. 110-113); on a bronze statuette of a warrior from Khurvin (Iran): Dezsö 1993, Chart 2, no. 53 (Vanden Berghe 1959, p. 124, pls. 156b-c); on a horse's breastplate from Urartu - NW Iran (Dezsö 1993, Chart 2, nos. 114-115); bronze statuettes from Toprak-Kale (Dezsö 1993, Chart 2, no. 116); bronze statuette of a warrior from Marash (Dezsö 1993, Chart 2, no. 117); Zinçirli relief (first half of 8th century B.C., Dezsö 1993, Chart 2, no. 130).
201 Dezsö 1993, Cat. nos. 48-52, Group nos. H.2.1-H.2.5, pp. 46-50, 131-134, pls. 68-76.
202 Dezsö 1993, Chart 2, no. 130; von Luschan et al. 1902, fig. 102, pl. XXXIX; Maxwell-Hyslop 1959, pl. III; Orthmann 1971, p. 538, pl. 57a.

type.[203] If so, there was a change in the helmet tradition of Carchemish under Sangara. The early 9th century B.C. conical crested helmets of the sculptures of Katuwash (ca. 900-873 B.C.) were, possibly under Urartian influence, replaced with this hemispherical type of crested helmet, known from Hasanlu[204] or most probably the two types of helmet were used together. The short history of the hemispherical crested helmet in North Syria did not have any effect on the flourishing North Syrian conical crested helmet tradition. Finally this hemispherical type of crested helmet was replaced in Urartu by conical/pointed helmets coming from Assyria[205], and by conical crested helmets spreading from North Syria in the late 9th century B.C.[206]

The place of the development of later conical crested helmets - originating from the Late Bronze Age and early 9th century B.C. Carchemish crested helmets - is not likely to have been confined to Carchemish. Other North Syrian states also possibly played an important role in the evolution of the conical type of crested helmets. On the basalt sculptures of Karatepe[207] there are local warriors wearing this type of crested helmet fighting with Assyrian(?) soldiers wearing pointed helmets. These crested helmets (*Ill. 5, nos. O.2.20-23*) may be traced back to the Late Bronze Age helmet tradition from which the Carchemish helmets are also derived, and are late examples of the same North Syrian helmet tradition to which the Carchemish helmets (*Ill. 5, nos. O.2.1-4*) also belonged. Their shape is similar to two half a century earlier Assyrian[208] and to an Urartian crested helmet[209] inscribed with the name of Ishpuini (ca. 830-810 B.C.). Karatepe was probably one of the Neo-Hittite states which transmitted the early conical crested helmet tradition to Assyria. The earliest representation of the developed version of this type of helmet is shown on an Urartian wall-painting from Erebuni, on which possibly the Urartian king, Argishti I (789-766 B.C.) himself wears the helmet[210]. This helmet is very similar to the conical crested helmet of Ishpuini, king of Urartu mentioned above. This type of crested helmet remained in use in Urartu through the 8th-7th centuries B.C.[211] or even in the 6th-5th centuries B.C. as well[212].

The first appearance of crested helmets in the Assyrian army is on the palace-reliefs of Tiglath-Pileser III (745-727 B.C.). Unfortunately between the reigns of Shalmaneser III (858-824 B.C.) and Tiglath-Pileser III there are no Assyrian representations available. Only the two crested helmets, the Munich[213] and Karlsruhe[214] crested helmets, said to be found in Urartu (Eastern Anatolia), but

---

203 **King 1915**, pl. 42; **de Schauensee 1988**, p. 55.

204 See note 82.

205 The earliest known Urartian examples are inscribed with the name of Ishpuini, king of Urartu (ca. 830-810 B.C.): London, BM 135061 (**Barnett - Curtis 1973**, pp. 133, 136; **Frankel 1979**, p. 20, fig. 12; **Vanden Berghe - De Meyer 1982**, p. 128, no. 17 (fig.); **Dezsö 1993**, Cat. no. 57, Group no. U.4.1, pl. 83); Mainz, Römisch-Germanisches Zentralmuseum (2 examples) (**Kellner 1980**, p. 205, pl. 1; **Egg 1984**, pp. 618, 621, 649, fig. 39; **Dezsö 1993**, Cat. nos. 58-59, Group nos. U.4.2-U.4.3, pls. 84-85.

206 The earliest known Urartian conical crested helmet inscribed with name of Ishpuini, king of Urartu (ca. 830-810 B.C.): Mainz, Römisch-Germanisches Zentralmuseum, O 39702; **Vanden Berghe - De Meyer 1982**, p. 132, no. 24 (fig.); **Yesaian 1986**, p. 23, pl. 13:9; **Maass 1987**, p. 69, note 22; **Pflug 1988a**, pp. 23-24, note 74, fig. 11; **Egg - Waurick 1990**, pl. 7; **Dezsö - Curtis 1991**, pp. 114-121, pl. 19; **Dezsö 1993**, Cat. no. 53, Group no. U.1, pp. 17, 51-52, 134, pls. 77-78.

207 The dating of the Karatepe sculptures is questionnable. Th. Bossert (**Bossert et al. 1950**, p. 62) dated them to the reign of Tiglath-Pileser III (745-727 B.C.). On the other hand D. Ussishkin (**Ussishkin 1969**, pp. 121-137) proposed a middle of 9th century B.C. date. For detailed description of the problem see **Ussishkin 1969**. Following **Orthmann 1971**, the present writer follows a first half of 8th century - middle of 8th century B.C. date.

208 1. Munich, Prähistorische Staatssammlung, PS 1979/1181; **Dezsö 1993**, Cat. no. 9, Group no. A.3.2, pp. 17, 21-22, 111, pls. 16-17; 2. Karlsruhe, Badisches Landesmuseum, Inv. no. 89/12; **Dezsö 1993**, Cat. no. 10, Group no. A.3.3, pp. 17, 22-24, 111-112, pls. 18-20.

209 Mainz, Römisch-Germanisches Zentralmuseum, O 39702; **Vanden Berghe - De Meyer 1982**, p. 132, no. 24 (fig.); **Yesaian 1986**, p. 23, pl. 13:9; **Maass 1987**, p. 69, note 22; **Pflug 1988a**, pp. 23-24, note 74, fig. 11; **Egg - Waurick 1990**, pl. 7; **Dezsö - Curtis 1991**, pp. 114-121, pl. 19; **Dezsö 1993**, Cat. no. 53, Group no. U.1, pp. 17, 51-52, 134, pls. 77-78.

210 **Hodjash et al. 1979**, pls. 40, 46; **Yesaian 1986**, pl. 9:9.

211 Paravakar: Chart 2, nos. 123-126, **Yesaian 1976**, figs. 148:1-3, 149:2; **Yesaian 1986**, pls. 2:1-2, 2:4, 9:10-12.

212 For example the helmets of the bronze statuettes from Ayrum (Armenia) dated to the 6th-5th centuries B.C.: **Yesaian 1976**, fig. 146:3; **Yesaian 1986**, pls. 2:3, 9:14.

213 Munich, Prähistorische Staatssammlung, PS 1979/1181; **Kellner 1980**, pp. 212-213, pls. 15-16; **Pflug 1988a**, p. 24, note 75;

attributed by the present author to Assyria[215], show that this type of crested helmet should have appeared in Assyria by at least the last quarter of the 9th century B.C. However, there is a 50 year gap which cannot be filled, between these helmets and the first Assyrian representations of the type on the sculptures of Tiglath-Pileser III, on which there are at least 15 developed forms of crested helmets (*Ill. 5, nos. O.2.8-18*[216]). A special type of crested helmet (with pointed crest-support and crescent-shaped crest) visible on the Til-Barsip wall-paintings (*Ill. 5, no. O.2.19*) has its best parallels on the palace-reliefs of Tiglath-pileser III (*Ill. 5, nos. O.2.17-18*) and together with an example of this type now in the British Museum[217] can be dated to that period.

As is shown on Assyrian sculptures, crested helmets are always worn by spearmen carrying round shields and wearing breastplates (*kardio phylakes*). Not only the Assyrian light infantry, or troops said to be North Syrian allies or associated with Anatolian[218] or Phrygian[219] auxiliaries of the Assyrian army, but also their enemies, recruited when defeated as auxiliary units, wore crested helmets[220]. But, while at the end of the 9th century B.C. - first half of 8th century B.C. the crested helmet indicated the nationality of its wearer (Syrian, Anatolian or Phrygian troops), later, from the reign and army reform of Tiglath-Pileser III (745-727 B.C.) it simply indicated/demonstrated membership of a special service, the light infantry of the Assyrian "new model imperial army". The Assyrian horsemen, charioteers and chariot warriors, and even the heavy infantry always wore conical/pointed helmets. From that time soldiers of any nationality could be recruited to the light infantry, the auxiliary units of the Assyrian army. This is the reason why the fragments of the Nimrud crested iron helmet[221] from the last quarter of the 8th century B.C. can be identified as Assyrian helmets.

After the reign of Tiglath-Pileser III (745-727 B.C.) the types and forms of crested helmets became standardized, and in the reigns of Sargon II (721-705 B.C.) and Sennacherib (705-681 B.C.) only variants of two major types remained in use: 1. with crest curving forward (*Ill. 5, nos. O.2.24-25, O.2.27-29; O.2.34-41*); 2. with a crescent-shaped crest on the top of a pointed crest support (*Ill. 5, nos. O.2.26; O.2.30-33*). In the reign of Sennacherib the earflaps became permanent parts of the helmets. Representations of the two major types of crested helmets mentioned above are known not only from Assyria[222] and elsewhere in the Near East, but also from the Eastern Mediterranean under strong Oriental/Assyrian influence from the middle of the 8th century B.C. through the 7th century B.C. The best example of the first type (crest curving forward) is the orientalizing helmet from Praisos. Several representations of such helmets are known from the Aegean/Eastern Mediterranean[223] (e.g. *Ill. 5, no.*

Calmeyer 1991a, no. 10, pl. 10; Dezső - Curtis 1991, pp. 114-121, pl. 17; Dezső 1993, Cat. no. 9, Group no. A.3.2, pp. 17, 21-22, 111, pls. 16-17.

214 Karlsruhe, Badisches Landesmuseum, Inv. no. 89/12; Kellner 1980, pp. 211-212, pls. 13-14; Gröschel 1986, p. 74, notes 229-233; Maass 1987, pp. 65-71, pls. 1:2, 2, 3; Maass 1988, p. 170, no. 97, fig. 97; Pflug 1988a, p. 24, note 75; Maass 1989, p. 195; Dezső - Curtis 1991, pp. 114-121, pl. 18; Dezső 1993, Cat. no. 10, Group no. A.3.3, pp. 17, 22-24, 111-112, pls. 18-20.

215 H.-J. Kellner, who published the Karlsruhe helmet (Dezső 1993, Cat. no. 10) first, attributed it to Urartu, and considered its decoration (regarded by the present writer as Assyrian) as "orientalisches Gemeingut auf in stark assyrierender Ausprägung" (Kellner 1980, p. 212). S.-G. Gröschel (Gröschel 1986, p. 74, notes 229-233) and M. Maass (Maass 1987, p. 68) considered the helmet Assyrian. Dezső 1993, p. 19.

216 11 Assyrian helmets (Chart 2, nos. O.2.8-18) and 4 different helmets depicted as worn by the enemies of Assyria (Dezső 1993, Chart 2, nos. 158-161).

217 London, British Museum, Walters's no. 2841; Walters 1899, p. 349, cat. no. 2841; British Museum 1929, pp. 77, 79, fig. 69, no. 229; Pflug 1988a, pp. 19-20, fig. 9, note 43; Dezső 1993, Cat. no. 11, Group no. A.3.4, pp. 19, 24-25, 112, fig. 3, pl. 21.

218 Barnett - Falkner 1962, p. xix, pls. XXXVI, XXXVIII, p. xxiii, pl. LI.

219 Barnett - Falkner 1962, p. xxiii, pl. LII.

220 Barnett - Falkner 1962, pp. xix-xx, fig. 2:1, pl. XLI (Eastern campaign of Tiglath-Pileser III, 2nd and 9th palu); pp. xx-xxiv, fig. 2:2, pl. LI (Anatolian [Phrygian?] campaign of Tiglath-Pileser III, 3rd palu); pp. xxii-xxiv, fig. 2:13, pl. LXV (Urartian warrior?), (Urartian campaign of Tiglath-Pileser III, 3rd palu) and pl. LXI.

221 London, British Museum, WA 48-11-4, 113-115; Dezső - Curtis 1991, pp. 105-122, figs. 1-20; Dezső 1993, Cat. nos. 12-27, Group nos. A.4.1-A.4.16, pp. 20, 25-33, 113-120, pls. 22-40.

222 First type: Assyrian helmet crest from Lacish (destruction level III, 701 B.C.): Tuffnell et al. 1953, p. 387, pl. 39:1-2; Wright 1958, p. 165, fig. 119; Ussishkin 1982, p. 57, fig. 49; Dezső 1993, Cat. no. 8, Group no. A.3.1, pp. 20-21, 110, pl. 15; Munich Assyrian crested helmet (see note 92); Karlsruhe Assyrian crested helmet (see note 93). Second type: London Assyrian crested helmet (see note 95).

M.4.2, see below). A well known example of the second type (crescent-shaped crest) is the Argos crested helmet of the Geometric Period[224], see below. In the reigns of Esarhaddon (680-669 B.C.) and Ashurbanipal (668-669 B.C.) the crested helmets became uniform (*Ill. 5, nos. O.2.42, O.2.43-48*) and for the first time in the history of Assyrian helmet representations the continuous arcs (semicircles) framing a scene of figures appeared on the front (*Ill. 5, no. O.2.46*) and on the back (*Ill. 5, no. O.2.48*) of the crested helmets. Previously it was an exclusive characteristic of conical/pointed helmets. This change was the last step in standardization of the Assyrian army, soldiers of which - at least in their uniform - finally lost the remains of their national characteristics. In spite of the only and late representation of this feature on the front of a crested helmet mentioned above, there are other examples proving its use on crested helmets. One of them is the late 9th - early 8th century B.C. Munich Asssyrian crested helmet with two curves and a vertical rib on the front. Its date is so early that the decorative system of crested helmets was not yet developed. The second example is one of the Nimrud iron helmet fragments[225] showing continuous arcs on the front of a possibly crested helmet, presumably from the last quarter of the 8th century B.C., when the standardization of Assyrian army equipment was undertaken.

The original or actual crests made of perishable materials (feathers, horsehair) and fastened between the bronze or iron crest-pieces by rivets[226] or similar methods have disappeared from helmets. The original function of horsehair or feather crests and plumes of the Late Bronze Age might have been to threaten the enemy with the help of becoming similar to a wild animal (bull, horse, etc.). Another original function of the crests on helmets might be the apotropaic function, which would be very appropriate on a helmet.

In the Assyrian imperial army of the second half of the 8th century B.C. (Tiglath-Pileser III) however, the crests of crested helmets might have had a new function, which can be connected to the uniformization (crested helmets = light infantry) of the "new model Assyrian army" and the standardization of its weaponry and helmets (reign of Sargon II and Sennacherib, see above): the different shapes of crested helmets, or at least the colour of their crests might indicate that their wearers belonged to certain units of the arm of light infantry. This might be the case with the crests of the horse trappings which are often visible on Assyrian palace reliefs, and which might demonstrate the different cavalry and chariot units of the Assyrian army.

Unfortunately there are only a few representations of crests in Assyrian art from which the colours can be reconstructed. On one of the palace reliefs of Sargon II (721-705 B.C.) from Khorsabad the red and blue paint of the feathers (or horsehair plumes) of a crested helmet remained visible at the time of the excavations[227]. The same colours appeared on three other slabs representing the red and blue crests of horsetrappings[228]. Another variant of crest decoration is known from the horses' crests on the Til-Barsip wall-paintings[229]: the characteristic black and white chequered motif which might be considered a local, North Syrian variant as it appears in the bronze inlay decoration of the Zinçirli conical iron helmet fragments[230].

As can be seen (*Ill. 4*), there were at least two phases in the influence exerted by the Near Eastern helmet tradition on the Mediterranean helmet tradition:

---

223 On modells and pendants: **Hoffmann 1972**, pl. 41; the incised representation of this kind of helmet can be seen on a "faceplate" attached secondarily to the helmet mentioned above.

224 Argos, Tomb 45, Argos, Archaeological Museum, H.: 48 cm; second half - last third of 8th century B.C.; **Borchhardt 1972**, p. 65, Kat. 13 I, pls. 33:1-3; **Pflug 1988a**, pp. 12-14, figs. 1-3.

225 **Dezsö - Curtis 1991**, pp. 105-122, no. 1, figs. 1, 16, 18; **Dezsö 1993**, Cat. no. 12, Group no. A.4.1, pp. 25-28, 113, figs. 4-6, pls. 22, 36, 38.

226 Holes for fastening the crest between crest-pieces of metal are visible around the edges of crestpieces of all the crested helmets: **Dezsö 1993**, Cat. nos. 8-11, 48, 51-52, 53, 116.

227 **Botta - Flandin 1849**, pl. 61.

228 **Botta - Flandin 1849**, pls. 62, 63, 65.

229 **Thureau-Dangin - Dunand 1936**, pl. LIII.

230 Zincirli, North Palace, Inv. no.: S.3964; **von Luschan - Andrae 1943**, pp. 76-79, 163, fig. 88, pl. 41; **Barnett 1953**, p. 102; **Borchhardt 1972**, p. 100, Kat. 22 B I 3; **Overlaet 1979**, p. 54, note 7, p. 55; **Curtis 1979**, vol. I, pp. 182-183; **Özgen 1982**, pp. 20, 52 note 5; **Dezsö - Curtis 1991**, pp. 124-125, fig. 22; **Dezsö 1993**, Cat. no. 28, Group no. NS.1, pp. 34-35, pls. 41-42.

1. The influence of the independent North Syrian ("Carchemish-type" and connecting) conical crested helmets[231].
   Second half of 9th century - early 8th century B.C.
   From: North Syria (Carchemish: *Ill. 5, nos. O.2.1-4*; Kültepe(?): *Ill. 5, no. O.2.5*; Zinçirli: *Ill. 5, nos. O.2.6-7*; and probably Karatepe: *Ill. 5, nos. O.2.20-23*)
   To: (almost exclusively to) Crete (Fortetsa: *Ill. 5, M.3.1-2, M.4.1*; Kato-Symi: *Ill. 5, no. M.3.3*; Khaniale Tekke: *Ill. 5, no. M.3.4*; Kavousi: *Ill. 5, no. M.3.5*)[232]

2a. The influence of the Syro-Assyrian or Assyrian conical crested helmets.
   Second half of 8th century - 7th century B.C.
   From: the Assyrian Empire (already including North Syria). Assyrian palace reliefs: Kalhu (Nimrud), reign of Tiglath-Pileser III (745-727 B.C.): *Ill. 5, nos. O.2.8-18*; Dur-Sharrukin (Khorsabad), reign of Sargon II (721-705 B.C.): *Ill. 5, nos. O.2.24-29*; Ninua (Nineveh), reign of Sennacherib (704-681 B.C.): *Ill. 5, nos. O.2.30-41*; reign of Esarhaddon (680-669 B.C.): *Ill. 5, no. O.2.42*; reign of Assurbanipal (668-627 B.C.): *Ill. 5, no. O.2.43-48*;
   Til-Barsip wall-paintings (Tiglath-Pileser III): *Ill. 5, no. O.2.19*
   To: Cyprus, Greece (islands and mainland), Western Anatolia: *Ill. 5, group M.4* (conical/pointed helmets with crest curving forward); *Ill. 5, group M.5* (conical/pointed helmets with unstilted crest curving forward); *Ill. 5, group M.6* (conical/pointed helmets with crescent-shaped crest).

2b. The influence of Assyrian conical/pointed helmets
   9th - 7th century B.C. (especially second half of 8th century - 7th century B.C.) (parallely with the Near Eastern spread of the helmet type)
   From: Assyria (later from the Assyrian Empire)[233].
   To: Eastern Mediterranean (*Ill. 5, group M.2*).

As can be seen, the first "wave of orientalization" reached Crete probably in the early 8th century B.C. The only evidence for the spread of Near Eastern helmet types in Crete - the pictorial representations of helmets on sheet metalwork - raises the question, whether these representations refer to the actual spread or use of Near Eastern helmet types only in this part of the Eastern Mediterranean and nowhere else, or just simply refer to a kind of artistic connection, the existence of a kind of Near Eastern, let us say North Syrian, artistic tradition in Crete in the first half or middle of the 8th century B.C. If these Near Eastern helmets were used on Crete in the 8th century B.C. - well out of the date of their Near Eastern use - it was a kind of archaizing helmet tradition[234]. However, therefore it is

---

[231] The origin of Mediterranean hemispherical crested helmets (hemispherical cap with a crest fitted centrally across the cap), (Chart 1, group M.7) is questionnable. As have been mentioned this type of helmets had a short life in North Syria (see above). The single early representation on the Fortetsa "belt" might be the result of this influence (**Brock 1957**, pl. 115; **Borchhardt 1972**, p. 70, Kat. 15 II 2; **Dezsö 1993**, Chart 2, no. 118.). But the fitting of a crest to a hemispherical cap might be a local feature as well. There is no reason to see for example Near Eastern (let us say Urartian) influence in the crest structure of the corinthian helmets furnished with this kind of crest. It might be for example a variant of the helmets with crescent-shaped crest without crest holder. The contemporary diversity of the early Mediterranean (Greek) helmet types is shown for example on the Mykonos relief pithos: helmets with high, forward curving crest (Chart 2, nos. M.4.3-4); their crest variants, the hemispherical crested helmets (Chart 2, nos. M.7.1-2); and probably an early variant of the helmet type, which survived almost exclusively in Corinthian helmets ("covered face tradition" originated from the oriental "open face tradition") (Chart 2, nos. M.8.1-2). For the early variants of the Greek "covered face tradition" see Fig. 10.

[232] It must be mentioned that - at least in its form - an almost similar type of helmet was used in the territories around the head of the Adriatic Sea from the late 8th century to the first half of the 7th century B.C. The exact origin of this Adriatic type is not known, but **Hencken 1972** (pp. 163-168, figs. 132-133) and **Egg 1988** (pp. 218-221, figs. 9-11) assumed, that this type was partly the result of Oriental influence, which spread indirectly via the Aegean. The geographically very limited use of it makes the origin of this type very curious.

[233] For the nearly hundred (mainly Assyrian) representations of the variants of this helmet type see **Dezsö 1993**, Chart 2. For detailed study see later.

much more probable that the connection between the Near East and Crete in the first half of 8th century existed only in the arts. But the level of artistic influence (these pieces, exclusively (sheet) metalwork 1. represent the actual presence of Near Eastern (North Syrian) craftsmen on Crete ("migration"); 2. represent the use of Near Eastern motifs (would have been depicted as "wandering motifs" from a set of stereotyped motifs, from "motif books" or wooden moulds used for sheet metalwork) on Crete; 3. or simply refers to Near Eastern trade contacts (in this case the metalwork was made in North Syria). The artistic connection may owe something to all three possibilities. In the present writers view this early phase of orientalization existed only in the "archaizing representations" of these helmets and not in the "archaizing - well out of the date of their Near Eastern - use" of them. There is no other type of evidence available for the existence of early (9th century B.C.) oriental helmet tradition in the Mediterranean, or especially on Crete. There is no sign that development of further helmet types originated in this early 8th century B.C. (and probably pictorial) Cretan helmet tradition. The two later helmets, the Fortetsa (*Ill. 5, no. M.4.1*) and Kavousi (*Ill. 5, no. M.4.2*) helmets, with a crest curving forward refer to the 8th century B.C. development of this helmet type (originated in the Carchemish and North Syrian conical crested helmet tradition, see above). These helmets would lower the date of the metalwork on which they were represented, but we know, that the evolution of this helmet type started in the late 9th - early 8th centuries B.C.[235]. It is possible that the evolution of the Eastern Mediterranean crested helmets started with this first stage of orientalization, but more probably that the helmet types of the 8th and 7th century B.C. Eastern Mediterranean originated in the influence of the complete set of Assyrian helmet variants, and consequently in the second (second half of 8th century B.C.) phase of orientalization.

The Praisos helmet represents a later phase of this evolution, the second phase of orientalization. Its best representational parallels are known mainly from Crete (open face helmets with high crestholder and neckguard): miniature votive bronze helmets from Gortyn (5 pieces) (*Ill. 5, no. M.5.2*); from Praisos (6 pieces) (*Ill. 5, nos. M.5.3*) and from Palaiokastro (*Ill. 5, no. M.5.4*). These votive helmets represent the same technique as the Praisos helmet, they were joined together from two similar halves. Further representational evidence is known from other media of Cretan art: from the incised decoration of a bronze corslet (*Ill. 5, no. M.4.7*), from a Late Orientalizing alabastron from Fortetsa (Sphinx, *Ill. 5, no. M.4.5*), from a Melian hydria from Rheneia (Sphinx, *Ill. 5, no. M.4.6*) and from an early orientalizing pithos from Knossos (*Ill. 5, no. M.5.18*). The recently discovered warrior stelai from Prinias (*Ill. 5, nos. M.4.8-13*) and a terracotta plaque of a warrior from Gortyn (*Ill. 5, no. M.4.14*) and a later bronze plaquette from the Geometric Period temple at Dreros, representing Athena (*Ill. 5, no. M.4.22*) show the same helmet type. All the representational evidence corresponds with the mid 7th century B.C. (second half of 7th century B.C.) date of the helmet. Snodgrass dated the use of this type, open faced crested helmet to the 7th century B.C., and emphasizes its primary Cretan distribution[236]. This or at least a very similar helmet type was known in the Greek Mainland and on the Greek Islands as well[237]. Its representations are known from a votive terracotta shield from Tiryns

---

234 For the chronological problems of the three different helmet types on the Fortetsa "belts" and the Kavousi bronze openwork see above. **Snodgrass 1964**, p. 12 wrote on the Kavousi bronze sheet that "it can perhaps be dated to the late eighth century, less by its provenance (a tholos of Late Geometric or Early Orientalizing date) than by its decorations". Furthermore he wrote on the Fortetsa girdle (**Snodgrass 1964**, p. 12): "which illustrates, along with helmets of Oriental type, a series of archers in what appear to be early Corinthian helmets, with cheek-pieces and ridge crest". The Cretan origin of the Corinthian helmets would be eliminated since the helmets mentioned above almost certainly represent the hemispherical crested helmets known from the Near East, second half of 9th - early 8th century B.C. date of which fits into the chronological framework of the Near Eastern helmets (**Dezső 1993**, pp. 47-48).

235 For example see the Munich, Karlsruhe and Mainz crested helmets mentioned above.

236 **Snodgrass 1964**, p. 17: "Its life seems to extend sporadically throughout the seventh century, but effectively it must be superseded by c. 650. From beginning to end Crete and the islands predominate in the distribution of the type, and it was retained there later than on the mainland."

237 This helmet type was in some way (perhaps because of its definite Oriental character) connected with the representations of sphinxes and Amazons, which themselves had some Oriental origins in the Greek world and mythology. **Snodgrass 1964**, p. 18 writes: "It is worth noticing the frequent association of this helmet with the Sphinx... This confirms the Oriental connections of the crest form, and also suggests, that the helmet had acquired semimythical associations, and might therefore be represented long after it was in actual use." As a unique helmet, one variant became the standard helmet of the early

(Amazonomacheia, *Ill. 5, nos. M.4.17-19*) and from a votive terracotta shield from Samos (Amazon, *Ill. 5, no. M.4.16*). A parallel helmet type without neckguard has the same distribution in the Greek Mainland and on the Greek Islands but this type is unknown on Crete. Its representations are known from a terracotta head from Amyklae, Sparta (*Ill. 5, no. M.4.20*), from a Lakonian Sub-Geometric sherd (Sphinx, *Ill. 5, no. M.4.15*), from a Theran rock carving (*Ill. 5, no. M.5.5*) and from the famous relief pithos from Mykonos (*Ill. 5, nos. M.4.3-4*). A similar helmet type, if not the same, is represented extensively in the bronzework of the Greek Mainland in the late 8th century and 7th century B.C. onwards. It can be seen with neckguard on a bronze statuette (*"Pferdeführer"*) from Olympia (*Ill. 5, no. M.5.12*) and on a bronze statuette now in New York (*Ill. 5, no. M.5.20*); without neckguard on a bronze statuette from Amorgos (*Ill. 5, no. M.5.15*), series of bronze statuettes from Olympia (*Ill. 5, nos. M.5.6-8, 13-14, 17*), from a bronze tripod leg from Olympia (*Ill. 5, no. M.5.21*), from a Samian bronze group (*Ill. 5, no. M.5.19*), from a Delphi bronze warrior (*Ill. 5, no. M.4.21*), from a bronze statuette of a warrior from the Acropolis, Athens (*Ill. 5, no. M.5.22*). One bronze handle attachment from Olympia shows this type of helmet without neckguard but furnished with elaborate earflaps covering parts of the face as well (*Ill. 5, no. M.5.24*). Another representation of a similar helmet on a bronze sheet - said to be Oriental in origin and in some details reworked in Greece - decorated in *repoussé* and incised figurative scenes, shows very similar helmets to the helmets of the 7th century B.C. Assyrian army (with small rounded earflaps, *Ill. 5, no. M.5.23*). The bronze sheet however is not an oriental work or at least not from the Assyrian Empire, since the helmets depicted on this sheet are worn by horsemen wearing scale armour as well. In the Assyrian army, however, horsemen never wore crested helmets only pointed ones, and the light infantry wearing crested helmets never wore scale armour, only small round breast plates (*kardio phylakes*). So the details of this bronze sheet are against the Near Eastern or at least the Assyrian tradition, and were probably made outside the Assyrian Empire, where such conventional details were not known. As can be seen later, the well known Greek Geometric helmet type with its characteristic earflaps and five piece construction[238] had two variants with a crest curving forward: the Ordona variant[239] with a hemispherical cap and a high crestholder curving forward and riveted onto the top of the helmet, and the conical variant with a small crest curving forward mounted onto the point of the helmet known from a miniature votive bronze helmet from Delos[240]. However, three bronze statuettes from Olympia (*Ill. 5, nos. M.5.9-11*) show a probable third variant of this type of Geometric Greek helmet with the characteristic earflaps, but with a high point probably curving forward[241].

These helmet representations show us a variety of technical differences as well: helmet with neckguard *versus* helmet without neckguard; helmet with earflaps *versus* helmet without earflaps; helmet made of a single piece of metal *versus* helmet with separately riveted crestholder; helmet with stilted crest *versus* helmet with unstilted crest. These technical differences vary almost from helmet to helmet and may refer to real (sometimes local) variants of helmets with crest curving forward or simply suggest technical variations in the execution of the same basic helmet type.

These were probably the local, Greek variants of the same Oriental helmet type, the helmet with a crest curving forward.

GREEK MAINLAND

As has already been mentioned there are three basic types of Late Geometric Greek helmets

---

representations of Athena (probably because of the "open face" tradition of representations of Greek deities - in most cases the face of an armoured Greek deity, i.e. Athena, has to be uncovered). As **Gröschel 1986**, pp. 71-78 has already pointed out, the idea of the figurative decoration of Athena's helmet in the Iliad (V, 743-744) can be found in the Near Eastern decorated helmet tradition. No doubt, the Near East, and especially the famous Assyria was far enough (several months of cruise) to become the home of certain semimythical elements in the Greek mythology and iconography.

238 And originated probably in Argos.
239 At least three examples from Italy.
240 **Deonna 1938**, p. 208, pl. 69:554.
241 So altogether there were at least five variants of the five-piece construction Geometric (Argive?) Greek helmet in use in the late 8th century B.C.: 1. pointed, 2. pointed with crescent-shaped crest, 3. pointed with a high point curving forward, 4. pointed with a small crest curving forward, 5. hemispherical cap with a high point curving forward. See later.

("*Kegelhelm*") made of five separate pieces (cap, front plate, back plate, and two pointed earflaps) known mainly from Argos, Olympia, and Italy (Ordona). The basic types are the same as the three basic helmet types of the Assyrian army in the 8th and 7th centuries B.C.[242]:

I. With pointed cap
II. With crescent-shaped crest
III. With crest curving forward
    A. With hemispherical cap and a separately added high crest curving forward
    B. With pointed cap and a separately added small crest curving forward
    C. With high pointed cap curving forward

Furtwängler[243], Kukahn[244] and Lorimer[245] proposed a Cypriote origin for this type of helmet ("*Kegelhelm*"). Courbin however located the origin of the type to the Argolid[246], while Kunze in 1938 claimed that it was a Greek form[247] and later suggested a Peloponnese-Argolid origin[248]. Müller-Karpe assumed[249] that the type is directly descended from the Bronze Age helmets of the type found at Knossos. He and Yalouris proposed a Greek origin for the crest types[250]. Similarly Borchhardt proposed that the *Kegelhelm* was an original Greek form[251]. Snodgrass however emphasized the parallels of this type of helmet on the Assyrian palace reliefs[252], and located the origin of the crest types in Assyria[253]. But, as he identified the Assyrian soldier on the Til-Barsip wall-paintings as an Anatolian soldier in charge of prisoners[254], he turned to Anatolia and Urartu: "*In view of the evidence at Karatepe and Carchemish for other types of conical helmet, it seems reasonable to conclude that Anatolia was the home of all these crested varieties, which perhaps have a common Bronze Age ancestor in the helmet of the Guardian of the Gate at Boghazköy. The likeliest medium for its transmission to the Iron Age will then be, not Assyria, but Urartu, where crested conical helmets are apparently characteristic in the ninth century. Assyria and Greece alike would be legatees independent of each other, and making different modifications: in this way the Greek type would become distinctive without being wholly original.*"[255] But as we have already seen, there is no evidence available for direct Anatolian influence, at least not in the helmet tradition. The transmitters were the North Syrian Neo-Hittite states, whose influence is known only in the first phase of orientalization (see above). The crescent-shaped crest for example <u>is not known</u> from <u>anywhere else</u> only from Assyrian art[256] (*Ill. 5, nos. O.2.16-18, 19*, reign of Tiglath-Pileser III [745-727 B.C.]), where it is always worn by soldiers of the Assyrian imperial army, in which - after the army reform of Tiglath-Pileser III - the equipment, especially the helmet of the soldier does not indicate any national origins, only the belonging of the soldier to an arm of the Assyrian Imperial army. On the Assyrian palace reliefs furthermore there is no any sign or evidence which would indicate that

---

242 For the crested helmets of the Assyrian army see Chart 2; for the pointed and crested helmets of the Assyrian army together see **Dezső 1993**, Chart 1.
243 **Furtwängler 1890**, p. 172.
244 **Kukahn 1936**, p. 14.
245 **Lorimer 1950**, p. 225, note 2.
246 **Courbin 1957**, p. 367.
247 **Kunze 1938a**, pp. 93-94.
248 **Kunze 1958**, pp. 123-124.
249 **Müller-Karpe 1962**, p. 272.
250 **Müller-Karpe 1962**, p. 272; **Yalouris 1960**, p. 60.
251 **Borchhardt 1972**, p. 64: "Die Helmmacher der assyrischen Armee setzten den herrkömmlichen Typen lediglich die Bügelkonstruktion auf.Die griechischen Waffenmeister dagegen Schufen einen neuen Helmtypus."
252 **Snodgrass 1964**, p. 14.
253 **Snodgrass 1964**, p. 194: "The two main types which stand up from the helmet (figure 1a-j) were both found to be closely linked to Assyria, in the eigth century at any rate; and although an ultimately Anatolian origin for these types is fairly likely, it was surely through Assyria that the Greeks acquired this new and conspicuous accoutrement ...".
254 **Snodgrass 1964**, p. 14.
255 **Snodgrass 1964**, p. 14.
256 Which is represented in the form of the Till-Barsip frescoes as well, dated to the reign of Tiglath-Pileser III (745-727 B.C.).

those soldiers wearing the helmets with crescent-shaped crest were definitely Anatolians. As has been mentioned before, the crested helmet as a phenomenon may be traced back to Late Bronze Age Anatolia and North-Syria[257], but the place of the evolution of Iron Age types was probably North-Syria and not Anatolia (see *Ill. 5*). The other problem is the role of Urartu. In Urartu, conical crested helmets were apparently not characteristic in the 9th century B.C. Urartian soldiers wore hemispherical crested helmets, as known from the bronze reliefs of the Balawat Gates of Shalmaneser III, king of Assyria (858-824 B.C.)[258]. In the last quarter of the 9th century B.C. Urartu started the new conical crested helmet tradition together with Assyria, and from the same source: North-Syria (see *Ill. 5*). Consequently we can eliminate the role of Urartu in any oriental influence exerted on the Eastern Mediterranean. Gröschel discussed the possible oriental origin of the helmet type and examining the description of the helmet of Athena in the *Iliad*[259] identified the piece with the Greek geometric *Kegelhelm*[260]. He emphasized the Oriental origin of the figural decoration - which was unknown in Greece - of the helmet of Athena[261].

I. Geometric pointed helmets with earflaps and made of five pieces

Budapest (Museum of Fine Arts, Inv. no. 8442; H.: 28 cm, Diam.: 20.3 cm; Last third of 8th century B.C.)[262] (*Ill. 16-17*)
Pointed bronze helmet made of five separate pieces, which were riveted and probably melded together: cap of the helmet, a front plate, a back plate (neck-guard) and two earflaps. The four protective parts (front and back plates, two earflaps) were joined to the rim of the cap and formed a horizontal rib around the cap to strengthen its rim. There is a horizontal *repoussé* rib along the lower rim of the front plate, and there are two horizontal *repoussé* ribs (one along the lower edge, the other in the middle) on the back plate of the helmet. Both of them to give additional strength to the bronze sheet. The two large earflaps (curving at the back and terminating in a point at the front) hold the cap, the front and back plates together, and secured the construction of the helmet. The point of the left earflap and the curved rim of the right earflap are broken. There is a series of rivet holes along the rim of the helmet and the earflaps for the attachment of a lining. There are three small holes on the cap of the helmet: one of them is in the front part of the point, the two others are at the rim of the cap, in the joining point of the earflaps on the front of the helmet. The three most probably ancient holes served to fix a kind of applique to the front of the helmet, or served to fix the lining inside the cap.

Argos, Odos Diomidous (Argos, Archaeological Museum; Last third of 8th century B.C.)[263] (*Ill. 18*)
Pointed bronze helmet with a similar shape and construction as the Budapest helmet discussed above.

The two helmets mentioned above are the best examples of pointed helmets of the Greek mainland. Their characteristic is the conical skull-piece hammered out from one piece of bronze, to which the other parts of the helmet (front plate, neck-guard and two pointed earflaps) were riveted.
The origin of the type can be undoubtedly found in Assyria. A.M. Snodgrass wrote: *"Though it*

---

[257] See the chapter **The evolution of Near Eastern and Aegean/Eastern Mediterranean crested helmets**, and **Dezső 1993**, pp. 18-34.

[258] **King 1915**, passim. For detailed study of the hemispherical crested helmets see **Dezső 1993**, pp. 47-51, fig. 8, Chart 2, nos. 109-117, 130; for detailed study of Urartian Iron Age helmets see **Dezső 1993**, pp. 52-69, Cat. nos. 53-103.

[259] Iliad, V, 743.

[260] **Gröschel 1986**, p. 63: "Vers V, 743 war, wie oben dargelegt, mit großer Wahrscheinlichkeit als Beschreibung des frühgriechisches Kegelhelms erkannt worden."

[261] **Gröschel 1986**, pp. 70-71. This fact emphasizes that in the Greek semimythical tradition the helmets of sphinxes, Amazons and Athena (and of Geryon as well) can be originated in the Near East.

[262] **Lipperheide 1896**, p. 88f., no. 434; **Courbin 1957**, pp. 364ff., fig. 48; **Kunze 1958**, pp. 118-125; **Kunze 1967**, pp. 112-113, fig. 38; **Pflug 1988a**, p. 14; **Dezső 1993**, p. 40, pls. 160-161.

[263] **Protonotariou-Deilaki 1971**, pp. 81-82, fig. 13, pl. ; **Protonotariou-Deilaki 1982**, pp. 33-48; **Pflug 1988a**, p. 14, fig. 4; **Dezső 1993**, p. 40.

undoubtedly acquired distinct Greek characteristics, and even exhibits a fleeting resemblance to Greek Bronze Age shapes, this important Geometric artefact cannot be considered a Mycenaean legacy, nor yet a spontaneous creation, at a time when the Greeks were in close touch, and occasionally hostile encounter, with the Assyrians. The Kegelhelm must either share a common ancestry with the Assyrian conical helmet portrayed on eight- and seventh-century reliefs, or derive directly from it. Since the fully developed form, with neck guard and ear- or cheek-pieces, seems a novelty in Assyria at this same period, it is easier to accept the former alternative."[264] But the earliest known representation of conical helmets is known from a Middle Assyrian cylinder seal impression on a cuneiform tablet from the reign of Ashur-nirari II (1424-1418 B.C.)[265]. It appears on the White Obelisk (*Ill. 4, no. O.1.1*) as well, which can be dated probably to the reign of Ashur-nasir-pal I (1050-1032 B.C.)[266]. From the reign of Ashur-nasir-pal II (883-859 B.C.) the representations of the Assyrian conical helmet are well known[267]. Only four contemporary North Syrian representations of conical helmets are known (*Ill. 4, nos. O.1.15-16, O.1.24-25*). Since their provenance, date and identification is doubtful, they should not be considered as evidence for the evolution of conical/pointed helmets. Altogether more than 60 variants in form and decoration are known from the palace reliefs of Ashur-nasir-pal II (*Ill. 4, nos. O.1.2-12*), from the Balawat Gates (*Ill. 4, nos. O.1.17-20*) of Shalmaneser III (858-824 B.C.), from late 9th - early 8th century B.C. ivory plaques from Nimrud (*Ill. 4, nos. O.1.21-23, 28*), from the palace reliefs (*Ill. 4, nos. O.1.29-37*) of Tiglath-Pileser III (745-727 B.C.), from wall-paintings of the same ruler from Nimrud (*Ill. 4, nos. O.1.38-40*), from the palace reliefs[268] of Sargon II (721-705 B.C.) (*Ill. 4, nos. O.1.55-58*), from the palace reliefs[269] of Sennacherib (704-681 B.C.) (*Ill. 4, nos. O.1.59-79*), from the palace reliefs of Esarhaddon (680-669 B.C.) (*Ill. 4, no. O.1.83*), from the palace reliefs of Ashurbanipal (668-627 B.C.) (*Ill. 4, nos. O.1.84-89*) and from several other representations from the Assyrian art in Assyria and North Syria as well[270]. So the Assyrian and Greek conical helmets did not share a common ancestry, but the Greek conical helmet tradition can be originated in the Assyrian conical/pointed helmet tradition. This Assyrian tradition was the source of several Near Eastern, e.g. North Syrian ("Syro-Assyrian")[271], Urartian[272], Caucasian[273], North-West Iranian (with Hasanlu)[274] and Persian[275] conical helmet traditions as well. Its unquestionnable impact on the Cypriote conical helmet tradition has already been discussed (*Ill. 4, nos. M.2.1-16, 17-20*).

The earliest representations of conical helmets from Greece can be dated to the second half (most probably to the last quarter) of the 8th century B.C. A certain type of conical helmet - with ear cut-outs and deep neckguard - which has exact parallels on the palace reliefs of Sargon II (721-705 B.C.)[276] is known from various bronze objects: e.g. on a Cretan bronze shield (*Ill. 4, no. M.2.21*)[277], on a bronze bowl from Delphi (*Ill. 4, no. M.2.22-23*)[278], on an other bronze bowl from "Olympia" (*Ill. 4, no. M.2.24*)[279] and on a bronze statuette of a warrior from Olympia (*Ill. 4, no. M.2.25*)[280]. The Assyrian influence is obvious. It must be emphasized, however, that the crest fitted centrally across the conical helmet of the hunter of the Cretan shield (*Ill. 4, no. M.2.21*) and of the Olympia warrior (*Ill. 4, no.*

---

264 **Snodgrass 1964**, p. 195.
265 From Ashur; Berlin, VAT 8951 (= Ass 14446n), **Beran 1957**, fig. 1; **Dezsö 1993**, p. 1, Chart 1, no. 41.
266 For the problem of dating see **Börker-Klähn 1982**, pp. 179-180.
267 For the evolution of the Assyrian conical/pointed helmet see **Dezsö 1993**, pp. 1-17, fig. 1, Charts 1-2.
268 Dur-Sharrukin (Khorsabad).
269 Nineveh.
270 **Dezsö 1993**, Chart 2.
271 **Dezsö 1993**, pp. 35-40.
272 **Dezsö 1993**, pp. 52-69.
273 **Dezsö 1993**, pp. 70-71.
274 **Dezsö 1993**, pp. 41-44.
275 **Dezsö 1993**, pp. 75-78.
276 **Dezsö 1993**, Chart 2, no. 193; **Botta - Flandin 1849**, pl. 76 and passim.
277 Crete, Zeus Cave, Mt. Ida; Iraklion, Archaeological Museum, Inv. no. 7; **Kunze 1931**, p. 8, fig. 1, pl. 14; **Dezsö 1993**, Chart 2, no. 187.
278 Delphi, Archaeological Museum, Inv. no. 4463; **Markoe 1985**, pp. 205-206, 320-323, G4; **Dezsö 1993**, Chart 2, nos. 188-189.
279 Oxford, Ashmolean Museum, G401; **Markoe 1985**, pp. 207, 326-327, G7; **Dezsö 1993**, Chart 2, no. 190.
280 Olympia Museum, Inv. B 4240.

M.2.25) is not the sign of a different type of helmet, only the local Greek variant of a basic type. These five helmets probably represent a certain phase of orientalization in the last quarter of 8th century B.C. Greek helmet tradition. A similar phase, on a similar (bronze) group of objects, has already been examined in the case of the early Cretan crested helmets[281] (see above). As there are no known examples of this type outside Assyria and these orientalizing objects in Greece, it may reflect a certain Oriental (Assyrian) influence, which reached Greece probably in the reign of Sargon II (721-705 B.C.), who conquered Cyprus.

More general orientalization can be detected in the second, early 7th century B.C. phase of the evolution of orientalizing Greek conical helmets, which is best described as simple "stimulus diffusion". The representations of this phase are mainly bronze statuettes of warriors wearing conical or pointed helmets: e.g. from Athens, Acropolis (*Ill. 4, no. M.2.26*)[282], from Delphi (*Ill. 4, no. M.2.27*)[283], Tegea (*Ill. 4, no. M.2.28*)[284], Thermon (*Ill. 4, no. M.2.29*)[285] and Karditsa (*Ill. 4, no. M.2.30*)[286]. The shapes - conical or pointed - simply reflect the new helmet type, which as a result of oriental influence or "stimulus diffusion" appeared in Greece as well in the late 8th - early 7th century B.C.

Unfortunately there are no representations of the "*Kegelhelm*" known. The three Olympian bronze statuettes of warriors ("Steiner bronzes")[287] (*Ill. 4, nos. M.5.9-11*), as Kunze has argued[288], can be dated to the early 7th century B.C. They are later than the last quarter of 8th century B.C., which date was suggested by Courbin after examining the grave goods found together with the Argos crested helmet[289] and was raised to around 740 B.C. by Kunze[290] (which seems a little high). Snodgrass describing the "*Kegelhelm*" as the experimental forerunner of the Corinthian helmet[291], wrote that the "Steiner bronzes" *show every sign of having observed an artistic convention too long for it to have corresponded throughout with contemporary life*"[292]. So there are no contemporary, Geometric Period representations even of the basic (made of five piece) structure type as well.

As has been quoted, Snodgrass argued that the neckguard and earflap was a new invention in the contemporary Assyrian army as well. And indeed, on the palace reliefs of Tiglath-Pileser III (745-727 B.C.) we can find a wide range of different types of earflaps[293]. There are rounded (*Ill. 4, nos. O.1.33-35, 37*) and pointed earflaps (*Ill. 4, no. O.1.36*) on the conical and crested helmets as well[294]. Moreover, there are representations of Assyrian conical and crested helmets with rounded or pointed earflaps and neckguard[295] from the reign of the same ruler. The conical/pointed and crested helmet with neckguard terminating in pointed earflap (*Ill. 4, no. O.2.23*) could be the forerunner of the Greek "*Kegelhelm*" variants. The only difference between them is that the Assyrian examples seem to be made from a single piece of metal. As has however been mentioned, the "*Kegelhelm*" as a basic type was a

---

281 First half or middle of 8th century B.C. - the first phase of orientalization - from Fortetsa, Kato-Symi, Khaniale Tekke and Kavousi.

282 Athens, National Museum, Inv. 6612, H.: 21.2 cm, **Schweitzer 1971**, pls. 164-165; **Lamb 1929**, pl. 20a.

283 Delphi, Archaeological Museum, Inv. 3649, H.: 13 cm; **Predrizet 1908**, p. 30, no. 16, pl. 1:4; **Rolley 1969**, p. 45, no. 28, pl. IX:28.

284 **Dugas 1921**, pp. 355-356, no. 53, fig. 19.

285 **Lamb 1929**, pl. 17a.

286 **Lamb 1929**, pl. 17b.

287 With high, unstilted crest or cap curving forward, type IIIC.

288 **Kunze 1958**, p. 124.

289 **Courbin 1957**, pp. 339-340.

290 **Kunze 1967a**, p. 114.

291 **Snodgrass 1964**, p. 15.

292 **Snodgrass 1964**, p. 16.

293 **Dezső 1993**, Chart 2, passim.

294 Assyrian crested helmets with rounded earflap: Chart 1, nos. O.2.19-20, 25; **Dezső 1993**, Chart 2, nos. 151-152, 157; **Barnett - Falkner 1962**, pls. LXI, XLI, XLII, XXXIII, XXXIV; Assyrian crested helmets with pointed earflap: Chart 1, nos. O.2.17, 21, 24; **Dezső 1993**, Chart 2, nos. 149, 153, 156; **Barnett - Falkner 1962**, L, LI, LXXIX, LXXIII.

295 Assyrian conical/pointed helmet with a neckguard ending in a pointed earflap: Til-Barsip wall-painting: Chart 1, no. O.1.48; **Amiet 1980**, pl. 105; Assyrian crested helmet with neckguard terminating in a rounded earflap: Chart 2, no. O.2.18; **Barnett - Falkner 1962**, pls. XXXV, XXXVI; Assyrian crested helmet with neckguard terminating in pointed earflap: Chart 2, no. O.2.23; **Barnett - Falkner 1962**, pl. LXII.

Greek product (at least in the "five piece" construction), and observed only the basic principles of the Oriental helmet tradition. But the fact that already 15 developed types of crested helmets can be seen on the palace reliefs of Tiglath-Pileser III (745-727), suggests that the evolution of crested helmets in the Assyrian army started in that 80 year gap, from which there are no well dated representations of Assyrian helmets available. Since the Assyrian army was the only army, which had all the varieties (one conical and four crested) of this basic helmet type ("*Kegelhelm*"), we cannot find a common source for the two productions outside Assyria. So it can be concluded that this basic type of helmet ("made of five pieces", or "*Kegelhelm*") derived from Assyria most probably in the second half of 8th century B.C.

It seems probable that the life of this - well documented - helmet type was very short. As Snodgrass wrote: "... *its life seems to have been extremely short. The simple lines and composite structure of the Kegelhelm could have been easily portrayed in the outline styles of the seventh-century painting, had it still been in use.*"[296].

Snodgrass assumed that the ridge in relief, which bisects the neckguard horizontally is a later evolution, and consequently the Budapest helmet[297] and helmet Olympia Inv. Br. 10533[298] are late in the series and can be dated to the early 7th century B.C. He is probably right, since the shape of the helmet is conical and the four separate parts attached vertically to the cap of the helmet do not brake the curving contour of the cap (with the exception of the joining rib) but follow it. These two helmets with their smooth curve may indeed represent a later evolution in the series. Felsch found a fragment in the sanctuary of Kalapodi with Late Geometric pottery[299]. The date of this production ranges between the last quarter of the 8th century and the first quarter of the 7th century B.C., when the later classical helmet forms, the Corinthian and Illyrian helmets gradually replaced it as the leading helmet type. Undoubtedly this type of helmet was the first important 1st millennium B.C. Greek helmet type, which became part of the heavy weaponry of the earliest Greek hoplites.

II. Geometric pointed helmets with a high, crescent-shaped crest

Argos, Tomb 45 (Argos, Archaeological Museum; Last third of 8th century B.C.)[300] (*Ill. 19*)
Variant of the conical type discussed above. The basic structure of the helmet is the same as the other helmets of the pointed and other groups: it consists of a conical skull-piece, a front and a back plate and two earflaps. The rims of the separate bronze sheets were strengthened by an embossed rib. The horizontal central rib of the back plate of the Budapest pointed helmet is missing from this helmet. On the top of the skull-piece however there is a tubular crest-support decorated with three bands of horizontal ribs (4-5-6 ribs). There is a crescent-shaped crest - curving almost back to the side of the skull-piece - riveted on the top of the crest-support. The two sides of the crest were decorated with an embossed rib and 8 pseudo-rivets. The actual horsehair plume was fixed into this crest. Last quarter of 8th century B.C.[301]

Olympia, South of the Heraion (Olympia Museum, Old Inv. Br. 10533; H.: 28.7 cm; H. of the frontplate: 7.6 cm; H. of the backplate: 10.2 cm; H. of the earflaps: 18.2 cm)[302] (*Ill. 20*)
Its construction is similar to the Argos helmet. The crest and the right earflap are missing. The right side of the front plate and the back plate is fragmentary. There is a joining fragment of the backplate published separately (H.: 5.4 cm; L.: 11.1 cm)[303]. The horizontal rib which bisects the back plate of the helmet dates it to the first quarter of the 7th century B.C.

---

296 Snodgrass 1964, pp. 15-16.
297 Snodgrass 1964, p. 15, A1.
298 Snodgrass 1964, p. 15, A2.
299 Felsch 1987, pp. 12-13, fig. 18.
300 Courbin 1957, pp. 322ff., figs. 19, 39-45, pls. 1, 4; Kunze 1958, p. 124; Kunze 1967a, pp. 113-114; Borchhardt 1977, pl. E IV b; Pflug 1988a, p. 12, figs. 1-3; Dezső 1993, p. 40.
301 Courbin 1957, p. 3 dated the two kantharoi found in the tomb together with the helmet to the last quarter of the 8th century B.C.
302 Furtwängler 1890, p. 172, no. 1031, pl. 62; Kunze 1958, p. 119, no. 1, pls. 33-34; Kunze 1967a, p. 112, note 1; Pflug 1988a, pp. 12-14, note 12; Dezső 1993, p. 40.
303 Kunze 1967a, p. 112, note 1.

Olympia, probably from the Alpheios (Olympia Museum, Inv. no.: without number; H.: 20.8 cm; H. of the frontplate: 8.3 cm; H. of the backplate: 10.7 cm; H. of the earflaps: 15.8 cm)[304] (*Ill. 21*)

Its construction is similar to the Argos helmet. Its fragmentary condition (the top of the conical skull-piece and the left earflap are missing) makes its identification doubtful: the upper structure of the helmet might be pointed or crested as well. The missing of the horizontal rib which bisects the back plates of the Budapest pointed helmet and helmet Old Inv. Br. 10533 dates it to the end of the 8th century B.C.

Olympia, from the North Wall of the Stadion (Olympia Museum, Inv. no. B 51; H.: 18 cm; H. of the frontplate: 7.2 cm)[305] (*Ill. 22*)

Fragmentary helmet, construction of which is similar to the Argos helmet. Its skull-piece and front plate is intact, but both earflaps and the back plate are missing. A tubular crest-support later added to the helmet.

Olympia, "Brunnen 23 im Stadion-Nordwall" (Olympia Museum, Inv. no. B 4714; H.: 9.7 cm; Diam.: 18.3-19.8 cm; Diam. of the crestbase hole: 1.9 cm)[306] (*Ill. 23*)

Skull-piece of a helmet of the Argos type. The crest, the front and back plates and the two earflaps are missing.

Athen, Kerameikos (Grab V) (H. of crest-support tube: 4.5 cm; Diam.: 1.45 - 2 cm)[307]

Tubular crest-support similar to the crest-support of the Argos helmet.

A further fragmentary example may be in Delos Museum.[308]

This kind of crested helmet was widespread in Assyria (*Ill. 5, nos. O.2.23-25*) and North Syria (*Ill. 5, nos. O.2.26*)[309] in the third quarter of the 8th century B.C. There is only a single, but unfortunately unprovenanced Assyrian or North Syrian example known of this type of crested helmet, now in the British Museum:

British Museum, Inv. no.: 2841 (Richard Payne Knight Bequest 1824), provenance unknown, H.: 24.6 cm, Diam.: 19.6 cm, middle of the 8th century B.C.[310] (*Ill. 24*)

Borchhardt suggested that the best parallel for the Argos helmet with crescent-shaped crest (*"Bügelhelm"*) is on the palace reliefs of Sennacherib[311] (704-681 B.C.), but as we have seen much better Assyrian parallels are known from the reign of Tiglath-Pileser III (745-727 B.C.), with earflaps and neckguard (*Ill. 5, no. O.2.23*) or with earflaps but without neckguard (*Ill. 5, nos. O.2.24-26*).

Several representations of this type of helmet are known from Greek late geometric and archaic art (*Ill. 5, nos. M.6.1-24*). However, in contradiction to the Near Eastern practice, where crested helmets were worn only by foot soldiers of the light infantry, in the Aegean this type of crested helmet was worn by warriors fighting on ship (*Ill. 5, no. M.6.1*), horsemen (*Ill. 5, nos. M.6.2, 18, 22*) and hoplites (*Ill. 5, nos. M.6.3, 5, 10, 12-13, 24*). This type of helmet was worn almost everywhere in the Eastern Mediterranean. Representations range from Cyprus (*Ill. 5, nos. M.6.18-21*) to Athens (*Ill. 5, nos. M.6.1-*

---

304 **Kunze 1938a**, p. 93, note 4; **Kunze 1941**, p. 106, pl. 36 upper; **Kunze 1958**, p. 119, no. 2, pl. 35; **Pflug 1988a**, pp. 12-14, note 12; **Dezső** (forthcoming), p. 40.

305 **Hampe - Jantzen 1936-1937**, p. 52, pl. 6 right; **Kunze 1958**, p. 119, no. 3; **Pflug 1988a**, pp. 12-14, note 12; **Dezső 1993**, p. 40.

306 **Kunze 1967a**, p. 111, no. 3a, pl. 50:1; **Pflug 1988a**, p. 12, note 12; **Dezső 1993**, p. 40.

307 **Brückner - Pernice 1893**, p. 108; **Borchhardt 1972**, p. 65, Kat. 13 III 1; **Pflug 1988a**, p. 20.

308 **Snodgrass 1964**, p. 13: "A possible sixth example is in the Museum at Delos (Inv. no. A.798), unpublished as far as I know: it is a much damaged bronze object of flat conical shape, whose dimensions (height 10 cm, diameter 16 cm) and form correspond well with the 'cap' sections of those listed above."

309 **Dezső 1993**, Chart 2, no. 174 (Tiglath-Pileser III [745-727 B.C.]), Chart 3, no. 174.

310 **Walters 1899**, p. 349, cat. no. 2841; **British Museum 1929**, pp. 77, 79, fig. 69, no. 229; **Pflug 1988a**, pp. 19-20, fig. 9, note 43; **Dezső 1993**, pp. 16-24, Cat. no. 11, pl. 21.

311 **Borchhardt 1972**, p. 64. Our Chart 2, nos. O.2.30-32.

3, 5, 10), the Peloponnese (*Ill. 5, nos. M.6.4, 7, 11, 14-15, 22-23*) and the Greek islands (*Ill. 5, nos. M.6.6, 8-9, 12-13, 16*).

There were several smaller fragments found in Olympia and ranged among the helmets of this group, but it is possible that these pieces belong to an other variant (III A or B) of this basic helmet type. We listed the fragments, helmet type of which is unidentified, under a separate title.

III.A. Geometric hemispherical helmet with a high crest curving forward

Ordona (South Italy) (Collection of A. Ceccanti, Florence, Inv. no. prov. CC 436)[312]
Hemispherical helmet basic structure of which is similar to the Budapest and Argos type made of five pieces. It was made of a hemispherical skull-piece, a front plate, a back plate and two earflaps. The most important characteristic of this type is the high crest curving forward and ending in an stylized animal's (bird's or probably a horse's) head. The crest was fixed to the top of the hemisphericalskull-piece by rivets. There were two attachments fixed to the sides of the helmet by hinges. These attachments might be the same as the attachment of the other Ordona helmet: a bull's horn and ear cut out from a bronze sheet.

Ordona (South Italy)[313] The fragmentary helmet consists of the hemispherical skull-piece, the frontplate and a bronze sheet attachment fixed to the right side of the skull-piece by hinges. The attachment represents a bull's horn and ear. The basic structure of the helmet is the same as the Ceccanti helmet discussed above.

Venice (Private Collection)[314] The third known helmet of the group, which has the same structure as the Ordona helmets.

These helmets are the only examples of the third variant: a high crest was riveted on to the top of a hemispherical skull-piece. The basic structure is the same as helmet types I and II made of five pieces. Kunze supposed that this type is a transitional form between the *Kegelhelm* and the Illyrian helmet[315]. According to Lepore this type might be a local (provincial), Italian variant of the basic type[316] (type I) but the overall shape is well known in Greece as well (*Ill. 5, groups M.4-M.5*)[317]. Like the Cretan crested helmet discussed above, its oriental prototypes are known from the the middle of the 8th century B.C. on Assyrian palace reliefs. Helmets with crest curving forward can be seen on the palace reliefs of Tiglath-Pileser III (745-727 B.C.): *Ill. 5, nos. O.2.8-13*, Sargon II (721-705 B.C.): *Ill. 5, nos. O.2.27-29*, Sennacherib (704-681 B.C.): *Ill. 5, nos. O.2.34-40*, Esarhaddon (680-669 B.C.): *Ill. 5, no. O.2.42* and Ashurbanipal (668-627 B.C.): *Ill. 5, nos. O.2.43-46, 48*. We can find all the basic types of crested helmets with crest curving forward in the Assyrian imperial army: there are crested helmets without earflaps (*Ill. 5, nos. O.2.8-9, 27*), with earflaps, and with earflaps and neckguard (*Ill. 5, nos. O.2.11-12* from the reign of Tiglath-Pileser III and *Ill. 5, no. O.2.28* from the reign of Sargon II) as well[318].

The two basic variants in manufacture - conical skull-piece or hemispherical skull-piece - of the same basic type developed in parallel. The difference between these two basic types might be a technical one: the conical shape might be hammered out from a single piece of bronze, while the crest of the hemispherical skull-piece might be riveted separately on the top of the helmet. As we can see the prototypes of the Greek crested helmets can be found on the Assyrian palace reliefs of the third quarter of the 8th century B.C. This almost one and half century development of Assyrian representational evidence shows an interesting difference between the Oriental and Mediterranean helmet

---

[312] **Lepore 1984**, pp. 329-332, pl. 1; **Pflug 1988a**, pp. 14-15, figs. 5-6; **Dezső 1993**, p. 41.
[313] **Egg 1986**, p. 15, pl. 17; **Pflug 1988a**, p. 15; **Dezső 1993**, p. 41.
[314] **Sotheby's Catalogue 19. 6. 1961**, p. 28, no. 117; **Kunze 1967a**, pp. 115f., fig. 39; **Lepore 1984**, p. 330, note 7; **Pflug 1988a**, p. 14; **Dezső 1993**, p. 41.
[315] **Kunze 1967a**, p. 116.
[316] **Lepore 1984**, p. 331.
[317] For the detailed discussion of Greek representational evidence see the chapter of Cretan crested helmet from Praisos.
[318] For detailed discussioin see th chapter of The evolution of Near Eastern crested helmets, pp. 24-29.

traditions. The tendency of standardization of Assyrian military equipment, especially of Assyrian helmets contrasts sharply with the Eastern Mediterranean development, which was characterized by the almost free variation or permutation of the different elements of the basic types of crested helmets. The Oriental standardization was a government policy, while the Aegean standardization of military equipment (hoplite equipment with Corinthian or Illyrian helmet and *hoplon* shield) was a spontaneous evolution.

Altogether four Oriental crested bronze helmets, a crest, and 16 iron helmet fragments of this type are known. The four crested bronze helmets can be dated to the late 9th century B.C. Two of them are Urartian, and are inscribed with the name of Ishpuini, king of Urartu (ca. 830-810 B.C.):

1. **Mainz, Römisch-Germanisches Zentralmuseum, Inv. no. O.39702, from "Urartu (Eastern Turkey)"**, H.: 29 cm, last quarter of 9th century B.C.[319] (*Ill. 25*)
2. **Mainz, Römisch-Germanisches Zentralmuseum, Inv. no. O.39703, from "Urartu (Eastern Turkey)"**, H.: 29 cm, last quarter of 9th century B.C.[320]

Further two helmets can be identified as Assyrian products:

3. **Munich, Prähistorisches Staatssammlung, Inv. no. P.S. 1979/1181, from "Urartu (Eastern Turkey)"**, H.: 30.8 cm, Diam.: 20.4-22.3 cm, last quarter of 9th - first quarter of 8th century B.C.[321] (*Ill. 26*)
4. **Karlsruhe, Badisches Landesmuseum, Inv. no. 89/12, from "Urartu (Eastern Turkey)"**, H.: 28.5 cm, Diam.: 19-22 cm, last quarter of 9th - first quarter of 8th century B.C.[322] (*Ill. 27*)

A fifth fragment, a crest was found in Lachish, in the destruction level of the Assyrian siege of 701 B.C.

5. **Jerusalem, The Israel Museum, Inv. no.: 34.133/1-2, Lachish, 701 B.C.**[323]

These helmets represent the two basic structural groups of crested helmets: the Mainz and Karlsruhe helmets were hammered out from a single piece of bronze sheet, while the crests of the Munich and Lachish helmets were riveted separately onto the top of the helmet. However, the Mainz and Karlsruhe helmets show the signs (e.g. pseudo-rivets) of the earliest construction of this type. The relatively complicated shape of crested helmets was formed by riveting the different parts of the helmet together.[324]

There are **16 fragments of Assyrian (crested) iron helmets** excavated by Layard at Nimrud, in the North-West Palace, Chamber I in the autumn of 1846, now in the British Museum[325] (*Ill. 28*). There are fragments at least from four helmets (from the 16 there are 4 crest fragments). These fragments together with an Assyrian pointed iron helmet (see above) from the same find are the earliest known iron helmets in the world. Furthermore these helmets were mass-produced helmets (decorated with bronze inlay, a unique technique), which emphasizes the skill of Assyrian blacksmiths and the high

---

319 Vanden Berghe - De Meyer 1982, p. 132, no 24 (fig.); Yesaian 1986, p. 23, pl. 13:9; Maass 1987, p. 69, note 22; Pflug 1988a, pp. 23-24, note 74, fig. 11; Egg - Waurick 1990, pl. 7; Calmeyer 1991, p. 123, fig. 7; Dezső - Curtis 1991, pp. 114-116, pl. 16; Dezső 1993, pp. 54-55, Cat. no. 54, Group no. U.1.1.

320 Unpublished. Dezső 1993, pp. 54-55, Cat. no. 55, Group no. U.1.2.

321 Kellner 1980, pp. 212-213, pls. 15-16; Pflug 1988a, p. 24, note 75; Calmeyer 1991, no. 10 (pl.); Dezső - Curtis 1991, pp. 114-121, pl. 17; Dezső 1993, pp. 16-24, Cat. no. 10, Group no. A.3.2.

322 Kellner 1980, pp. 211-212, pls. 13-14; Gröschel 1986, p. 74, notes 229-233; Maass 1987, pp. 65-71, pls. 1:2, 2, 3; Maass 1988, p. 170, no. 97, fig. 97; Pflug 1988a, p. 24, note 75; Maass 1989, p. 195; Dezső - Curtis 1991, pp. 114-121, pl. 18; Dezső 1993, pp. 16-24, Cat. no. 11, Group no. A.3.3.

323 Tuffnell 1953, p. 387, pl. 39:1-2; Wright 1958, p. 165, fig. 119; Ussishkin 1982, p. 57, fig. 49; Shanks 1984, fig. on p. 63; Dezső 1993, pp. 16-24, Cat. no. 9, Group no. A.3.1.

324 For detailed study of the development of Near Eastern crested helmets and their construction, see Dezső - Curtis 1991, pp. 107-122; Dezső 1993, pp. 16-24.

325 British Museum, 48-1-4, 113-115. Dezső - Curtis 1991, pp. 105-122, figs. 1-20; Dezső 1993, pp. 25-31, Cat. nos. 13-28, Group nos. A.4.1-16.

standard of the weaponry of the Assyrian imperial army in the second half of 8th century and throughout the 7th century B.C.[326]. The reconstructed shape of these crested iron helmets[327] follows the overall shape of the crested bronze helmets discussed above. The ribs on bronze helmets - both on the base and on the crest of the helmet - are to strengthen the bronze sheet. In case of iron helmets the ribs would have been redundant because of the greater strength of the iron. In the archaizing structure of these iron helmets therefore the ribs were replaced by inlaid bronze bands - as decoration replacing structural necessity. The inlaid bronze dots replacing the bronze rivets or pseudo-rivets of crested bronze helmets served probably the same archaizing decorative function.

Their decorative system, however, was much more complicated. The figural representations of deities on the front of some of these helmets - besides the common apotropaic function - served a special, not only decorative but practical purpose as well. As part of the standardization of the military equipment of the Assyrian imperial army, these representations probably indicated the status of its wearer[328], the unit or special service of the army, the origin of the unit[329], from which its wearer came, or even military rank. As has already been mentioned the helmets of the 8th-7th century Assyrian army expressed the arm, in which its wearer served (crested helmets were worn only by the soldiers of the light infantry equipped with round wooden shields, spears and *kardio phylakes*).[330]

These mass-produced Assyrian crested iron helmets represent a new development, a qualitative change in the history of ancient Near Eastern and Mediterranean helmet traditions. After the fall of the Assyrian Empire similarly mass-produced iron helmets did not reappear until the Hellenistic Age.

III.B. Geometric pointed helmet with a separately added small crest curving forward

The only surviving example of this type is a 6 cm high miniature bronze helmet[331]. It shows the distinctive traits of the basic type: it has a conical cap, two characteristic earflaps, a front plate and a back plate (neck guard). The characteristic feature of this type is, however, the separately added small crest curving forward. Parallels to this small crest are known from the Assyrian palace reliefs from the reign of Tiglath-Pileser III (745-727 B.C.): *Ill. 5, nos. O.2.8-10*, but mainly from the reign of Sennacherib (704-681 B.C.): *Ill. 5, nos. O.2.34-35*, Esarhaddon (680-669 B.C.): *Ill. 5, no. O.2.42* and Ashurbanipal (668-627 B.C.): *Ill. 5, nos. O.2.43-46, 48*, when (during the 7th century B.C.) the standardization of the crested helmets made progress as well. Representations of this type in Greek art cannot be separated from the representations of helmet type III. A. because these types are differently manufactured versions of the same basic type, the helmet with crest curving forward.

III.C. Geometric pointed helmet with a high cap curving forward

This group represents the helmet type of the so called Steiner bronzes found in Olympia:

Bronze statuette of a warrior, Olympia, Inv. no. B.2000, H.: 21 cm, Late or Sub-Geometric (first quarter of 7th century B.C.)[332]. *Ill. 5, no. M.5.9*

Bronze statuette of a warrior, Olympia, Inv. no. B.1999, H.: 17.3 cm, Late or Sub-Geometric (first quarter of 7th century B.C.)[333]. *Ill. 5, no. M.5.10*

Bronze statuette of a warrior, Olympia, Inv. no. B.1701, H.: 16.9 cm, Late or Sub-Geometric (first quarter of 7th century B.C.)[334]. *Ill. 5, no. M.5.11*

The basic structure of their helmets is the same as the helmets of groups discussed above: the characteristic earflaps, and neck-guard are clearly visible. Unfortunately the points of their helmets are

---

326 Dezsö - Curtis 1991, passim; Dezsö 1993, pp. 11-15, 24-31; For Assyrian ironwork see Curtis 1979; Curtis, et al. 1979.
327 Dezsö - Curtis 1991, figs. 16-20.
328 For example sa qurbute, royal bodygard.
329 Local deities, for example Ishtar of Arbela.
330 Dezsö - Curtis 1991, pp. 108-110; Dezsö 1993, pp. 12-13, 27.
331 Deonna 1938, p. 208, pl. 69:554; Kunze 1967a, pp. 114-115; Gröschel 1986, p. 64, note 166.
332 Kunze 1944, p. 120, pls. 38-39.
333 Kunze 1944, p. 122, pls. 43-44.
334 Kunze 1944, p. 122, pls. 45-46.

missing. Therefore we can only suppose that their helmets were furnished with a high point or an unstilted crest curving forward[335]. There is a further damaged example of the type known from Olympia (*Ill. 5, no. M.5.12*). There are, however, several other representations of the complete form of this type: from Olympia (*Ill. 5, nos. M.5.6-8, 13-14, 21*), from the Greek Mainland (*Ill. 5, nos. M.5.16-17, 20, 22*), from Crete (*Ill. 5, no. M.5.2-4, 18*) and from the Greek Islands (*Ill. 5, nos. M.5.5, 15, 19*). Kunze proposed a possible Argive manufacture for the "Steiner bronzes"[336].

There are further representations of this type known, first of which is a pair of linch pin figures from Salamis, Cyprus (*Ill. 5, no. M.5.1*). The helmet of these warriors is an Oriental unstilted crested helmet, but the figures wear scale armour, which combination (crested helmet of the light infantry and scale armour of the heavy infantry) is unknown in the Near East. This contradiction establishes the truth of our assumption, that the Oriental crested helmets were adopted in the Aegean out of their original context. The helmet of the warrior of a bronze handle attachment (*Ill. 5, no. M.5.24*) and the helmets of horseriders of an Orientalizing bronze sheet (*Ill. 5, nos. M.5.23*), both from Olympia, seem to be similarly original Oriental (Assyrian) helmets but their context is mixed. Namely crested helmets were never worn in the ranks of Assyrian horseriders, and as has been mentioned, soldiers wearing crested helmets (light infantry of the Assyrian standing army) were never equipped with scale armour. Kunze proposed a North-Syrian - South-Anatolian origin for this bronze sheet[337]. This phenomenon can be explained only by saying that the different types of Oriental (let us say Assyrian) helmets and other parts of the army equipment were adopted in the Eastern Mediterranean and in the Aegean out of their original context. They were borrowed by breaking the strict equipment rules of the different arms of the Assyrian imperial army. Another explanation might be, that these strict rules were valid till the last quarter of the 7th century B.C., and we do not know anything about the army equipment of the Neo-Babilonian Empire (612-539 B.C.). We can only suppose that the Babylonian armies used the same equipment as the Assyrian army.

The structure of the "crest" can be distinguished with difficulty from the high unstilted crest of the type of the Praisos helmet. Both types may be traced back to the Assyrian crested helmets, on representations of which we can find unstilted crests curving forward or high points curving forward together. On the palace reliefs of Tiglath-Pileser III (745-727 B.C.) crested helmets with unstilted crest curving forward were quite common (*Ill. 5, nos. O.2.8-12*), but in the armies of later rulers the unstilted crest seems to be superseded by stilted crests. The only later example of this crest type is a helmet on the palace reliefs of Sennacherib (704-681 B.C.): *Ill. 5, no. O.2.40*. This evolution can be explained by the importance of the crest (probably its colour) in the identification of the different units of light infantry of the Assyrian imperial army.

The date of this type is relatively late (first quarter of 7th century B.C.). As has already been noted Snodgrass interpreted the "Steiner bronzes" as part of artistic convention observed for too long for it to have corresponded throughout with contemporary life[338].

The possible pattern of the different levels of orientalization which I outlined in my present paper I hope can be used not only for helmets, but for other groups of objects, and as a general system eventually for other, theoretical fields of this or other multi-level cultural exchange.

---

335 **Snodgrass 1964**, p. 15: "... their crests (now lost) were apparently the unstilted, forward curving type in contrast with the Argos crest."

336 **Kunze 1944**, pp. 120-122.

337 **Kunze 1961-62**, p. 115: "Im Ganzen scheint sich aber vorerst der schon früher aus der Einzelnen Figur gewonnene Eindruck zu bestätigen, dass wir es mit einer provinziellen Brechnung assyrischer Kunst zu tun haben, deren Heimat im nordsyrisch-südanatolischen Raum zu suchen sein wird."

338 **Snodgrass 1964**, p. 16.

APPENDICES

APPENDIX I

FRAGMENTS OF GREEK GEOMETRIC HELMETS

In this chapter we simply list those fragments of Greek Geometric helmets made of five pieces, helmet type of which (I., II., III.A., III.B. or III.C.) we cannot identify from them.

Helmet front plate fragments:
1. Olympia (from *3. Stadion-Südwall*); Inv. B 1678; H.: 7.4 cm; L.: 18.5 cm[339]
2. Olympia (from *3. Stadion-Südwall*); Inv. B 1677; H.: 7.8 cm; L.: 18.2 cm[340]
3. Olympia (from *3. Stadion-Südwall*); Inv. B 2004; H.: 6.7 cm; L.: 24.9 cm[341]
4. Olympia (East of the Temple of Zeus); Old Inv. Br. 5596; H.: 7.6 cm; L.: 18.5 cm[342]
5. Olympia (from *Stadion-Nordwall, Quadrat G2 in spätarchaisches Füllung*); Inv. B 4557; H.: 8.1 cm; L.: 17.7 cm[343]

Helmet back plate fragments:
6. Olympia (from *Nordostecke der Festungsmauer*); Old Inv. Br. 2832; H.: 11.1 cm; L.: 19.5 cm[344]
7. Olympia (from *2. Stadion-Südwall*); Inv. B 3440; H.: 10.7 cm; L.: 26 cm[345]
8. Olympia (from Alpheios); Without Inv. number; H.: 9 cm; L.: 24.7 cm[346]
9. Kalapodi; Lamia Mus., Inv.-Nr. B 2361[347]

Left earflaps:
10. Olympia (from South of the Metroon); Old Inv. Br. 6244; H.: 19.2 cm; W.: 11.6 cm[348]
11. Olympia (from Alpheios); Without Inv. number; H.: 9 cm; W.: 12 cm[349]
12. Olympia (from *Stadion-Nordwall*); Inv. B 52; H.: 18.2 cm; W.: 12 cm[350]
13. Olympia (from Alpheios); Inv. B 2277; H.: 18.4 cm; W.: 11.7 cm[351]
14. Olympia (from *3. Stadion-Südwall*); Inv. B 2254; H.: 19.6 cm; W.: 12.7 cm[352]
15. Olympia (from *Stadion-Westwall*); Inv. B 851; H.: 19.2 cm; W.: 11 cm[353]
16. Olympia (from *4. Stadion-Südwall*); Inv. B 1514; H.: 16.1 cm; W.: 12.2 cm[354]
17. Olympia (from *Stadion-Nordwall, Quadrat K4*); Inv. B 4531; H.: 18.2 cm; W.: 11.5 cm[355]
18. Olympia (from *Brunnen 5 Stadion-Nordwall, Quadrat K3*); Inv. B 4459; H.: 19.5 cm; W.: 11.6 cm[356]
19. Olympia (from *Südöstl. vom Mosaiksaal der Erweiterung des Nerohauses*); Inv. B 6095; H.: 18 cm; W.: 11.9 cm[357]
20. Olympia[358]

---

[339] **Kunze 1958**, p. 119, no. 4, pl. 36:2a.
[340] **Kunze 1958**, p. 119, no. 5, pl. 36:2b.
[341] **Kunze 1958**, p. 119, no. 6.
[342] **Kunze 1958**, p. 119, no. 7, pl. 36:1.
[343] **Kunze 1967a**, p. 111, no. 7a, pl. 50:2.
[344] **Kunze 1958**, p. 119, no. 8.
[345] **Kunze 1958**, p. 120, no. 9, fig. 94.
[346] **Kunze 1967a**, pp. 111-112, no. 9a.
[347] **Felsch 1987**, pp. 12-13, fig. 18; **Pflug 1988a**, p. 17.
[348] **Furtwängler 1890**, p. 172; **Kunze 1958**, p. 120, no. 10, pl. 37:1a.
[349] **Kunze 1958**, p. 120, no. 11, pl. 37:1b.
[350] **Kunze 1941**, pp. 106-107, fig. 95 right; **Kunze 1958**, p. 120, no. 12.
[351] **Kunze 1958**, p. 120, no. 13, pl. 37:2b.
[352] **Kunze 1958**, p. 120, no. 14, pl. 38:2b.
[353] **Kunze 1941**, p. 106; **Kunze 1958**, p. 120, no. 15.
[354] **Kunze 1941**, pp. 106-107, fig 95 left.
[355] **Kunze 1967a**, p. 112, no. 15a, pl. 51:1a.
[356] **Kunze 1967a**, p. 112, no. 15b, pl. 51:1b.
[357] **Kunze 1967a**, p. 112, no. 15c, pl. 50:4.

21. Thermos Museum, H.: 18 cm, W.: 11.2-12.6 cm[359]

Right earflaps:
22. Olympia (from *Südwestecke des Zeustempels*); Old Inv. Br. 2722; H.: 18.9 cm; W.: 10.8 cm[360]
23. Olympia; Without Inv. number; H.: 20.2 cm; W.: 10.5 cm[361]
24. Olympia (*Südlich von der Echohalle*); Inv. B 303; H.: 20.1 cm; W.: 11.3 cm[362]
25. Olympia (*4. Stadion-Südwall*); Inv. B 901; H.: 17.8 cm; W.: 13 cm[363]
26. Olympia (*Botros in der Südwestecke des Stadions*); Inv. B 1947; H.: 19.6 cm; W.: 12.8 cm[364]
27. Olympia (*Mosaiksaal des Nerohauses*); Inv. B 3339; H.: 18.3 cm; W.: 11 cm[365]
28. Olympia (*3. Wall in der Südwestecke des Stadions*); Inv. B 3308; H.: 18.5 cm; W.: 11.1 cm[366]
29. Olympia (*3. Stadion-Südwall*); Inv. B 4057; H.: 19 cm; W.: 11 cm[367]
30. Olympia (*Stadion-Nordwall, Quadrat H2*); Inv. B 4057; H.: 19.4 cm; W.: 11.4 cm[368]

The Lindos earflaps:
Lindos, Acropolis, (right side earflap); H.: 14.5 cm; W.: 11.6 cm[369]
Lindos, Acropolis (left side earflap); H.: 13.4 cm; W.: 10.9 cm[370]
Lindos, Acropolis; H.: 13.3 cm; W.:[371]
Lindos, Acropolis; H.: 13 cm; W.:[372]
Lindos, Acropolis[373]
Lindos, Acropolis[374]

---

358 Papathanasopoulos 1969, p. 146, pl. 144a.
359 Mastrokostas 1961-62, p. 131, note 10.
360 Furtwängler 1890, p. 172; Kunze 1958, p. 120, no. 17, pl. 38:1b.
361 Kunze 1958, p. 120, no. 18, pl. 38:1a.
362 Kunze 1938a, p. 93; Kunze 1958, p. 120, no. 19, pl. 38:2a.
363 Kunze 1941, p. 106; Kunze 1958, p. 120, no. 20, pl. 37:2a.
364 Kunze 1958, p. 120, no. 21, fig. 95.
365 Kunze 1958, p. 120, no. 22, fig. 96a.
366 Kunze 1958, p. 120, no. 23, fig. 96b.
367 Kunze 1961a, p. 22; Kunze 1967a, p. 112, no. 24, pl. 51:2a.
368 Kunze 1961b, pp. 74f., note 23; Kunze 1967a, p. 112, no. 25, pl. 51:2b.
369 Blinkenberg 1931, pp. 189-190, no. 571, pl. 22.
370 Blinkenberg 1931, p. 190, no. 572, pl. 22.
371 Blinkenberg 1931, p. 190, no. 573.
372 Blinkenberg 1931, p. 190, no. 574, pl. 23.
373 Blinkenberg 1931, p. 190, no. 575.
374 Blinkenberg 1931, p. 190, no. 576.

APPENDIX II

ANATOLIAN COMPOSITE BRONZE AND IRON HELMETS[375]

The type of two composite iron and bronze helmets which were furnished with bronze knob, earflaps, neckguard and eyebrow cutouts found in western Anatolia was previously unknown. Two examples are known from Sardis[376] (*Ill. 29-30*) and Old-Smyrna (Bayrakli)[377]. Unfortunately the Old-Smyrna helmet no longer exists[378], the only information is a short note which mentioned the finding of the helmet[379]. Probably fragments of a third similar helmet were found on the Lindos Acropolis, but the identification of this piece is impossible. We know only the fact that there were three iron fragments of a helmet excavated on the Acropolis of Lindos, and one of them, probably an earflap fragment was decorated with a bronze cord (W.: 0.8 cm)[380].

The examination of the Sardis helmet (probably of the same type) revealed the structure and construction of this type of helmet: it was made of eight triangular plates of iron placed in radial arrangement and fastened to an interior armature of eight iron bands or ribs. On the top of the cap the ends of the plates and ribs were masked underneath an iron disk. On the front of the helmet, at the brows there was a pair of scallops evidently meeting in a point above the nose. There was no nose-guard on the helmet. The edges of the helmet were perforated with small holes for the attachment of a lining. The cheek-pieces - which were attached to the helmet by hinges - have a triangular semilunate shape. Their edges were similarly perforated for the attachment of a lining. Near the point of each cheek-piece there was a bigger hole for the chin-strap. The fragmentary neck-guard is a narrow strip of iron sheet with an everted lip at the bottom. The method of attachment to the cap of the helmet is unclear. The helmet was decorated with bronze. The finial was made of bronze with an iron cotter-pin which secured it to the cap of the helmet. The cap of the helmet and the cheek-pieces were decorated with cords contouring the edges of all and on the cap of the helmet radiating from the rim of the finial plate to the contour cords. On the cap of the helmet the cord occur in groups of three, on each cheek-pieces the top edge is contoured by two rods, the side edges by one. The cords were made of bronze except of the central cords of the triplets of the cap of the helmet, which are iron.

The helmet was found in the destruction level (Brick Fall deposit of Colossal Lydian Structure) which can be associated with the siege and partial sack of Sardis by Cyrus the Great of Persia[381]. So the helmet should belong to one of the troops of Croesus or Cyrus. As Greenewalt has argued[382], the cultural identity of the helmet is obscure, since the armies of Croesus and Cyrus included soldiers from other eastern Mediterranean and Near Eastern territories[383], Persia and Lydia are not the only cultural homes possible for this type of helmet.

The representational evidence for both Persian and Lydian helmets is very slight[384]. A Graeco-

---

[375] This chapter is based on my earlier study on the Near Eastern helmets of the Iron Age. **Dezsö 1993**.

[376] **Greenewalt 1989**, pp. 183-184; **Greenewalt 1991**, pp. 11-12, figs. 14-17; **Greenewalt - Heywood 1992**, pp. 1-31, figs. 1-27; **Greenewalt 1992**, pp. 260-269, figs. 12-19; **Dezsö 1993**, Cat. no. 127, Group no. P.2.1, pls. 156-159.

[377] **Cook 1952**, p. 106, fig. 12; **Cook - Akurgal 1952**, p. 23: "...between the pithoi and the floor of the seventh century pylon, a large cache of iron weapons was uncovered; this cache also consisted largely of spearheads, some of considerable length, but also contained an iron helmet with a bronze plume-knob"; **Greenewalt 1991**, p. 12; **Greenewalt - Heywood 1992**, p. 12, note 19; **Greenewalt 1992**, p. 265, note 31; **Dezsö 1993**, Cat. no. 128, Group no. P.2.2.

[378] C.H. Greenewalt, personal communication; **Greenewalt - Heywood 1992**, p. 12, note 19.

[379] **Cook - Akurgal 1952**, p. 23. See **Greenewalt - Heywood 1992**, p. 12, note 19; **Greenewalt 1992**, p. 265, note 31.

[380] **Blinkenberg 1931**, p. 189, no. 569: "569 GD. Trois fragments d'un casque en fer, comprenant le sommet avec la partie frontale at une partie des couvre-joues fixes. L'état incomplet ne permet pas de déterminer précisément la forme du casque, mais ce qui en reste fait penser qu'il a été du type corinthien. La partie frontale est reinforcée par un morceau de fer fixé à l'aide de rivets; au couvre-joue sont appliquées par dehors des bandes de bronze (larg. 0.008)."

[381] **Greenewalt 1991**, p. 12. Greenewalt dated the destruction of the Colossal Lydian Structure ca. 550 B.C.

[382] **Greenewalt - Heywood 1992**, pp. 16-17.

[383] **Greenewalt - Heywood 1992**, pp. 16-17, notes 37-40: Xenophon (*Cyroupaideia* 6.2.10) listed 12 non-Lydian auxilliary troops: Thrace, Egypt, Cyprus, Cilicia, Phrygia, Lycaonia, Paphlagonia, Cappadocia, Arabia, Phoenicia, Assyria, Ionia and Aeolis; and Egyptians (6.3.19-20; 7.1.30-45) Indians and Chaldaeans (6.2.9, 11; 7.2.2-8) in Cyrus's army.

Persian stele[385] shows a horseman wearing a helmet, but his helmet is crested with a tassel. A limestone statue from Golgoi, Cyprus[386] shows a headdress with radial structure at the front. But this headdress can not be considered as a helmet. Two iron earflaps with bronze cord decoration similar to that of the Sardis helmet were found at Idalion, Cyprus[387].

Various features of this type of helmet can be traced back to three different Near Eastern helmet types and/or traditions:

1. The earliest known examples of the eyebrow cutouts on helmets in the ancient Near East are Middle Elamite[388]. This feature appears on Scythian cast bronze helmets of "Kuban" type[389] (late 7th - early 6th centuries B.C.), where the eyebrow cutout is bordered by a rib and follows the line of the pair of curves on the front of the earlier Near Eastern conical helmets, to which it harks back.

2. The closest parallels for the shape are the Scythian bronze helmets of "Kuban" type as well. These helmets derived probably from the Near Eastern (Assyrian) conical helmet tradition: the eyebrow cutouts and the vertical rib on the front of the Scythian helmets may be traced back to the pair(s) of curve(s) and the vertical rib between them on the front of Near Eastern conical helmets (Assyria, North Syria, Urartu, North-West Iran). Most of these Scythian helmets bear a knob of conical shape or in the form of a ring. The vertical rib of the Near Eastern helmets is similarly changed on the Marlik helmets (Northern Iran)[390] as well. So these Scythian helmets can be derived from various Near Eastern helmet traditions (Assyrian - Urartian tradition and North-West Iranian - Transcaucasian tradition) and played an important role through direct connections in the evolution of the Sardis type of composite helmets.

3. The closest parallel or archetype of the structure of the Sardis helmet is a Transcaucasian helmet found at Safar-Haraba, Trialeti, Mogila 13[391], which was made from triangular bronze plates placed in radial arrangement(?) and furnished with long earflaps. Unfortunately the possible inner structure of this helmet is unknown.

All these three features mentioned above prove the theory already suggested by Greenewalt[392] that the most likely cultural home for the Sardis type of composite helmets would be late 7th - early 6th century B.C. northern Iran (eyebrow cutouts) and the Transcaucasian - Caucasian region (radial structure). The role of the Scythians in the emergence of this type of helmet may have been very important since the shape of Scythian helmets of "Kuban" type is the closest parallel to the shape of the Sardis helmet[393]. This Iranian-Caucasian(-Scythian) inspiration does not signify that Lydia or Persia was the most likely place for it to have been made. This type of helmet could be considered as the product of a

---

384 There are altogether three bronze helmets which can be identified as "Persian". For detailed discussion see **Dezső 1993**, pp. 77-81. 1. Mainz, RGZM, O.39606: **Schaaff 1973**, pl. 49; **Kellner 1976**, p. 78, Cat. no. 143; **Dezső 1993**, Cat. no. 129, Group no. P.1.1; 2. Mainz, RGZM, O.39585: **Schaaff 1973**, pl. 48; **Kellner 1976**, p. 79, Cat. no. 151; **Dezső 1993**, Cat. no. 130, Group no. P.1.2; 3. Olympia, B 5100: **Kunze 1961c**, pp. 129-137, pls. 56-57, **Schaaff 1973**, pl. 50; **Dezső 1993**, Cat. no. 131, Group no. P.1.3.

385 Manisa, Archaeological Museum, Inv. no. 3389, **Greenewalt - Heywood 1992**, figs. 25-26.

386 New York, Metropolitan Museum of Art, MMA 74.51.2466; **Greenewalt - Heywood 1992**, fig. 23.

387 **Gjerstad 1935**, pl. CLXXVIII:14 (no. 505), 15 (no. 1071); **Gjerstad 1948**, pp. 132-133, fig. 20:8. These earflaps were for long time identified as the earflaps of Cypriote examples of Greek "Kegelhelm", (**Tatton-Brown 1979**, p. 283). Similar shape of earflaps is known from the "Tamassos type" of Cypriote conical helmets, from Greek "Kegelhelm" of Geometric Age and from Illyrian helmets.

388 **Dezső 1993**, Cat. nos. 113-118, Group nos. I.1.1-5.

389 **Dezső 1993**, p. 80 lists 11 helmets of this type with measures and bibliography.

390 **Dezső 1993**, Cat. nos. 125-127, Group nos. I.4.1-3.

391 **Kuftin 1941**, pp. 68, 159, 224, note 265, pls. 11, 40; **Piotrovsky 1955**, p. 26, note 1; **Belinsky 1990**, p. 194; **Dezső 1993**, Cat. no. 109, Group no. C.3.

392 **Greenewalt - Heywood 1992**, pp. 12-14, esp. 17.

393 The Kuban type of Scythian helmet itself is the latest example of the canonical decorative system of 9th and early 8th centuries B.C. Assyrian, 8th-7th centuries B.C. North-West Iranian conical helmets. The conical shape became mostly hemispherical (early Iranian local tradition). Only the knob-like projection on the top of this Kuban type of Scythian helmets reminds us of the earlier shape. The vertical rib on the front of these helmets still exists, but the pair of curves bending to the centre on the front of the helmets lost its original function and became simply the border of two eyebrow cutouts (which was similarly an early Iranian feature: see **Dezső 1993**, pp. 68-69, Cat. nos. 109-113).

region of Anatolia or Transcaucasia under Scytho-Iranian (Median and/or Persian) influence. The general principle of construction may be seen as a prototype of the later Sassanian composite *Bandhelm* and the late Roman, early medieval *Strebenhelm* and *Spangenhelm* types[394].

---

[394] **Greenewalt - Heywood 1992**, pp. 12-14, notes, 22-23.

APPENDIX III

THE DEVELOPMENT OF EARLY CORINTHIAN HELMETS

The aim of this chapter is not to discuss the development of the classical form of Corinthian helmets which was studied in great detail by Kunze[395] and others[396], most recently by Pflug[397], but to trace the genesis of the form of Corinthian and the connecting "pseudo-Corinthian"[398] helmets.

The complexity of the problem is clearly visible on *Ill. 3*. The "official line of development" of the classical form of Corinthian helmets is represented at **Olympia**. The 2nd column of the diagram shows this sequence: 1. the archaic form with high, unstilted crest curving forward (from two bronze statuettes, *B 5700* and *B 6177*); 2. archaic helmet form with short nose-guard (*B 55*); 3a. helmet with *Seitenzwickeln* (*B 2185*); 3b. helmet with *Seitenausschnitten* (so called *Myros-Gruppe*). But there is an alternative, "unofficial" line of development not only outside the Peloponnese, but in Olympia and in Sparta as well. This "unofficial" line is characterized by archaic elements, which first became redundant on the Greek Mainland, then later on the islands as well.

The first phase of the development was probably the Oriental hemispherical helmet with a high crest curving forward. This basic type was furnished in the Aegean with two local features: separate faceguard with eye and mouth cutouts (covered face tradition) and separate neck guard. These two features occur separately or together.

The alternative (and redundant) line of development was present in Olympia as well: 1. helmet *M.8.5* is an Oriental type high crested helmet which was furnished with a face-guard and neck-guard complex. The overall shape is already Corinthian. 2. Two face-guards (*B 4228* and *B 357*) show the presence of probably composite Corinthian helmets with the separate face-guard furnished with redundant eye and mouth cutouts. 3. The hole on the face-guard of helmets *B 2196* and *B 4150* is an archaizing feature, reminiscent of the earlier mouth cutout. The classical form of Corinthian helmet with separately added face-guard with a developed, elongated point (*M.8.11*) remained in use in Olympia for a while (probably until the last quarter of 7th century B.C.).

Pseudo-Corinthian helmets

Sparta, the other important centre of the Peloponnese shows a quite different helmet tradition which points in the direction of the archaic tradition of the Greek islands[399]. There are five types of pseudo-Corinthian helmets represented on various objects from Sparta:

1. Pseudo-Corinthian helmet with neck- and face-guard made of a single piece. High, stilted crest curving forward. There is no nose-guard and the face-guard (without mouth cutout) is small (*M.8.7*).
2. Pseudo-Corinthian helmet with neck- and face-guard made of a single piece. Stilted crest attached to the cap of the helmet. There is no nose-guard and the face-guard (without mouth) cutout is small (*M.8.9*).
3. Pseudo-Corinthian helmet with face-guard without neck-guard made of a single piece. High, orientalizing crescent-shaped stilted crest. The rounded face-guard was furnished with eye- and mouth cutouts as well. The nose-guard is missing (*M.8.3*).
4. Pseudo-Corinthian helmet with face-guard and neck-guard made of a single piece. High, stilted crest curving forward. Its main characteristic is the ear-cutout. The rounded face-guard was furnished with eye- and mouth cutouts. The nose-guard is missing (*M.8.6*).

---

395 **Kunze 1941**, pp. 108-113, figs. 96-100, pls. 38-45; **Kunze 1956**, pp. 69-74, pls. 34-39; **Kunze 1961b**, pp. 56-128, pls. 13-55; **Kunze 1967c**, pp. 83-110, figs. 28-37, pls. 39-40.

396 **Amandry 1949**, pp. 437-446, figs. 1-7, pls. 22-25; **Neeft 1977**, pp. 443-449; **Weiss 1977**, pp. 195-207; **Despini 1981**, pp. 246-250; **Dörig 1981**, pp. 109-110, pl. 12; **Cialowicz 1983**, pp. 47-52; **Jackson 1987**, pp. 107-114, pl. 17; **Bottini 1988**, pp. 107-136.

397 **Pflug 1988c**, pp. 65-106.

398 Named here by the present author.

399 This fact is emphasized by the objects, on which the helmet representations occure: ivory carving and relief pythoi.

5. Pseudo-Corinthian helmet with face-guard made of a single piece. The neck-guard was added separately. Stilted crest attached to the cap of the helmet. The rounded face-guard was furnished with eye- and mouth-cutouts as well. The nose-guard is missing (*M.8.8*).

Samos was probably an other important centre of the Eastern Aegean helmet tradition. The helmet of Geryon (*M.8.10*) from a horse's bronze breastplate is a composite pseudo-Corinthian helmet with all the features of the Spartan helmets discussed above. The only difference is the pointed shape of the face-guard, which was added separately to the cap of the helmet. The neck-guard - similarly to helmet *M.8.8* - was added separately as well.

Lindos - similarly to Samos - represents the Eastern Aegean - Eastern Mediterranean covered face helmet tradition. The characteristic Lindos face-guards[400] (which were added separately to the cap of the helmet and were furnished with eye and mouth cutouts) belonged probably a to basically Oriental type of crested helmet (*M.8.4* with small crest curving forward). The construction of this type of helmet is unknown. Helmet representation *M.8.4* does not give the details of construction. We do not know whether the cap of the helmet was made of a single piece of bronze sheet or followed the five part construction of the Greek Geometric helmets discussed above in detail. These face-guards transformed the open face Oriental helmets to characteristic Eastern Aegean covered face helmets. Similar pseudo-Corinthian helmets were known not only in Lindos and Samos, but in Olympia as well (*B 4228* and *B 357*). For the special, intermediatory role of Lindos between the Oriental and Aegean helmet types see Appendix II.

Mykonos. On the famous Mykonos relief pithos[401] there are interesting helmets representing the early development of the Aegean covered face (pseudo-Corinthian) helmets (*M.8.1* and *M.8.2*), and their forerunners, the plain Oriental crested helmets (*M.4.3-4, M.7.1* and *M.7.2*). These Oriental crested helmets were furnished with a separately added bronze sheet, forming the neck- and face-guard. The high, tasselled crest have parallels both in Anatolia (*O.2.56*) and the Near East as well (*O.2.1-4, 25-30*).

Prinias. This Cretan pseudo-Corinthian helmet represents the local development of covered face helmets of the last quarter of 7th century B.C. The most important archaizing features of the Cretan helmets are the riveted construction (helmets made of two similar halves riveted together)[402] and the mouth cutout characteristic of the Eastern Aegean pseudo-Corinthian helmets (*M.8.12*).

The following diagram shows the differences between the Corinthian and pseudo-Corinthian line of evolution.

	face-guard	face-guard added sep.	neck-guard	neck-guard added sep.	nose-guard	eye cutout	mouth cutout	ear cutout	crest
B 5700	+		+		+	+			+
B 6177	+		+		+	+			+
B 55	+		+		+	+			
B 2185	+		+		+	+			
B 4170	+		+		+	+			
M.8.5		+	+			+	+		+
B 4228		+		+		+	+		
B 357		+		+		+	+		
B 2196	+			+	+	+	+		
B 4150	+			+	+	+	+		
M.8.7	+		+			+			+

---

400 **Blinkenberg 1931**, nos. 571-576.
401 **Ervin 1963**, pls. 18-19.
402 **Hoffmann 1972**, passim.

ID	1	2	3	4	5	6	7
M.8.9	+		+		+		+
M.8.11		+	+		+	+		+
M.8.3	+				+	+	+
M.8.6	+		+		+	+	+
M.8.8	+			+	+	+	+
M.8.10		+		+	+	+	+
L 571		+			+	+	
M.8.4		+			+	+	+
M.8.1		+		+	+		+
M.8.2		+		+	+		+
M.8.12	+		+		+	+	+

As can be seen the most important pseudo-Corinthian features are: separately added face-guard, rounded face-guard, separately added neck-guard, the missing of nose-guard and mouth cutout. These elements gradually became redundant, and the Corinthian and other type of classical helmets (Illyrian and Chalkidian) replaced them by the end of the 7th century B.C. This pseudo-Corinthian tradition or at least one of its features (detachable faceguard) survived in the Ionian helmet tradition of the late 7th and 6th centuries B.C.

This brief discussion I hope sheds light on the tendency, in which the Corinthian (and Illyrian) type of helmet was only one alternative in the evolution of the covered face helmets, whilst several other traditions flourished mainly in the Aegean islands and on the Greek Mainland, at least in Sparta, in the 7th century B.C.

APPENDIX IV

CATALOGUE OF NEAR EASTERN AND MEDITERRANEAN HELMET REPRESENTATIONS

O = Oriental
M = Mediterranean

O.1 = Oriental conical/pointed helmets
O.2 = Oriental crested helmets

M.1 = Local Geometric helmets
M.2 = Conical helmets
M.3 = Conical crested helmets
M.4 = Conical/pointed helmets
 with crest curving forward
M.5 = Conical/pointed helmets
 with unstilted crest curving forward
M.6 = Conical/pointed helmets
 with crescent-shaped crest
M.7 = Hemispherical crested helmets
M.8 = "'Pseudo Corinthian'/unknown Greek/
 Cretan"
M.X = Unclassified

O.1.1
White Obelisk
Ninive
Ashur-nasir-pal I (1050-1032 B.C.)
London, British Museum, WA 118807
H.: 290 cm
Börker-Klähn 1982, pp. 179-180, no. 132, pls. 132a-d
Dezsö 1993, no. 75

O.1.2
Palace relief
Kalhu (Nimrud)
Ashur-nasir-pal II (883-859 B.C.)
London, British Museum, N.G. no. 7b
Budge 1914, pl. XXI:1
Dezsö 1993, no. 76

O.1.3
Palace relief
Kalhu (Nimrud)
Ashur-nasir-pal II (883-859 B.C.)
London, British Museum, N.G. no. 4a
Budge 1914, pls. XII:2, XIII:1-2, XVIII:1, XX:2
Dezsö 1993, no. 77

O.1.4
Palace relief
Kalhu (Nimrud)
Ashur-nasir-pal II (883-859 B.C.)
London, British Museum, N.G. no. 10a
Budge 1914, pls. XV:2, XXIV:1-2
Dezsö 1993, no. 78

O.1.5
Palace relief
Kalhu (Nimrud)
Ashur-nasir-pal II (883-859 B.C.)
London, British Museum, N.G. no. 15b
Budge 1914, pl. XVIII:2
Dezsö 1993, no. 79

O.1.6
Palace relief
Kalhu (Nimrud)
Ashur-nasir-pal II (883-859 B.C.)
London, British Museum, N.G. no. 1b
Budge 1914, pl. XXIII:2
Dezsö 1993, no. 80

O.1.7
Palace relief
Kalhu (Nimrud)
Ashur-nasir-pal II (883-859 B.C.)
London, British Museum, N.G. no. 3a
Budge 1914, pls. XII:1, XIII:1, XVII
Dezsö 1993, no. 81

O.1.8
Palace relief
Kalhu (Nimrud)
Ashur-nasir-pal II (883-859 B.C.)
London, British Museum, N.G. no. 16b(2)
Budge 1914, pl. XXV:2
Dezsö 1993, no. 82

O.1.9
Palace relief
Kalhu (Nimrud)
Ashur-nasir-pal II (883-859 B.C.)
London, British Museum, N.G. no. 9a
Budge 1914, pls. XV:1, XXI:2
Dezsö 1993, no. 83

O.1.10
Palace relief
Kalhu (Nimrud)
Ashur-nasir-pal II (883-859 B.C.)
London, British Museum, N.G. no. 9a
Budge 1914, pls. XV:1, XVII:1-2, XVIII:2, XXI:1, XXIII:2, XXV:2
Dezsö 1993, no. 84

O.1.11
Palace relief

Kalhu (Nimrud)
Ashur-nasir-pal II (883-859 B.C.)
London, British Museum, N.G. no. 14b
Budge 1914, pl. XXIV:1
Dezsö 1993, no. 85

O.1.12
Palace relief
Kalhu (Nimrud)
Ashur-nasir-pal II (883-859 B.C.)
London, British Museum, N.G. no. 15b
Budge 1914, pls. XVIII:2, XXIV:1
Dezsö 1993, no. 86

O.1.13
Fragments of a coloured brick orthostat
Ashur
9th c. B.C. (Shalmaneser III?)
Ass. 10756
Andrae 1925, pl. 9e
Dezsö 1993, no. 88

O.1.14
Throne base, panel f
Nimrud, Fort Shalmaneser, great throne room T1
Shalmaneser III (858-824 B.C.), Mushallim-Marduk
Baghdad, Iraq Museum, ND 11000
Mallowan 1966, vol. 2, pp. 446-448
Dezsö 1993, no. 89

O.1.15
Bronze statuette
Beqaa (Lebanon)
10th-9th (?) c. B.C.
Beirut, National Museum
Seeden 1980, p. 109, no. 1723, pl. 102
Dezsö 1993, no. 90

O.1.16
Bronze model of a chariot
"Tartous"
10th-9th (?) c. B.C.
Paris, Louvre, AO 22265
Collon - Crouwel - Littauer 1976, pls. XIA-B
Seeden 1980, pp. 109-110, no. 1725, pls. N and 103
Dezsö 1993, no. 91

O.1.17
Reliefs from bronze gate
Balawat
Shalmaneser III (858-824 B.C.)
London, British Museum
King 1915, pl. IX, band II.3, lower register
Dezsö 1993, no. 92

O.1.18
Reliefs from bronze gate
Balawat
Shalmaneser III (858-824 B.C.)
London, British Museum
King 1915, pl. III, band I.3, lower register
Dezsö 1993, no. 93

O.1.19
Reliefs from bronze gate
Balawat
Shalmaneser III (858-824 B.C.)
London, British Museum
King 1915, pl. III, band I.3, lower register
Dezsö 1993, no. 94

O.1.20
Reliefs from bronze gate
Balawat
Shalmaneser III (858-824 B.C.)
London, British Museum
King 1915, pls. XIV, band III.2, lower register
XXIV, band IV.6, lower register
Dezsö 1993, no. 95

O.1.21
Ivory
Kalhu (Nimrud), NW Palace, ZT. 25
9th c. B.C.
ND 3266
Mallowan - Davies 1970, pl. VI, no. 14
Dezsö 1993, no. 96

O.1.22
Ivory
Kalhu (Nimrud), Nabu Temple, Throneroom (SEB II)
Early 8th c. B.C.
ND 5612
Mallowan - Davies 1970, pl. XVIII, no. 62
Dezsö 1993, no. 97

O.1.23
Ivory
Kalhu (Nimrud), Nabu Temple, Throneroom (SEB II)
9th c. B.C.
ND 5612
Mallowan - Davies 1970, pl. XVIII, no. 62
Dezsö 1993, no. 98

O.1.24
Relief slab (basalt orthostat)
Zinçirli, "Südtor der Stadt"
10th-9th c. B.C.

Berlin, Staatliche Museen zu Berlin
H.: 128 cm
Bittel 1976b, fig. 297
Dezsö 1993, no. 99

O.1.25
Relief slab (basalt orthostat)
Tell Halaf
9th c. B.C.
Berlin, Staatliche Museen zu Berlin
Klengel-Brandt 1986, pl. on the back cover
Dezsö 1993, no. 100

O.1.26
Basalt orthostat
Zinçirli, Southern Gate of the City
First half of 8th c. B.C.
Berlin, Vorderasiatisches Museum
H.: 130 cm
von Luschan et al. 1902, fig. 96, pls. XXXIVc, XXXV
Orthmann 1971, pp. 537-538, pl. 55b
Dezsö 1993, no. 133

Basalt orthostat
Zinçirli, Western Walls of the Outer Walls of the Acropolis
First half of 8th c. B.C.
Istanbul, Archaeological Museum, Inv. no. 7780
H.: 116 cm
von Luschan et al. 1902, fig. 130, pl. XLIV
Orthmann 1971, p. 543, pl. 60c

O.1.27
Basalt orthostat
Zinçirli, outer front of the Eastern Walls of the Gate of Acropolis
First half of 8th c. B.C.
Berlin, Vorderasiatisches Museum, VA 2647
H.: 137 cm
von Luschan et al. 1902, fig. 103, pl. XL
Orthmann 1971, p. 541, pl. 58f
Dezsö 1993, no. 134

O.1.28
Ivory
Kalhu (Nimrud), Ezida: Temple of Nabu, N.T. 14
8th c. B.C.
ND 5395
Mallowan -Davies 1970, pl. XVII, no. 61a
Dezsö 1993, no. 135

O.1.29
Palace reliefs
Kalhu (Nimrud), SW Palace
Tiglath-pileser III (745-727 B.C.)
London, British Museum, BM 118908
Smith 1938, pl. IX
Barnett - Falkner 1962, pls. LXIX, LXX
London, British Museum, BM 118934
Smith 1938, pl. X
Dezsö 1993, no. 136

Palace reliefs
Kalhu (Nimrud), Central Palace
Tiglath-pileser III (745-727 B.C.)
London, British Museum
Barnett - Falkner 1962, pls. IX, X, XIII, XIV
(BM 118878 = *Smith 1938, pl. XIX*), *XXVII, XXVIII* (Istanbul, Inv. no. 23), *XXXI, XXXII* (Bombay, Inv. no. 7), *LII* (Leningrad, Hermitage, Inv. no. 3943), *LIV, LV* (Paris, de Clerq Coll.),
with unknown provenance:
Barnett - Falkner 1962, pls. LXXII (Zürich, Inv. no. 1918), *LXXIII* (Zürich, Inv. no. 1917), *LXXIV* (Berlin, VA 984), *LXXV* (Louvre, AO 19854), *LXXVI* (Bristol, H.3175)

O.1.30
Palace relief
Kalhu (Nimrud), "Between Central Palace and Upper Chambers
Tiglath-pileser III (745-727 B.C.)
London, British Museum, Or. Dr. I, pl. XIII
Barnett - Falkner 1962, pl. LVIII
Dezsö 1993, no. 137

Palace relief
Kalhu (Nimrud)
Tiglath-pileser III (745-727 B.C.)
Private collection
Barnett - Falkner 1962, pl. LXXVII

O.1.31
Palace relief
Kalhu (Nimrud), Central Palace
Tiglath-pileser III (745-727 B.C.)
London, British Museum, BM 115634
Smith 1938, pl. XIII
Barnett - Falkner 1962, pl. XXXVIII
Dezsö 1993, no. 138

O.1.32
Palace relief
Kalhu (Nimrud), Central Palace
Tiglath-pileser III (745-727 B.C.)
London, British Museum, BM 118903
Smith 1938, pl. XIV
Barnett - Falkner 1962, pls. XXXIX, XL, XLVIII, XLIX
Dezsö 1993, no. 139

O.1.33
Palace relief
Kalhu (Nimrud), SW Palace
Tiglath-pileser III (745-727 B.C.)
London, British Museum, BM 118934
Smith 1938, pl. X
Dezsö 1993, no. 140

O.1.34
Palace reliefs
Kalhu (Nimrud), Central Palace
Tiglath-pileser III (745-727 B.C.)
Bombay, V.A.M. 78
Barnett - Falkner 1962, pl. XVI (= pl. XV, Or. Dr. III, Central XI)
Paris, De Clerq Collection
Barnett - Falkner 1962, pl. LV (= pl. LIV, Or. Dr. III, Central XXIV)
London, British Museum, BM 118934+118931
Barnett - Falkner 1962, pls. XCII, XCIII
Dezsö 1993, no. 141

O.1.35
Palace relief
Kalhu (Nimrud), "Between Central Palace and Upper Chambers"
Tiglath-pileser III (745-727 B.C.)
London, British Museum, Or. Dr. I, pl. IX
Barnett - Falkner 1962, pl. LIX
Dezsö 1993, no. 142

O.1.36
Palace relief
Unknown provenance
Tiglath-pileser III (745-727 B.C.)
Private collection
Barnett - Falkner 1962, pl. LXXVII
Dezsö 1993, no. 143

O.1.37
Palace relief
Kalhu (Nimrud), SW Palace
Tiglath-pileser III (745-727 B.C.)
London, British Museum, BM 118907
Smith 1938, pl. XVIII
Barnett - Flakner 1962, pls. LXVI (= Or. Dr. III, S.W. XV), LXVII
Dezsö 1993, no. 144

O.1.38
Coloured brick
Ashur, façade of the Temple of Ashur
Tiglath-Pileser III (745-727 B.C.)
Andrae 1925, pl. 6
Dezsö 1993, no. 162

O.1.39
Wall-painting
Nimrud, "Zentrum des Hügels"
Tiglath-pileser III (745-727 B.C.)
H.: 0.31 m
W.: 0.225 m
Nunn 1988, pl. 124
Dezsö 1993, no. 163

O.1.40
Wall-painting
Nimrud, "Acropolis Palace"
Tiglath-pileser III (745-727 B.C.)
H.: 0.17 m
W.: 0.10 m
Nunn 1988, pl. 123
Dezsö 1993, no. 164

O.1.41
Wall-painting
Til-Barsip, Room XXIV
Tiglath-pileser III (745-727 B.C.)
Thureau-Dangin - Dunand 1936, pl. XLIX, upper register
Dezsö 1993, no. 165

O.1.42
Wall-painting
Til-Barsip, Room XXIV
Tiglath-pileser III (745-727 B.C.)
Thureau-Dangin - Dunand 1936, pl. LI
Dezsö 1993, no. 166

O.1.43
Wall-painting
Til-Barsip, Room XXIV
Tiglath-pileser III (745-727 B.C.)
Thureau-Dangin - Dunand 1936, pl. L
Dezsö 1993, no. 167

O.1.44
Wall-painting
Til-Barsip
Tiglath-pileser III (745-727 B.C.)
Parrot 1961, fig. 339
Dezsö 1993, no. 168

O.1.45
Wall-painting
Til-Barsip
Tiglath-pileser III (745-727 B.C.)
Thureau-Dangin - Dunand 1936, pl. XLIX, lower register
Dezsö 1993, no. 169

O.1.46

Wall-painting
Til-Barsip, Room XXIV
Tiglath-pileser III (745-727 B.C.)
Thureau-Dangin - Dunand 1936, pl. XLIX
Dezsö 1993, no. 170

O.1.47
Wall-painting
Til-Barsip, Room XXIV
Tiglath-pileser III (745-727 B.C.)
Thureau-Dangin - Dunand 1936, pl. LI
Dezsö 1993, no. 171

O.1.48
Wall-painting
Til-Barsip
Tiglath-pileser III (745-727 B.C.)
Aleppo Museum
Amiet 1980, pl. 105
Dezsö 1993, no. 172

O.1.49
Wall-painting
Til-Barsip
Tiglath-pileser III (745-727 B.C.)
Aleppo Museum
Amiet 1980, pl. 105
Dezsö 1993, no. 173

O.1.50
Reliefs
Hadatu (Arslan-Tash), Western gate
Tiglath-pileser III (745-727 B.C.)
Istanbul, Archaeological Museum, Inv. no. 7-9
Thureau-Dangin et al. 1931, pls. IX:1, XI:1-2
Dezsö 1993, no. 175

O.1.51
Basalt relief
Karatepe, "Obere Grabung"
1st half of the 8th c. B.C ("Sph III")
H.: 135 cm
Bossert et al. 1950, pl. XIII, no. 64
Orthmann 1971, p. 494, pl. 18f
Dezsö 1993, no. 176

O.1.52
Basalt relief
Karatepe, "Obere Grabung"
1st half of the 8th c. B.C ("Sph III")
H.: 135 cm
Bossert et al. 1950, pl. XIII, no. 64
Orthmann 1971, p. 494, pl. 18f
Dezsö 1993, no. 177

O.1.53
Basalt reliefs
Karatepe, "Rampe der Untere Grabung"
1st half of the 8th c. B.C. ("Sph. IIIb")
Bossert et al. 1950, pls. 82, 83
Orthmann 1971, p. 493, pl. 18a
Dezsö 1993, no. 178

O.1.54
Relief
Tell Ta'yinat
Ca. 750-725 B.C. (Amuq Phase O)
Chicago, Oriental Institute Museum, A.27854
Marfoe et al. 1982, no. 32
Dezsö 1993, no. 191

O.1.55
Palace relief
Dur-Sharrukin (Khorsabad)
Sargon II (721-705 B.C.)
Botta - Flandin 1849, pl. 49 (Salle 1, slab 2)
Dezsö 1993, no. 192

O.1.56
Palace relief
Dur-Sharrukin (Khorsabad)
Sargon II (721-705 B.C.)
Botta - Flandin 1849, pl. 76 (Salle 2, slab 1)
and passim
Dezsö 1993, no. 193

O.1.57
Palace relief
Dur-Sharrukin (Khorsabad)
Sargon II (721-705 B.C.)
Botta - Flandin 1849, pl. 58 (Salle 2, slab 10)
Dezsö 1993, no. 194

O.1.58
Palace relief
Dur-Sharrukin (Khorsabad)
Sargon II (721-705 B.C.)
Botta - Flandin 1849, pls. 62-67 (Salle 11, slabs 15-21) and passim
Dezsö 1993, no. 195

O.1.59
Palace relief
Ninive (Quyunjik, SW Palace, Room XIV)
Sennacherib (705-681 B.C.)
London, British Museum, BM 124787
Smith 1938, pl. XLIII
Dezsö 1993, no. 203

O.1.60
Palace relief
Ninive (Quyunjik, SW Palace, Room XII)

Sennacherib (705-681 B.C.)
London, British Museum, BM 124783
Smith 1938, pl. XLIV
Dezsö 1993, no. 204

O.1.61
Palace relief
Ninive (Quyunjik, SW Palace, Court VI)
Sennacherib (705-681 B.C.)
London, British Museum, BM 124773
Smith 1938, pl. XXXVII
Dezsö 1993, no. 205

Palace relief
Ninive (Quyunjik, SW Palace, Court XIX)
Sennacherib (705-681 B.C.)
London, British Museum, BM 124782
Smith 1938, pl. XLVII

O.1.62
Palace relief
Ninive (Quyunjik)
Sennacherib (705-681 B.C.)
Boston, Museum of Fine Arts
Terrace 1962, no. 22
Dezsö 1993, no. 206

O.1.63
Palace relief
Ninive (Quyunjik, SW Palace)
Sennacherib (705-681 B.C.)
London, British Museum, BM 124789
Smith 1938, pl. XLI
Dezsö 1993, no. 207

O.1.64
Palace relief
Ninive (Quyunjik, SW Palace, Room XIV)
Sennacherib (705-681 B.C.)
London, British Museum, BM 124787
Smith 1938, pl. XLIII
Dezsö 1993, no. 208

O.1.65
Palace relief
Ninive (Quyunjik, SW Palace, Room XII)
Sennacherib (705-681 B.C.)
London, British Museum, BM 124783
Smith 1938, pl. XLIV
Dezsö 1993, no. 209

O.1.66
Palace relief
Ninive (Quyunjik, SW Palace, Court LXIV)
Sennacherib (705-681 B.C.)
Paterson 1912, pl. 91

Dezsö 1993, no. 210

O.1.67
Palace relief
Ninive (Quyunjik, SW Palace, Court XIX)
Sennacherib (705-681 B.C.)
London, British Museum, BM 124782
Smith 1938, pl. XLVII
Dezsö 1993, no. 211

O.1.68
Palace relief
Ninive (Quyunjik, SW Palace)
Sennacherib (705-681 B.C.)
London, British Museum, BM 124786
Smith 1938, pl. XLII
Dezsö 1993, no. 212

O.1.69
Palace relief
Ninive (Quyunjik, SW Palace)
Sennacherib (705-681 B.C.)
London, British Museum, BM 124775
Smith 1938, pl. XXXVIII:1
Dezsö 1993, no. 213

Palace relief
Ninive (Quyunjik, SW Palace, Room XLV)
Sennacherib (705-681 B.C.)
London, British Museum, BM 124777
Smith 1938, pl. XXXIX

O.1.70
Palace relief
Ninive (Quyunjik, SW Palace, Room XIV)
Sennacherib (705-681 B.C.)
London, British Museum, BM 124784
Smith 1938, pl. LVII
Dezsö 1993, no. 214

O.1.71
Palace relief
Ninive
Sennacherib (705-681 B.C.)
Madrid, Real Academia de la Historia
Reade 1972, pl. XXXVIIa
Dezsö 1993, no. 215

O.1.72
Palace relief
Ninive (Quyunjik, SW Palace, Room XII)
Sennacherib (705-681 B.C.)
London, British Museum, BM 124780
Smith 1938, pl. XLVI
Dezsö 1993, no. 216

O.1.73
Palace relief
Ninive (Quyunjik, SW Palace, Room V)
Sennacherib (705-681 B.C.)
Paterson 1912, pl. 12
Dezsö 1993, no. 217

O.1.74
Palace relief
Ninive (Quyunjik, SW Palace, Room XIV)
Sennacherib (705-681 B.C.)
London, British Museum, BM 124784
Smith 1938, pl. LVII
Dezsö 1993, no. 218

O.1.75
Palace relief
Ninive (Quyunjik, SW Palace, Room XII)
Sennacherib (705-681 B.C.)
London, British Museum, BM 124779
Smith 1938, pl. XLV
Dezsö 1993, no. 219

O.1.76
Palace relief
Ninive
Sennacherib (705-681 B.C.)
London, British Museum, BM 124775
Smith 1938, pl. XXXVIII:1
Dezsö 1993, no. 220

Palace relief
Ninive
Sennacherib (705-681 B.C.)
London, British Museum, BM 124776
Smith 1938, pl. XXXVIII:2

O.1.77
Palace relief
Ninive (Quyunjik, SW Palace)
Sennacherib (705-681 B.C.)
London, British Museum, BM 124789
Smith 1938, pl. XLI
Dezsö 1993, no. 221

O.1.78
Palace relief
Ninive (Quyunjik, SW Palace)
Sennacherib (705-681 B.C.)
Oxford, Ashmolean Museum, 1950.240
Moorey 1987, fig. 11
Dezsö 1993, no. 222

O.1.79
Palace relief
Ninive (Quyunjik, SW Palace, Court XIX)
Sennacherib (705-681 B.C.)
London, British Museum, BM 124782
Smith 1938, pl. XLVII
Dezsö 1993, no. 223

O.1.80
Cylinder seal
Ashur-nadin-shumi (700-695 B.C.)
London, British Museum, BM 77611+2
Collon 1988, pp. 129-130, no. 555
Dezsö 1993, no. 236

O.1.81
Wall-painting
Ninive
Sennacherib (705-681 B.C.) or Ashurbanipal (668-627 B.C.)
Fundnr. 1930-5.8-216
H.: 0.13 m
W.: 0.22 m
Nunn 1988, pl. 130
Dezsö 1993, no. 237

O.1.82
Stele A of Asarhaddon
Til-Barsip
Esarhaddon (680-669 B.C.)
Aleppo, Archaeological Museum
Thureau-Dangin - Dunand 1936, pp. 151-155 pl. XII
Dezsö 1993, no. 238

Stele B of Asarhaddon
Til-Barsip
Esarhaddon (680-669 B.C.)
Aleppo, Archaeological Museum, Inv. no. 31
Thureau-Dangin - Dunand 1936, pp. 155-156, pl. XIII

O.1.83
Palace relief
Ninive
Esarhaddon (680-669 B.C.)
Venice, Museuo Archeologica, no. 46
Reade 1972, pl. XLb
Dezsö 1993, no. 239

O.1.84
Palace relief
Ninive, North Palace, Room I
Ashurbanipal (668-627 B.C.)
London, British Museum, BM 124929-124930
Barnett 1976, pl. XVI and passim
Dezsö 1993, no. 241

Palace relief

Ninive
Ashurbanipal (668-627 B.C.)
Oxford, Ashmolean Museum, 1940.202
Reade 1972, pl. XXXIXa

O.1.85
Palace relief
Ninive, North Palace, Room V^1-T^1
Ashurbanipal (668-627 B.C.)
Paris, Louvre, AO 19909
Barnett 1976, pl. LXIX
Dezsö 1993, no. 242

O.1.86
Palace relief
Ninive, North Palace
Ashurbanipal (668-627 B.C.)
Berlin, Vorderasiatisches Museum, VA 961
Barnett 1976, pl.LXXa
Dezsö 1993, no. 243

O.1.87
Palace relief
Ninive, North Palace, Room V^1-T^1
Ashurbanipal (668-627 B.C.)
Paris, Louvre, AO 19908, 19904
Barnett 1976, pl. LXVIII
Dezsö 1993, no. 244

O.1.88
Palace relief
Ninive, North Palace
Ashurbanipal (668-627 B.C.)
London, Royal Geographical Society, Inv. no. 1
Barnett 1976, pl. LXXIm
Dezsö 1993, no. 245

O.1.89
Palace relief
Ninive, North Palace
Ashurbanipal (668-627 B.C.)
London, British Museum, BM 124956
Dezsö 1993, no. 246

O.2.1
Relief slab (limestone)
Carchemish, Back wall of the Processional Entry, (King's Gate), no. 12
Katuwash (c. 900-873 B.C.)
Ankara, Archaeological Museum, Inv. no. 9651
H.: 90 cm
Woolley 1921, pl. B.26c
Orthmann 1971, p. 512, H/12, pl. 34c
Dezsö 1993, no. 101

O.2.2
Relief slab (limestone)
Carchemish, King's Gate
Katuwash (c. 900-873 B.C.)
Ankara, Archaeological Museum, Inv. no. 115
H.: 130 cm
Hogarth 1914, pl. B.2a
Orthmann 1971, p. 505, F/1, pl. 28e
Dezsö 1993, no. 102

Relief slab (limestone)
Carchemish, King's Gate
Katuwash (c. 900-873 B.C.)
Ankara, Archaeological Museum, Inv. no. 117
H.: 130 cm
Hogarth 1914, pl. B.3a
Orthmann 1971, p. 507, F/3, pl. 29a
Dezsö 1993, no. 102

Relief slab
Carchemish, King's Gate
Katuwash (c. 900-873 B.C.)
Ankara, Archaeological Museum, Inv, no. 9664
H.: 135 cm
Hogarth 1914, pl. B.3b
Orthmann 1971, p. 507, F/4, pl. 29b
Dezsö 1993, no. 102

Relief slab (limestone)
Carchemish, Long wall of sculptures
Suhish II
H.: 157 cm
Woolley - Barnett 1952, pl. B.44b
Orthmann 1971, p. 503, C/11, pl. 25b
Dezsö 1993, no. 102

O.2.3
Relief slab
Carchemish, King's Gate
Katuwash (c. 900-873 B.C.)
Ankara, Archaeological Museum, Inv. no. 116
H.: 135 cm
Hogarth 1914, pl. B.2b
Orthmann 1971, pp. 505-507, F/2, pl. 28f, 71c
Dezsö 1993, no. 103

O.2.4
Relief slab
Carchemish, King's Gate
Katuwash (c. 900-873 B.C.)
Ankara, Archaeological Museum, Inv. no. 117
H.: 130 cm
Hogarth 1914, pl. B.3a
Orthmann 1971, p. 507, F/3, pl. 29a

Dezsö 1993, no. 104

Relief slab
Carchemish, King's Gate
Ankara, Archaeological Museum, Inv. no. 9664
H.: 135 cm
Hogarth 1914, pl. B.3b
Orthmann 1971, p. 507, F/4, pl. 29b
Dezsö 1993, no. 104

Relief slab
Carchemish, Long wall of sculptures
Suhish II
H.: 165 cm
Woolley - Barnett 1952, pl. B.46a
Orthmann 1971, p. 503, C/14, pl. 25d
Dezsö 1993, no. 104

O.2.5
Relief slab
Kanish (Kültepe)
9th c. B.C.
Kayseri, Archaeological Museum
H.: 92 cm
Bittel 1976b, fig. 321
Dezsö 1993, no. 105

O.2.6
Basalt orthostat
Zinçirli, Eastern Wall of the Outer Gate of teh Acropolis
First half of 8th c. B.C.
Berlin, Vorderasiatisches Museum, VA 2711
H.: 100 cm
von Luschan et al. 1902, figs. 122-123, pl. XXXVIIIc
Orthmann 1971, p. 542, pl. 59g
Dezsö 1993, no. 131

O.2.7
Basalt orthostat
Zinçirli, Eastern Wall of the Outer Gate of the Acropolis
First half of 8th c. B.C.
Berlin, Vorderasiatisches Museum, VA 2713
H.: 90 cm
von Luschan et al. 1902, fig. 135, pl. XXXVIIIb
Orthmann 1971, p. 543, pl. 61b
Dezsö 1993, no. 132

O.2.8
Palace reliefs
Kalhu (Nimrud), Central Palace
Tiglath-pileser III (745-727 B.C.)
London, British Museum, BM 115634
Smith 1938, pl. XIII
Barnett - Falkner 1962, pls. XXXVII, XXXVIII
Dezsö 1993, no. 147

O.2.9
Palace relief
Kalhu (Nimrud), Central Palace
Tiglath-pileser III (745-727 B.C.)
London, British Museum, BM 115634
Barnett - Falkner 1962, pls. XXXVII (Or. Dr. III. Central XXVII), XXXVIII
Dezsö 1993, no. 148

O.2.10
Palace relief
Kalhu (Nimrud), Central Palace
Tiglath-pileser III (745-727 B.C.)
Zürich, Archäologisches Institut der Universität, Inv. no. 1920
Barnett - Falkner 1962, pls. L (Or. Dr. III. Central XXVIII), LI
Dezsö 1993, no. 149

O.2.11
Palace relief
Kalhu (Nimrud), Central Palace
Tiglath-pileser III (745-727 B.C.)
Zürich, Archäologisches Institut der Universität, Inv. no. 1916
Barnett - Falkner 1962, pls. XXXV (Or. Dr. III. Central I), XXXVI
Dezsö 1993, no. 150

O.2.12
Palace relief
Unknown provenance
Tiglath-pileser III (745-727 B.C.)
Minneapolis, Institute of Arts
Barnett - Falkner 1962, pl. LXI
Dezsö 1993, no. 151

O.2.13
Palace relief
Kalhu (Nimrud), Central Palace
Tiglath-pileser III (745-727 B.C.)
Leyden, Rijksmuseum van Oudheden, Inv. no. A.1952/12.1
Barnett - Falkner 1962, pls. XLI (Or. Dr. III. Central XXI), XLII
Dezsö 1993, no. 152

O.2.14
Palace relief
Unknown provenance
Tiglath-pileser III (745-727 B.C.)
London, British Museum, BM 119402
Barnett - Falkner 1962, pl. LXXIX

Dezsö 1993, no. 153

O.2.15
Palace reliefs
Kalhu (Nimrud), SW Palace
Tiglath-pileser III (745-727 B.C.)
London, British Museum, BM 118934
Smith 1938, pl. X
Barnett - Falkner 1962, pls. LXXXVIII, XC (Or. Dr. III. S.W. XVIII), XCI
Dezsö 1993, no. 154

O.2.16
Palace relief
Kalhu (Nimrud), SW Palace
Tiglath-pileser III (745-727 B.C.)
London, British Museum, Or. Dr. III. S.W. XIX
Barnett - Falkner 1962, pl. LXII
Dezsö 1993, no. 155

O.2.17
Palace relief
Unknown provenance
Tiglath-pileser III (745-727 B.C.)
Zürich, Archäologisches Institut der Universität, Inv. no. 1917
Barnett - Falkner 1962, pl. LXXIII
Dezsö 1993, no. 156

O.2.18
Palace relief
Kalhu (Nimrud), Central Palace
Tiglath-pileser III (745-727 B.C.)
London, British Museum, BM 118902
Smith 1938, pl. XVI
Barnett - Falkner 1962, pls. XXXIII (Or. Dr. Central XIX), XXXIV
Dezsö 1993, no. 157

O.2.19
Wall-painting
Til-Barsip, Room XXIV
Tiglath-pileser III (745-727 B.C.)
Thureau-Dangin - Dunand 1936, pl. XLIX, lower register
Dezsö 1993, no. 174

O.2.20
Basalt relief
Karatepe, "Westwand der westliche Nebenkammer,
Untere Grabung
1st half of the 8th c. B.C. ("Sph. IIIb")
H.: 110 cm
Bossert et al. 1950, pl. XX, no. 100
Orthmann 1971, p. 491, pl. 16c
Dezsö 1993, no. 179

O.2.21
Basalt relief
Karatepe, "Obere Grabung"
1st half of the 8th c. B.C.
Bossert et al. 1950, pl. XIII, no. 69
Dezsö 1993, no. 180

O.2.22
Basalt reliefs
Karatepe, "Rampe der Untere Grabung"
1st half of the 8th c. B.C. ("Sph. IIIb")
Bossert et al. 1950, pl. XVI, nos. 82-83
Orthmann 1971, p. 493, pls. 18a
Dezsö 1993, no. 181

O.2.23
Basalt relief
Karatepe, "Obere Grabung"
1st half of the 8th c. B.C. ("Sph. IIIB")
Bossert et al. 1950, pl. XIII, no. 64
Orthmann 1971, p. 494, pl. 18f
Dezsö 1993, no. 182

O.2.24
Palace relief
Dur-Sharrukin (Khorsabad)
Sargon II (721-705 B.C.)
Botta - Flandin 1849, pl. 55 (Salle 11, slab 7)
Dezsö 1993, no. 197

O.2.25
Palace relief
Dur-Sharrukin (Khorsabad)
Sargon II (721-705 B.C.)
Botta - Flandin 1849, pl. 70 (Salle 11, slab 28)
Dezsö 1993, no. 198

O.2.26
Palace relief
Dur-Sharrukin (Khorsabad)
Sargon II (721-705 B.C.)
Botta - Flandin 1849, pl. 145 (Salle 14, slab 2)
Dezsö 1993, no. 199

O.2.27
Palace relief
Dur-Sharrukin (Khorsabad)
Sargon II (721-705 B.C.)
Botta - Flandin 1849, pl. 98 (Salle 5, slab 25)
Dezsö 1993, no. 200

O.2.28
Palace relief
Dur-Sharrukin (Khorsabad)

Sargon II (721-705 B.C.)
Botta - Flandin 1849, pls. 61-62 (Salle 11, slabs 14, 22)
Dezsö 1993, no. 201

O.2.29
Palace relief
Dur-Sharrukin (Khorsabad)
Sargon II (721-705 B.C.)
Botta - Flandin 1849, pl. 90 (Salle 5, slab 6)
Dezsö 1993, no. 202

O.2.30
Palace relief
Nineveh (Quyunjik, SW Palace, Room XIV)
Sennacherib (705-681 B.C.)
London, British Museum, BM 124786
Smith 1938, pl. XLII
Dezsö 1993, no. 224

O.2.31
Palace relief
Nineveh (Quyunjik, SW Palace, Room XIV)
Sennacherib (705-681 B.C.)
London, British Museum, BM 124784
Smith 1938, pl. LIX
Dezsö 1993, no. 225

Palace relief
Nineveh (Quyunjik, SW Palace, Room XIV)
Sennacherib (705-681 B.C.)
London, British Museum, BM 124785
Smith 1938, pls. LXIII-LXIV
Dezsö 1993, no. 225

O.2.32
Palace relief
Nineveh (Quyunjik, SW Palace, Room V)
Sennacherib (705-681 B.C.)
Paterson 1912, pl. 15
Dezsö 1993, no. 226

O.2.33
Palace relief
Nineveh (Quyunjik, SW Palace, Room XIV)
Sennacherib (705-681 B.C.)
Paterson 1912, pl. 39
Dezsö 1993, no. 227

O.2.34
Palace relief
Nineveh (Quyunjik, SW Palace, Room XIV)
Sennacherib (705-681 B.C.)
London, British Museum, BM 124784
Smith 1938, pl. LXII
Dezsö 1993, no. 228

Palace reliefs
Nineveh (Quyunjik, SW Palace, Room XXVIII)
Sennacherib (705-681 B.C.)
London, British Museum, BM 124774
Smith 1938, pls. L-LIII

O.2.35
Palace relief
Nineveh (Quyunjik, SW Palace, Room XIV)
Sennacherib (705-681 B.C.)
London, British Museum, BM 124786
Smith 1938, pl. XLII
Dezsö 1993, no. 229

O.2.36
Palace relief
Nineveh (Quyunjik, SW Palace)
Sennacherib (705-681 B.C.)
Oxford, Ashmolean Museum, 1933.1575
Moorey 1987, fig. 10
Dezsö 1993, no. 230

O.2.37
Palace relief
Nineveh (Quyunjik, SW Palace, Room V)
Sennacherib (705-681 B.C.)
Paterson 1912, pl. 14
Dezsö 1993, no. 231

O.2.38
Palace relief
Nineveh (Quyunjik, SW Palace, Great Hall)
Sennacherib (705-681 B.C.)
Paterson 1912, pl. 9
Dezsö 1993, no. 232

O.2.39
Palace relief
Nineveh
Sennacherib (705-681 B.C.)
Paterson 1912, pl. 7
Dezsö 1993, no. 233

O.2.40
Palace relief
Nineveh
Sennacherib (705-681 B.C.)
Paterson 1912, pl. 7
Dezsö 1993, no. 234

O.2.41
Palace relief
Nineveh (Quyunjik, SW Palace, Great Hall)
Sennacherib (705-681 B.C.)
Paterson 1912, pl. 7

Dezsö 1993, no. 235

O.2.42
Palace relief
Nineveh
Esarhaddon (680-669 B.C.)
Venice, Museo Archeologico, no. 46
Reade 1972, pl. XLb
Dezsö 1993, no. 240

O.2.43
Palace relief
Nineveh, North Palace, Room F
Ashurbanipal (668-627 B.C.)
London, British Museum, BM 124931-124932
Barnett 1976, pl. XVII
Dezsö 1993, no. 247

O.2.44
Palace relief
Nineveh, North Palace, Room C
Ashurbanipal (668-627 B.C.)
London, British Museum, BM 124860-124861
Barnett 1976, pl. VI
Dezsö 1993, no. 248

O.2.45
Palace relief
Nineveh, North Palace, Room F
Ashurbanipal (668-627 B.C.)
London, British Museum, BM 124933-124934
Barnett 1976, pl. XVIII
Dezsö 1993, no. 249

O.2.46
Palace relief
Nineveh, North Palace, Room C
Ashurbanipal (668-627 B.C.)
London, British Museum, BM 124861
Barnett 1976, pl. VI
Dezsö 1993, no. 250

O.2.47
Palace relief
Nineveh, North Palace, Room S[1]
Ashurbanipal (668-627 B.C.)
London, British Museum, BM 124788
Barnett 1976, pl. LXVI
Dezsö 1993, no. 251

O.2.48
Palace relief
Nineveh, North Palace
Ashurbanipal (668-627 B.C.)
London, British Museum, BM 124957
Dezsö 1993, no. 252

O.2.49
Architectural terracotta
Gordion, 2801 A 129
First half of 7th century B.C.
Akerström 1966, pl. 79

O.2.50
Architectural terracotta
Gordion
First half of 7th century B.C.
Akerström 1966, pl. 90

O.2.51
Architectural terracotta
Gordion
First half of 7th century B.C.
Akerström 1966, pl. 91

M.1.1
Warrior with Dipylon shield and two spears
Vase painting from an Attic sherd
Late Geometric
Lorimer 1950, fig. 12

M.1.2
Warriors with or without Dipylon shield
Vase painting of an Athenian Geometric Vase
Late Geometric
Richter 1934, figs. 1-2

M.2.1
Terracotta chariot group
Ayia Irini, Cyprus
Nicosia, Cyprus Museum
Gjerstad et al. 1935, pl. CCXXXIV:5, no. 2000

M.2.2
Terracotta chariot group
Ayia Irini, Cyprus
Second half of Cypro-Archaic I
Gjerstad et al. 1935, pl. CCXXXIV:6, no. 1046

Terracotta chariot group
Ayia Irini, Cyprus
Second half of Cypro-Archaic I
Gjerstad et al. 1935, pl. CCXXXV:5, no. 1998

Terracotta warrior with shield
Ayia Irini, Cyprus
Second half of Cypro-Archaic I
Gjerstad et al. 1935, pl. CCXXXII:7, no. 1032

Terracotta head of a warrior
Ayia Irini, Cyprus
Second half of Cypro-Archaic I

Gjerstad et al. 1935, pl. CCXXXII:15, no. 2384

Terracotta horseman
"Cyprus"
Edinburgh, Royal Scottish Museum, 1921.354
Second half of Cypro-Archaic I
Crouwel - Tatton-Brown 1988, pl. XXVI:4

M.2.3
Terracotta chariot group
Ayia Irini, Cyprus
Second half of Cypro-Archaic I
Gjerstad et al. 1935, pl. CCXXXIV:6, no. 1046

Terracotta horseman
"Cyprus"
London, British Museum, 1876.4.9.92
Second half of Cypro-Archaic I
Crouwel - Tatton-Brown 1988, pl. XXVI:2

M.2.4
Terracotta chariot group
Ayia Irini, Cyprus
Nicosia, Cyprus Museum
Second half of Cypro-Archaic I
Gjerstad et al. 1935, pl. CCXXXV:3, no. 1781+798

Terracotta chariot group
Ayia Irini, Cyprus
Nicosia, Cyprus Museum
Second half of Cypro-Archaic I
Gjerstad et al. 1935, pl. CCXXXV:4, no. 1170

M.2.5
Terracotta warrior
"Cyprus"
Early 7th century B.C.
Heuzey 1880, fig. F

M.2.6
Terracotta warrior
"Cyprus"
Early 7th century B.C.
Heuzey 1880, fig. G

M.2.7
Terracotta warrior with spiked shield
Ayia Irini, Cyprus
Nicosia, Cyprus Museum
Second half of Cypro-Archaic I
Gjerstad et al. 1935, pp. 721-722, pl. CXCIV, no. 1385+1530

M.2.8
Geryon terracotta
Pyrgia, Cyprus
H.: 24 cm, W.: 23 cm
London, British Museum, 1917.7-1.13
670/660-600 B.C.
Tatton-Brown 1979, pl. XXXII

M.2.9
Terracotta warrior
Tamassos, Cyprus
670/660-600 B.C.
Pflug 1988b, fig. 13

M.2.10
Terracotta chariot warrior
"Cyprus"
670/660-600 B.C.
Heuzey 1880, fig. H

M.2.11
Terracotta archer
Salamis, Cyprus
Nicosia, Cyprus Museum, Sal. 6471 = Tc. 2112
Second half of 7th century B.C.
Monloup 1984, pp. 182-183, (fig.), pl. 33, no. 663

M.2.12
Terracotta archer
Salamis, Cyprus
Nicosia, Cyprus Museum, Sal. 3535 = Tc. 1038
Second half of 7th century B.C.
Monloup 1984, p. 184, (fig.), pl. 33, no. 665

M.2.13
Terracotta archer
Salamis, Cyprus
Nicosia, Cyprus Museum, Sal. 4992 = Tc. 1839
Second half of 7th century B.C.
Monloup 1984, p. 184, pl. 33, no. 666

M.2.14
Terracotta horseman
Salamis, Cyprus
Nicosia, Cyprus Museum, Sal. 5022 = Tc. 1909
Second half of 7th century B.C.
Monloup 1984, p. 184, no. 668, (fig.)

M.2.15
Terracotta warrior drawing a sword from scabbard
"Cyprus"
H.: 10.5 inch
Myres 1914p. 157, no. 1049

M.2.16
Terracotta chariot group
Kourion, Sanctuary of Apollo Hylates
H.: 19.5 cm

University Museum, Philadelphia (?), T. 1700
"Close to the seventh century"
Young - Young 1955, pp. 55-56, no. 1055, pl. 60

M.2.17
Bronze statuette of Geryon
"Etruscan"?
de Chanot 1880, pl. 22

M.2.18
Terracotta head of a warrior
Idalion (?), Cyprus
Berlin, 499X
Mid-7th century B.C.
Schmidt 1968, pl. 44
Pflug 1988b, figs. 7-8

M.2.19
Terracotta head of a warrior
Samos
Samos Museum, T.2637
Mid-7th century B.C.
Schmidt 1968, pl. 44
Pflug 1988b, figs. 5-6

M.2.20
Terracotta head of a warrior
Samos
Samos Museum, T.2741
Mid-7th century B.C.
Schmidt 1968, pls. 44, 46

M.2.21
Bronze shield
Crete, Zeus Cave, Mt. Ida
Late 8th - early 7th c. B.C.
Iraklion, Archaeological Museum, Inv. no. 7
Kunze 1931, p. 8, fig. 1, pl. 14
Dezsö 1993, Chart 2, no. 187

M.2.22
Bronze bowl
Delphi
Late 8th century B.C.
Delphi, Archaeological Museum, Inv. no. 4463
Markoe 1985, pp. 205-206, 320-323, G4
Dezsö 1993, Chart 2, no. 188

M.2.23
Bronze bowl
Delphi
Late 8th century B.C.
Delphi, Archaeological Museum, Inv. no. 4463
Markoe 1985, pp. 205-206, 320-323, G4
Dezsö 1993, Chart 2, no. 189

M.2.24
Bronze bowl
"Olympia"
Oxford, Ashmolean Museum, G401
Late 8th century B.C.
Markoe 1985, pp. 207, 326-327, G7
Dezsö 1993, Chart 2, no. 190

M.2.25
Bronze statuette of a warrior
Olympia
Olympia Museum, Inv. B 4240
Late 8th - early 7th century B.C.

M.2.26
Bronze statuette of a warrior
Athens, Acropolis
Athens, National Museum, Inv. 6612
H.: 21.2 cm
Early 7th century B.C.
Schweitzer 1971, pls. 164-165
Lamb 1929, pl. 20a

M.2.27
Bronze statuette of a warrior
Delphi
Inv. 3649
H.: 13 cm
Early 7th century B.C.
Perdrizet 1908, p. 30, no. 16, pl. 1:4
Rolley 1969, p. 45, no. 28, pl. IX:28

Bronze statuette of a warrior
Delphi
H.: 18.5 cm
7th century B.C.
Perdrizet 1908, p. 32, no. 23, pl. 1:8

M.2.28
Bronze statuette
Tegea
H.: 6.5 cm
7th century B.C.
Dugas 1921, pp. 355-356, no. 53, fig. 19

M.2.29
Bronze statuette
Thermon
Early 7th century B.C.
Lamb 1929, pl. 17a

M.2.30
Bronze statuette
Karditsa
Early 7th century B.C.
Lamb 1929, pl. 17b

M.2.31
Plate fibula: Herakles and Iolaios killing the Hydra
Philadelphia, private collection
H.: 14 cm
Early 7th century B.C.
Schweitzer 1969, fig. 119

M.2.32
Terracotta horseman with round shield and sword
"Cyprus"
Cesnola Collection
New York, MMA 74.51.1778
Myres 1914, p. 344, no. 2093

M.3.1
Bronze "belt"
Fortetsa, Tomb P, no. 1568
Middle of the 8th c. B.C.
Iraklion, Archaeological Museum, Inv. no. 1568
Brock 1957, pl. 115
Borchhardt 1972, p. 70, Kat. 15 II 2
Dezsö 1993, Charts 2-3, no. 106

M.3.2
Bronze "belt"
Fortetsa, Tomb P, no. 1569
Middle of the 8th c. B.C.
Iraklion, Archaeological Museum, Inv. no. 1569
Brock 1957, pl. 116
Borcchardt 1972, pp. 69-70, Kat. 15 II 1, pl. 25:5
Dezsö 1993, Charts 2-3, no. 107

M.3.3
Bronze openwork
Kato-Symi (Symi-Biannou)
Middle of the 8th c. B.C.
Lempesi 1985, pl. 57, G4
Dezsö 1993, Charts 2-3, no. 184

M.3.4
Gold band
Khaniale Tekke
Middle of the 8th c. B.C.
Dunbabin 1944, p. 85
Borchhardt 1972, p. 70, Kat. 15 IV, pl. 25:3
Dezsö 1993, Charts 2-3, no. 185

M.3.5
Bronze plaque (lion hunter)
Kavousi
Middle of the 8th c. B.C.
Boyd 1901, pp. 147-148, figs. 10-11
Kunze 1931, p. 218, fig. 31, pl. 56e

M.4.1
Bronze belt
Fortetsa, Tomb P, no. 1569
Middle of the 8th c. B.C.
Iraklion, Archaeological Museum, Inv. no. 1569
Brock 1957, pl. 116
Borchhardt 1972, pp. 69-70, Kat. 15 II 1, pl. 27:1
Dezsö 1993, Charts 2-3, no. 183

M.4.2
Sphinx
Bronze plaque
Kavousi
Middle of the 8th c. B.C.
Boyd 1901, pp. 147-148, figs. 10-11
Kunze 1931, p. 218, fig. 31, pl. 56e
Dezsö 1993, Charts 2-3, no. 186

M.4.3
Warriors
Relief pithos (the Wooden Horse at Troy)
Mykonos
Around 675 B.C.
Ervin 1963, pls. 18, 20

M.4.4
Warriors
Relief pithos (the Wooden Horse at Troy)
Mykonos
Around 675 B.C.
Ervin 1963, pl. 18

M.4.5
Sphinx
Late Orientalizing alabastron
Fortetsa, Tomb P, no. 1299
Iraklion, Archaeological Museum, Inv. 1299
680-630 B.C.
Brock 1957, pp. 111-112, pl. 101

M.4.6
Sphinx
Melian hydria
Rheneia
Middle of 7th century B.C.
Kunze 1930, pl. 55a

M.4.7
Warrior with small round shield
Bronze corslet
"Crete"
Hamburg, Museum für Kunst und Gewerbe, Inv. 1970, 26a
Middle of the 7th century B.C. / 640 B.C.
Hoffmann 1972, pp. 7-8, pls. 19-23, esp. 21

M.4.8
Stele of a warrior (with hoplite equipment)
Prinias, Sidérospila
Iraklion, Archaeological Museum, ar. 399
H.: 1.06 m
670-660 B.C.
Lempesi 1976, B1, pls. 14-15

M.4.9
Stele of a warrior (with hoplite equipment)
Prinias, Sidérospila
Iraklion, Archaeological Museum, ar. 398
H.: 0.93 m
660-650 B.C.
Lempesi 1976, B2, pls. 16-17

M.4.10
Stele of a warrior (with hoplite equipment)
Prinias, Sidérospila
Iraklion, Archaeological Museum, ar. 402
H.: 0.4 m
660-650 B.C.
Lempesi 1976, B3, pls. 18-19

M.4.11
Stele of a warrior (with hoplite equipment)
Prinias, Sidérospila
Iraklion, Archaeological Museum, ar. 401
H.: 0.835 m
640 B.C.
Lempesi 1976, B4, pls. 20-21

M.4.12
Stele of a warrior (with hoplite equipment)
Prinias, Sidérospila
Iraklion, Archaeological Museum, ar. 481
H.: 0.725 m
640 B.C.
Lempesi 1976, B5, pls. 22-23

M.4.13
Stele of a warrior (with hoplite equipment)
Prinias, Sidérospila
Iraklion, Archaeological Museum, ar. 400
H.: 1.04 m
620-610 B.C.
Daux 1960, p. 840, fig. 2
Lempesi 1976, B7, pls. 26-27

M.4.14
Terracotta plaque of a warrior (with hoplite equipment)
Gortyn
Middle of the 7th century B.C.
Lempesi 1976, pl. 47b

M.4.15
Sphinx
Laconian Sub-Geometric sherd
First half of 7th century B.C.
Droop 1926-1927, p. 54, fig. 4

M.4.16
Amazon
Terracotta shield
Samos, Heraion
Early 7th century B.C.
Eilmann 1933, p. 120, fig. 66, pl. 37:1

M.4.17
Warrior
Terracotta shield
Tiryns
Early 7th century B.C.
Lorimer 1950, pl. IX:1

M.4.18
Amazon
Terracotta shield
Tiryns
Early 7th century B.C.
Lorimer 1950, pl. IX:1

M.4.19
Amazon
Terracotta shield
Tiryns
Early 7th century B.C.
Lorimer 1950, pl. IX:1

M.4.20
Terracotta head
Sparta, Amyklaion
Athen, National Museum, Tc. Inv. 4381
H.: 11.5 cm
Middle of the 7th century B.C.
Schweitzer 1971, pls. 161-162

M.4.21
Bronze statuette (Zeus?)
Munich, Antikensammlung, Inv. 4315
H.: 14.5 cm
Lullies 1962, pp. 627-628, no. 14, figs. 25-26

M.4.22
Bronze plaquette (Athena)
Dreros
Ca. 600 B.C.
Marinatos 1936, fig. 42, pl. 30

M.4.23

Head of a terracotta warrior
Salamis, Cyprus
Nicosia, Cyprus Museum, Sal. 4923 = Tc. 1840
Late 7th - early 6th century B.C.
Monloup 1984, p. 184, no. 668, (fig.)

M.5.1
Bronze warrior (linch pin)
Salamis, Tomb 79
Nicosia, Cyprus Museum, T.79, 129/220/5+5a and 188/220/4+4a
End of the 8th century B.C.
Törnkvist 1973, figs. 9-10

M.5.2
Miniature votive bronze helmets (5 pieces)
Gortyn
Iraklion, Archaeological Museum
First half of 7th century B.C.
Hoffmann 1972, p. 2, pl. 41:4

M.5.3
Miniature votive bronze helmets (5 complete and fragments of others)
Praisos, Altar Hill
Candia Museum
First half of 7th century B.C.
Bosanquet 1901-1902, p. 258, pl. 10
Benton 1939-1940, pl. 31:17

M.5.4
Miniature votive bronze helmet
Palaikastro
First half of 7th century B.C.
Benton 1939-1940, pl. 28:31

M.5.5
Rock carving
Thera
Middle of the 7th century B.C.
von Gaertringen - Wilski 1904, p. 79, fig. 64

M.5.6
Bronze statuette of a warrior
Olympia, Heraion
Second quarter of the 7th century B.C.
Steiner 1906, pl. 18
Kunze 1944, pp. 119-123, pl. 42

M.5.7
Bronze statuette of a warrior
Olympia, Inv. 5834
Athens, National Museum, Inv. 6094
Second quarter of the 7th century B.C.
Furtwängler 1890, p. 39, no. 245, pl. 16:245-245a

M.5.8
Bronze warrior cauldron attachement
Olympia
H.: 17 cm
Second quarter of the 7th century B.C.
Hampe - Jantzen 1936-1937, p. 66, fig. 29

M.5.9
Bronze statuette of a warrior
Olympia, Inv. B 2000
H.: 21 cm
Early 7th century B.C.
Kunze 1944, p. 120, pls. 38-39

M.5.10
Bronze statuette of a warrior
Olympia, Inv. B 1999
H.: 17.3 cm
Early 7th century B.C.
Kunze 1944, p. 122, pls. 43-44

M.5.11
Bronze statuette of a warrior
Olympia, Inv. B 1701
H.: 16.9 cm
Early 7th century B.C.
Kunze 1944, p. 122, pls. 45-46

M.5.12
Bronze statuette of a warrior
Olympia, Inv. B 5600
Early 7th century B.C.
Kunze 1967b, pls. 108-109

M.5.13
Bronze statuette of a warrior
Olympia
Early 7th century B.C.
Kunze 1944, p. 113, pl. 36:3

M.5.14
Bronze statuette of a warrior
Olympia, Inv. 1671
Early 7th century B.C.
Kunze 1944, p. 109, fig. 90, pl. 34

M.5.15
Bronze statuette of a warrior
Amorgos
Berlin, Inv. 10388
H.: 8.5 cm
Early 7th century B.C.
Neugebauer 1922, p. 61, no. 4
Kunze 1967b, fig. 78

M.5.16

Bronze statuette of a warrior
Delphi
Athens, National Museum, Inv. 7415
Early 7th century B.C.
Casson 1922, p. 213, fig. 7b

M.5.17
Bronze statuette of a warrior
Athens, Carapanos Collection
Early 7th century B.C.
Bequignon 1929, fig. 3

M.5.18
Warrior
Early Orientalizing pithos
Knossos, Inv. 6391
2nd quarter of the 7th century B.C.
Payne 1927-1928, p. 240, no. 38, pls. XI:10-11, XII

M.5.19
Bronze Group
Samos
Formerly Samos Museum, Inv. B.190
H.: 9 cm
Early 7th century B.C
Karo 1930, fig. 27
Schweitzer 1971, pls. 186-187

M.5.20
Bronze statuette of an armourer
New York, MMA, Inv. 42.11.42
H.: 5.2 cm
Early 7th century B.C
Schweitzer 1971, pl. 200

M.5.21
Scene from a tripod cauldron leg
Olympia
Plympia Museum, Inv. B 1730
L.: 46.7 cm
Early 7th century B.C
Schweitzer 1971, pl. 213

M.5.22
Bronze statuette of a warrior
Athens, Acropolis
Athens, national Museum, Inv. 6613
H.: 20.5 cm
Lullies - Hirmer 1960, p. 53, no. 2, pl. 2
Schweitzer 1971, pls. 159-161

M.5.23
Horsemen on a bronze relief
Olympia, "Brunnen 17"
Olympia Museum, Inv. B 5085a
Kunze 1961-1962, pp. 115-116, pl. 130b

M.5.24
Handle attachement from a bronze vessel
Olympia
Olympia Museum, Inv. B 4774

M.6.1
Warrior fighting on ship
Athenian Geometric (Dipylon) Ware
Late 8th century B.C.
Richter 1934, figs. 1-2

M.6.2
Horserider
Crater-fragment
Athens, "Piräusstrasse"
Athens, National Museum
Late 8th century B.C.
Pernice 1892, pl. 10
Borchhardt 1972, p. 65, Kat. 13 III 2, pl. 32:4

M.6.3
Foot soldier with round shield and two spears
Crater-fragment
Athens, "Piräusstrasse"
Athens, National Museum
Late 8th century B.C.
Pernice 1892, pl. 10
Borchhardt 1972, p. 65, Kat. 13 III 3, pl. 33:4

M.6.4
Pyxisfragment
Argos, Heraion
Athens, National Museum
Late 8th century B.C.
Lorimer 1950, p. 233, pl. 17:2

M.6.5
Warrior (hoplite)
Geometric amphora
Athens
Daux 1958, fig. 8

M.6.6
Warrior (Geometric gem)
Siphnos
Late 8th early 7th century B.C.
Lorimer 1950, pl. VI:5

M.6.7
Warrior (votive terracotta shield)
Tiryns
Late 8th early 7th century B.C.
Lorimer 1950, pl. X:1

M.6.8
Warriors (hoplites)
Reliefpithos
Tenos
700-675 B.C.
Kontoleon 1969, pls. 52-53

M.6.9
Warrior
Pottery sherd
Lindos, Acropolis
First half of 7th century B.C.
Blinkenberg 1931, pl. 37:867

M.6.10
Warrior (hoplite)
Late Geometric pottery sherd
Athens, Kerameikos, Inv. 112
First half of 7th century B.C.
Tölle 1963, p. 650, no. 7, fig. 5

M.6.11
Scene from a tripod cauldron leg
Olympia
Olympia Museum, Inv. B 1730
L.: 46.7 cm
Early 7th century B.C
Schweitzer 1971, pl. 213

M.6.12
Warrior with small round shield
Bronze helmet aplique
"Crete"
Hamburg, Museum für Kunst und Gewerbe
Middle of the 7th century B.C.
Hoffmann 1972, p. 6, fig. 1
Gröschel 1986, p. 72, fig. 5

M.6.13
Warrior (hoplite)
"Melian amphora"
Late 7th century B.C.
Conze 1862, pl. 3

M.6.14
Warrior
Proto-Corinthian ivory seal
Perachora, Sanctuary of Hera Akraia
First quarter of 7th century B.C.
ILN, 2 May 1931, p. 748

M.6.15
Bronze statuette of a warrior
Olympia, Inv. 2914
Early 7th century B.C.
Furtwängler 1890, p. 39, no. 243, pl. 16:243-243a

M.6.16
Rock carving
Thera
Middle of the 7th century B.C.
von Gaertringen - Wilski 1904, p. 79, fig. 63

M.6.17
Bronze statuette of a warrior
Delphi
Inv. 7733
Early 7th century B.C.
Rolley 1969, p. 38, no. 17, pl. VII:17

M.6.18
Terracotta horseman
"Cyprus"
Nicosia, Cyprus Museum
Second half of 7th century B.C.
Törnkvist 1973, p. 25, fig. 21

M.6.19
Terracotta warrior with shield
Kaloriziki, Cyprus
Museum of Episkopi, Cyprus
Second half of 7th century B.C.
Törnkvist 1973, p. 25, fig. 22-23

M.6.20
Terracotta warrior with shield
Kaloriziki, Cyprus, K.1144
Second half of 7th century B.C.
Benson 1973, pl. 41

M.6.21
Terracotta warrior with "figure-of-eight" shield
"Cyprus"
Pierides Foundation Museum
H.: 13.5 cm
End of 7th century B.C.
Karageorghis 1985, p. 216, no. 214 (pl.)

M.6.22
Warrior leading a horse
Argive Late geometric pottery sherd
Early 7th century B.C.
Waldstein 1905, pl. 57:4

M.6.23
Warrior
Argive Late geometric krater fragment
Early 7th century B.C.
Charitonidis 1954, p. 413, fig. 4

M.6.24

Warriors (hoplites)
Vase of Aristonothos
7th century B.C.
Lorimer 1950, pl. X:1

M.7.1
Warriors (hoplites)
Relief pithos (the Wooden Horse at Troy)
Mykonos
Around 675 B.C.
Ervin 1963, pls. 19, 21

M.7.2
Warriors (hoplites)
Relief pithos (the Wooden Horse at Troy)
Mykonos
Around 675 B.C.
Ervin 1963, pls. 19, 20, 21

M.7.3
Not warlike context
Lakonian sherd
Amyklaion
Late 8th - early 7th century B.C.
Wide 1899, fig. 42
Snodgrass 1964, p. 8

M.7.4
Bronze statuette of a warrior
Olympia, Inv. 9788
Early 7th century B.C.
Furtwängler 1890, p. 38, no. 242, pl. 16:242

M.7.5
Warriors
Terracotta plaques (2 pieces)
Praisos (?)
New York, Metropolitan Museum of Art
Dohan 1930-1931, figs. 1-2

M.7.6
Hoplite
Bone relief
Sparta
Late 7th century B.C.(?)
Richards 1891, pl. 11

M.7.7
Terracotta warrior
"Cyprus"
H.: 15.3 cm
Cypro-Archaic Period
Karageorghis 1985, p. 204, no. 199 (pl.)

M.8.1
Warriors (hoplites)
Relief pithos (the Wooden Horse, Troy)
Mykonos
"Around 675 B.C."
Ervin 1963, pls. 18

M.8.2
Warriors (hoplites)
Relief pithos (the Wooden Horse, Troy)
Mykonos
"Around 675 B.C."
Ervin 1963, pls. 19

M.8.3
Spartan warrior
Ivory plaque
Sparta, Sanctuary of Artemis Orthia
Second quarter - middle of 7th century B.C.
Dawkins 1929, pl. CVIII

M.8.4
Miniature votive bronze helmet
Lindos, Acropolis
H.: 6.3 cm
Middle of 7th century B.C.
Blinkenberg 1931, p. 391, no. 1564, pl. 63:1564

M.8.5
Bronze statuette of a hoplite
Olympia
Olympia Museum, Inv. B 6800
H.: 16 cm
Early 7th century B.C.
Furtwängler 1890, p. 17-18, no. 41, pl. 7:41

M.8.6
Fallen hoplite
Lakonian reliefpithos
Sparta, Heroon
Second quarter - middle of 7th century B.C.
Dawkins 1929, Pl. XVI

M.8.7
Hoplite (chariot warrior)
Lakonian reliefpithos
Sparta, Heroon
Second quarter - middle of 7th century B.C.
Dawkins 1929, Pl. XVI

M.8.8
Warrior
Lakonian reliefpithos
Sparta, Heroon
Sparta Museum
Second quarter - middle of 7th century B.C.
Dawkins 1929, Pl. XVI

Warrior
Lakonian reliefpithos
Sparta
Sparta Museum, Inv. 3099
Second quarter - middle of 7th century B.C.

Warrior
Lakonian reliefpithos
Sparta
Sparta Museum, Inv. 5395
Second quarter - middle of 7th century B.C.

M.8.9
Warrior (chariot rider)
Lakonian reliefpithos
Sparta, Heroon
Second quarter - middle of 7th century B.C.
Dawkins 1929, Pl. XVI

M.8.10
Geryon (with hoplite equipment)
Bronze horse's pectorale
Samos
Samos, Museum Vathy, Inv. B.2518
Last quarter of 7th century B.C.
Brize 1985, pls. 15-17, 20:1
Pflug 1988b, fig. 12

Geryon (with hoplite equipment)
Ivory plaque
Samos
Samos, Museum Vathy, Inv. E.127
Last quarter of 7th century B.C.
Brize 1985, pl. 22:2

Kaineus
Bronze plaque
Olympia
Olympia Museum, Inv. BE 11a
Middle of 7th century B.C.
Brize 1985, pl. 24:2

M.8.11
Hoplite
Bronze sheet
Olympia, M 78
"Early 6th century B.C."
Yalouri 1971, pl. 64

M.8.12
Stele of a hoplite (Cretan helmet)
Prinias, Sidérospila
Iraklion, Archaeological Museum, ar. 403
H.: 0.64 m
630-620 B.C.
Lempesi 1976, B6, pls. 24-25

M.8.13
Hoplite on chariot
Wall-painting
Kizilbel, West Wall
"Second half of 6th century B.C."
Mellink 1976, pl. 5

M.X.1
Bronze statuette of a chariot rider
Olympia
Late 8th - early 7th century B.C.
Kunze 1944, pp. 110-111, fig. 91, pl. 35

Bronze statuette of a chariot rider
Olympia, Inv. 7042
Late 8th - early 7th century B.C.
Furtwängler 1890, p. 38, no. 240, pl. 16:240

Bronze statuette
Olympia, Inv. 9000 (+ Inv. 8900, 5630)
Late 8th - early 7th century B.C.
Furtwängler 1890, p. 39, no. 241, pl. 16:241

Bronze statuette
Olympia, Inv. 13100
Late 8th - early 7th century B.C.
Furtwängler 1890, p. 39, no. 244, pl. 16:244

Bronze statuette
Olympia, Inv. 6507
Late 8th - early 7th century B.C.
Furtwängler 1890, p. 40, no. 249, pl. 15:249

Bronze statuette
Olympia, Inv. 3680 (+ Inv. 6800)
Late 8th - early 7th century B.C.
Furtwängler 1890, p. 40, no. 251, pl. 16:251

Bronze statuette
Olympia, Inv. 9626
Late 8th - early 7th century B.C.
Furtwängler 1890, p. 40, no. 251a (fig.)

M.X.2
Kentauromachia
Bronze group
Olympia
New York, MMA 17.190.2072
H.: 11 cm
Late 8th - early 7th century B.C.
Schweitzer 1971, pl. 185

BIBLIOGRAPHY

Ahlberg, G., 1971
  Fighting on Land and Sea in Greek Geometric Art, (Skrifter Utgivna av Svenska Institutet i Athen, 4°, XVI), Lund, Berlingska Boktryckeriet

Akerström, A., 1966
  Die architektonischen Terrakotten Kleinasiens, (Skrifter Utgivna av Svenska Institutet i Athen, 4°, XI), Lund, C.W.K. Gleerup

Akurgal, E., 1962
  The Art of the Hittites, New York

Almagro, M., 1958
  "Deposito de la Ría de Huelva", *Inventaria Arch. Espana 1-4 E.1* 39, p. 273ff.

Almagro-Gorbea, M., 1973
  "Cascos del Bronze Final en la Peninsula Iberica", *Trabajos de Prehistorica* 30, 349ff.

Amandry, P., 1949
  "Casques grecs à decor gravé", *BCH* 73, pp. 437-446, figs. 1-7, pls. 22-25

Amiet, P., 1980
  Art of the Ancient Near East, New York, Abrams

Andrae, W., 1925
  Coloured Ceramics from Ashur and Earlier Ancient Assyrian Wall Paintings. From Photographs and Water-Colours by Members of the Ashur Expedition Organized by the Deutsche Orient-Gesellschaft, London, Kegan Paul, Trench, Trubner & CO. LTD.

Aubet, M.E., 1993
  The Phoenicians and the West. Politics, Colonies and Trade, Cambridge, University Press

Barnett, R.D., 1953
  "An Assyrian Helmet", *The British Museum Quarterly* 18, pp. 101-102, pls. 31-32

Barnett, R.D., 1967
  The British Museum Report of the Trustees 1966, London, The Trustees of the British Museum

Barnett, R.D., 1976
  Sculptures from the North Palace of Ashurbanipal at Nineveh (668-627 B.C.), London, The Trustees of the British Museum

Barnett, R.D. - Curtis, J.E., 1973
  "A Review of Acquisitions 1963-1970 of Western Asiatic Antiquities, 2", *The British Museum Quarterly* 37, pp. 119-137

Barnett, R.D. - Falkner, M., 1962
  The Sculptures of Assur-nasir-apli II (883-859 B.C.), Tiglath-pileser III (745-727 B.C.), Esarhaddon (681-669 B.C.) from the Central and South-West Palaces at Nimrud, London, The Trustees of the British Museum

Belinskiy, A.B., 1990
  "K voprosu o vremeni poyavleniya shlemov Assiriyskogo tipa na Kavkaze (About the Date the Assyrian-type Helmets First Appeared in the Caucasus", *SA* 1990/IV, pp. 190-195

Benson, J.L., 1973
  The Necropolis of Kaloriziki, (Studies in Mediterranean Archaeology 36), Göteborg, Paul Aströms Vörlag

Benton, S., 1939-40
  "The Dating of Helmets and Corselets in Early Greece", *BSA* 40, pp. 78-82

Béquignon, Y., 1929
  "Études thessaliennes III: statuette de guerrier trouvée à Phères", *BCH* 53, pp. 101-116

Beran, T., 1957
  "Assyrische Glyptik des 14. Jahrhunderts", *ZA* 52, pp. 141ff.

Bittel, K., 1976
  Die Hethiter, (Universum der Kunst), München, C.H. Beck

Blinkenberg, Chr., 1931
  Lindos. Fouilles de l'Acropole 1902-1904. I. Les petits objects, Berlin, W. de Gruyter

Boardman, J., 1970
  "Orientalen auf Kreta", in: Hoffmann, H., ed., *Dädalisch Kunst auf Kreta*, Hamburg, pp. 14-25

Boardman, J., 1980
  The Greeks Overseas: Their Early Colonies and Trade, (new and enlarged edition), London

Bol, P.C., 1989
Argivische Schilde, (Olympische Forschungen XVII), Berlin, Walter de Gruyter

Borchhardt, J., 1972
Homerische Helme. Helmformen der Ädäis in ihren Beziehungen zu orientalischen und europäischen Helmformen in der Bronze- und frühen Eisenzeit, Mainz am Rhein, Philipp von Zabern

Borchhardt, J., 1977
"Helme", in: H.G. Buchholz - J. Wiesner, eds., *Kriegswesen, vol. I: Schutzwaffen und Wehrbauten*, (Archaeologia Homerica, Band 1, Kapitel E), Göttingen, Vandenhoeck & Ruprecht, pp. E57-E74

Bosanquet, R.C., 1901-02
"Excavations at Praisos, I.", *BSA* 8, pp. 231-270

Bossert, H.Th., et al., 1950
Karatepe Kazilari (Die Ausgrabungen auf dem Karatepe, Erster Vorbericht), (Türk Tarih Kurumu Yayinlarindan V. seri - No. 9), Ankara, Türk Tarih Kurumu Basimevi

Botta, M.P.E. - Flandin, M.E., 1849-1850
Monument de Ninive, vols. I-V, Paris, Imprimerie Nationale

Bottini, A., 1988
"Apulisch-korinthische Helme", in: A. Bottini, *et al., Antike Helme. Sammlung Lipperheide und andere Bestände des Antikenmuseums Berlin*, (Römisch-Germanisches Zentralmuseum, Monographien 14), Mainz, Verlag des Römisch-Germanisches Zentralmuseums, pp. 107-136

Boyd, H.A., 1901
"Excavations at Kavousi, Crete, in 1900", *American Journal of Archaeology* 5, pp. 125-158

Börker-Klähn, J., 1982
Altvorderasiatische Bildstelen und vergleichbare Felsreliefs, (Baghdader Forschungen, Band 4), Mainz am Rhein, Philipp von Zabern

Briquel-Chatonnet, F., 1992
Les relations entre les cités de la Cote Phénicienne et les Royaumes d'Israël et de Juda, (Studia Phoenicia 12, Orientalia Lovaniensia Analecta 46), Leuven, Peeters, esp. pp. 141-226

British Museum, 1929[3]
British Museum. A Guide to the Exhition illustrating Greek and Roman Life, London

Brize, P., 1985
"Samos und Stesichoros. Zu einem früharchaischen Bronzeblech", *AM* 100, pp. 53-90

Brock, J.K., 1957
Fortetsa. Early Greek Tombs near Knossos, (BSA Supplementum, 2), Cambridge, Cambridge University Press

Brückner, A. - Pernice, E., 1893
"Ein attischer Friedhof", *AM* 18, pp. 73-191

Buchholz, H.G., 1972
"Politiko-Tamassos, 1971", *RDAC* 1972, pp. 183-186

Buchholz, H.G., 1973
"Tamassos, Zypern, 1970-1972", *Arch.Anz.* 1973, pp. 295-388

Buchholz, H.G., 1978
"Tamassos, Zypern, 1974 bis 1976. 3. Bericht", *Archäologischer Anzeiger* 93, 155-230

Budge, E.A.W., 1914
Assyrian Sculptures in the British Museum. Reign of Ashur-nasir-pal, 885-860 B.C., London

Calmeyer, P., 1969
Datierbare Bronzen aus Luristan und Kirmanshah, (Untersuchungen zur Assyriologie und Vorderasiatischen Archäologie 5), Berlin, Walter de Gruyter

Calmeyer, P., 1975
"Helm", *Reallexikon der Assyriologie und Vorderasiatischen Archäologie* IV, Berlin, Walter de Gruyter, pp. 313-317

Calmeyer, P., 1991
"Helmets and Quivers", in: R. Merhav, ed., *Urartu. A Metalworking Center in the First Millennium B.C.E.*, Jerusalem, Israel Museum, pp. 123-133

Casson, S., 1922
"Bronze Work of the Geometric Period", *JHS* 42, pp. 207-219

Catling, H.W., 1964
　　Cypriote Bronzework in the Mycenaean World, (Oxford Monographs on Classical Archaeology), Oxford, Clarendon Press
Charitonidis, S., 1954
　　"Recherches dans le quartier Est d'Argos", *BCH* 78, pp. 410-426
Cialowicz, K.M., 1983
　　"Casques corinthiens dans les collections polonaises", *Études et Travaux* 13, pp. 47-52
Coldstream, J.N., 1977
　　Geometric Greece, (A Benn Study: Archaeology), London
Coldstream, J.N., 1982
　　"Greeks and Phoenicians in the Aegean", in: Niemeyer, H.G., ed., *Phönizier im Westen. Die Beiträge des Internationalen Symposiums über die phönizische Expansion im Westlichen Mittelmeerraum in Köln vom 24. bis 27. April 1979*, (Madrider Beiträge, 8), Mainz am Rhein, pp. 261-275
Coldstream, J.N., 1983
　　"Gift Exchange in the Eighth Century B.C.", in: Hägg, R., ed., *The Greek Renaissance in the Eighth Century B.C.: Tradition and Innovation*, (Skrifter Utgivna av Svenska Institutet i Athen 4, XXX), Stockholm, P. Aströms Vörlag, pp. 201-206
Collon, D., 1988
　　First Impressions. Cylinder Seals in the Ancient Near East, Chicago, The University of Chicago Press
Collon, D. - Crouwel, J. - Littauer, M.A., 1976
　　"A Bronze Chariot Group from the Levant in Paris", *Levant* 8, pp. 71-81
Conze, A., 1862
　　Melische Thongefässe, Leipzig, Breitkopf und Härtel
Cook, J.M., 1952
　　"Archaeology in Greece, 1951", *JHS* 72, pp. 92-112
Cook, J.M. - Akurgal, E., 1952
　　"Archaeological Work in Turkey, 1951: Old Smyrna (Bayrakli)", *AnSt* 2, pp. 23-24
Courbin, P., 1957
　　"Une tombe géométrique d'Argos", *BCH* 81, pp. 322-386
Crouwel, J.H., 1987
　　"Chariots in Iron Age Cyprus", *RDAC* 1987, pp. 101-118
Crouwel, J.H. - Tatton-Brown, V., 1988
　　"Ridden Horses in Iron Age Cyprus", *RDAC* 1988/II, pp. 77-87
Curtis, J.E., 1979
　　An examination of Late Assyrian metalwork with special reference to material from Nimrid, vols. I-II, Unpublished Ph. D. Diss., University of London
Curtis, J.E., 1994
　　"Mesopotamian Bronzes from Greek Sites: the Workshops of Origin", *Iraq* 56, pp. 1-25
Curtis, J.E. - Wheeler, T.S. - Muhly, J.D. - Maddin, R., 1979
　　"Neo-Assyrian Ironworking Technology", *PAPS* 123, pp. 369-390

Daux, G., 1958
　　"Chronique des fouilles et découvertes archéologiques en Grèce en 1957: Athènes", *BCH* 82, pp. 656-669, Tiryns, p. 707, fig. 26
Daux, G., 1960
　　"Chronique des fouilles et découvertes archéologiques en Grèce en 1959", *BCH* 84, pp. 617-868
Dawkins, R.M., ed., 1929
　　The Sanctuary of Artemis Orthia at Sparta, London, Macmillan
de Chanot, E., 1880
　　"Géryon. Bronze Étrusque", *Gazette Archéologique* 6, pp. 136-138
de G. Davies, N. and N., 1933
　　The Tomb of Menkheperrasonb, Amenmose, and Another (Nos. 86, 112, 42, 226), (Theban Tomb Series, Fifth Memoir), London
Deonna, W., 1938

Le mobilier Délien, (Délos XVIII), Paris, de Boccard

de Schauensee, M., 1988
"Northwest Iran as a Bronzeworking Centre: the View from Hasanlu", in: J. Curtis ed., *Bronzeworking Centres of Western Asia c. 1000-539 B.C.*, London, Kegan Paul, pp. 45-62, pls. 13-56

Despini, K., 1981
"Korinthiako kranos apo te Khalkidike" ("Ein archaischer Helm aus Chalkidike"), *Athens Annals of Archaeology* 14, pp. 246-250

Dezsö, T., 1993
Near Eastern Helmets of the Iron Age, Ph.D. dissertation, Budapest

Dezsö, T. - Curtis, J.E., 1991
"Assyrian Iron Helmets from Nimrud now in the British Museum", *Iraq* 53, pp. 105-126, pls. 15-20

Dikaios, P., 1969
Enkomi. Excavations 1948-1958. Vol. I., Mainz, Philipp von Zabern

Dohan, E.H., 1930-31
"Archaic Cretan Terracottas in America", *Metropolitan Museum Studies* 3, 209-228

Dörig, J., 1981
"Ein korinthischer Helm in Athener Privatbesitz", in: A. Mallwitz, *X. Bericht über die Ausgrabungen in Olympia*, (Fs. E. Kunze), Berlin, Walter de Gruyter, pp. 109-110, pl. 12

Droop, J.P., 1926-27
"Excavations at Sparta, 1927. The Native Pottery from the Acropolis", *BSA* 28, pp. 49-81

Dugas, Ch., 1921
"Le Sanctuaire d'Aléa Athéna a Tégée", *BCH* 45, pp. 335-435

Dunbabin, T.J., 1957
The Greeks and Their Eastern Neighbors. Studies in the Relations between Greece and the Countries of the Near East in the Eight and Seventh Centuries BC., (Society for the Promotion of Hellenic Studies, Supplementary Paper 8), London

Dyson, R.H. - Muscarella, O.W., 1989
"Constructing the Chronology and Historical Implications of Hasanlu IV", *Iran* 27, pp. 1-27

Egg, M., 1984
"Neuerwerbungen für die Sammlungen", *Jahrbuch des Römisch-Germanischen Zentralmuseums Mainz* 31, pp. 647-655

Egg, M., 1986
Italische Helme (RGZM Monographien 11, 1-2), Mainz, Verlag des RGZM

Egg, M., 1988
"Die ältesten Helme der Hallstattzeit", in: Bottini, A., et al., *Antike Helme. Sammlung Lipperheide und andere Bestände des Antikenmuseums Berlin. Handbuch mit Katalog*, (Römisch-Germanisches Zentralmuseum, Monographien 14), Mainz, Verlag des Römisch-Germanisches Zentralmuseums, pp. 212-221

Egg, M. - Waurick, G., 1990
Antike Helme. Ausstellungskatalog, Speyer, Mainz, Verlag des RGZM

Eilmann, R., 1933
"Frühe Griechische Keramik im Samischen Heraion", *AM* 58, pp. 47-145

Elayi, J., 1983
"Les cités phéniciennes et l'empire assyrien à l'époque d'Assurbanipal", *RA* 77, pp. 45-58

Elayi, J., 1985a
"Les relations entre les cités phéniciennes et l'empire assyrien sous le régne de Sennacherib", *Semitica* 35, pp. 19-26

Elayi, J., 1985b
Byblos et la domination assyro-babylonienne", *BaM* 16, pp. 393-397

Ervin, M., 1963
"A Relief Pithos from Mykonos", *Arch.Delt.* 18, pp. 37-75

Falsone, G., 1988
"Phoenicia as a Bronzeworking Centre in the Iron Age", in: Curtis, J.E., ed., *Bronzeworking Centres of Western Asia c. 1000-539 BC*, London, Keegan and Paul, pp. 227-250

Felsch, R.C.S., 1987
"Kalapodi", *Arch.Anz.* 1987, pp. 1-25
Frankel, D., 1979
The Ancient Kingdom of Urartu, London
Frankenstein, S., 1979
"The Phoenicians in the Far West: A Function of Neo-Assyrian Imperialism", in: Larsen, T., ed., *Power and Propaganda*, (Mesopotamica, Copenhagen Studies in Assyriology, 7), Copenhagen, pp. 263-294
Friedrich, J. - Meyer, R. - Ungnad, A. - Weidner, E., 1940
Die Inschriften vom Tell Halaf. Keilschrifttexte und aramäische Urkunden aus einer assyrischen Provinzhauptstadt, (Archiv für Orientforschung, Beiheft 6), Graz
Fuchs, H. - Kellner, H.-J., 1978
"Von den Aufgaben des Museums", in: B. Hrouda ed., *Methoden der Archäologie. Eine Einführung in ihre naturwissenschaftlichen Techniken*, München, C.H. Beck, pp. 372-390
Furtwängler, A., 1890
Olympia IV, Die Bronzen, Berlin, A. Asher
Gamber, O., 1978
Waffe und Rüstung Eurasiens, Frühzeit und Antike, (Bibliothek für Kunst- und Antiquitätenfreunde 51), Braunschweig, Klinkhard & Biermann
Garelli, P., 1983
"Remarques sur les rapports entre l'Assyrie et les cités phéniciennes", in: *Atti del I Congresso Internazionale di Studi Fenici e Punici*, vol. I, Rome, pp. 61-66
Gjerstad, E., et al., 1935
The Swedish Cyprus Expedition. Finds and Result of the Excavations in Cyprus, 1927-1931, vol. II, Stockholm, The Swedish Cyprus Expedition
Gjerstad, E., et al., 1948
The Sweidsh Cyprus Expedition, IV/2, Stockholm, The Swedish Cyprus Expedition
Greenewalt, C.H., Jr., 1989
"Recent Archaeological Research in Turkey: Sardis, 1988", *AnSt* 39, pp. 182-184
Greenewalt, C.H., Jr., 1991
"The Sardis Campaign of 1987", in: W.E. Rast, ed., *Preliminary Reports of ASOR-Sponzored Excavations of 1982-1989*, Baltimore, The Johns Hopkins University Press, pp. 1-28
Greenewalt, C.H., Jr., 1992
"When a Mighty Empire was Destroyed: The Common Man at the Fall of Sardis, Ca. 546 B.C.", *PAPS* 136/II, pp. 247-271
Greenewalt, C.H., Jr. - Heywood, A.M., 1992
"A Helmet of the Sixth Century B.C. from Sardis", *BASOR* 285, pp. 1-31
Gröschel, S.-G., 1986
"Der goldene Helm der Athena (Ilias V, 743/44)", *AMI* 19, pp. 43-78, pls. 13-20
Guralnick, E., 1988
"Greece and the Near East: Art and Archaeology", in: Sutton, R.F., ed., *Daidalikon: Studies in Memory of Raymond V. Schoder, S.J.*, Wauconda, Illinois, pp. 151-176
Guralnick, E., 1992
"East to West: Near Eastern Artifacts from Greek Sites", in: Charpin, D. - Joannès, F., eds., *La circulation des biens, des personnes et des idées dans le Proche-Orient ancien, XXXVIIIe R.A.I.*, (Editions Recherche sur les Civilisations), Paris, pp. 327-340
Hampe, R. - Jantzen, U., 1936-1937
"Eisengeräte und Waffen", in: *Bericht über die Ausgrabungen in Olympia*, Berlin, W. de Gruyter, pp. 49-64
Hawkins, J.D., 1976-1980
"Karkamis", *Reallexikon der Assyriologie und Vorderasiatischen Archäologie* V, Berlin, de Gruyter, pp. 426-446
Heuzey, L., 1880
"Sur un petit vase en forme de téte casquée prtant une inscription hiéroglyphique", *Gazette Archéologique* 6, pp. 145-160
Hodjash, S.I. - Trukhtanova, N.S. - Hovhannissian, K.L., 1979

Erebuni. Pamyatnik Urartskogo zodtshestva VIII-VI v. do n.e., Moskva, Iskusstvo

Hoffmann, H., 1972
Early Cretan Armorers, Mainz, Zabern

Hogarth, D.G., 1914
Charchemish I, Introductory, London

Horn, H.G. - Rüger, C.B., 1979
Die Numider, Bonn, Rheinisches Landesmuseum

Jackson, A.H., 1987
"An Early Corinthian Helmet in the Museum of the British School at Athens", *BSA* 82, pp. 107-114, pl. 17

Jantzen, U., 1962
"Phrygishe Fibeln", in: Hanfman, G.M.A., et al., *Festschrift für Friedrich Matz*, Mainz, Ph. von Zabern, pp. 39-43

Karageorghis, V., 1966
"Chronique des fouilles et découvertes archéologiques a Chypre en 1965", *Bulletin de correspondance hellénique* 90, pp. 287-389

Karageorghis, V., 1967
"Nouvelles tombes de guerriers a Palaepaphos", *Bulletin de correspondance hellénique* 91, pp. 202-245

Karageorghis, V., 1973
"Chronique des fouilles et découvertes archéologiques à Chypre en 1972", *BCH* 97, pp. 601-689

Karageorghis, V., 1985
Ancient Cypriote Art in the Pierides Foundation Museum, Larnaca

Karageorghis, V., 1988
"Chronique des fouilles et découvertes archéologiques a Chypre en 1987", *Bulletin de correspondance hellénique* 112, pp. 793-855

Karo, G., 1930
"Archäologische Funde aus dem Jahre 1929 und der Ersten Hälfte von 1930: Inseln", *Arch.Anz.* 45, pp. 128-165

Kellner, H.-J., 1976
Urartu, ein wiederentdeckter Rivale Assyriens, Katalog der Ausstellung, München, Prähistorische Staatssammlung

Kellner, H.-J., 1979
"Eisen in Urartu", in: *Akten des VII. Internationalen Kongresses für Iranische Kunst und Archäologie, München 7-10. September 1976*, (Archäologische Mitteilungen aus Iran, Ergänzungsband 6), Berlin, Dietrich Reimer Verlag, pp. 151-156

Kellner, H.-J., 1980
"Bemerkungen zu den Helmen in Urartu", *Anadolu Arastirmalari* 8, pp. 205-213, pls. 1-16

Kellner, H.-J., 1993
"Ein assyrische Beutehelm?", in: M.J. Mellink - E. Porada - T. Özgüç, eds., *Nimet Özgüçe Armagan. Aspects of Art and Iconography: Anatolia and its Neighbours. Studies in Honour of Nimet Özgüç*, Ankara, Türk Tarih Kurumu Basimevi, pp. 325-331

Kendall, T., 1975
Warfare and Military Matters in the Nuzi Tablets, Ph.D. Diss., Brandeis University, Ann Arbor 1979, University Microfilms

Kestemont, G., 1983
"Tyr et les Assyriens", *Studia Phoenicia* 1-2, pp. 53-78

Kilian-Dirlmeyer, I., 1985a
"Fremde Weihungen in griechischen Heiligtümern vom 8. bis zum Beginn des 7. Jahrhunderts v. Chr.", *JRGZM* 32, pp. 215-254

Kilian-Dirlmeyer, I., 1985b
"Noch einmal zu den "Kriegergräbern" von Knossos", *JRGZM* 32, pp. 196-214

King, L.W., 1915
Bronze Reliefs from the Gates of Shalmaneser, London

Klengel-Brandt, E., 1986
 Syrien, Kleinasien, (Vorderasiatisches Museum, Kleine Schriften, 6), Berlin, Staatlichen Museen zu Berlin

Kontoleon, N.M., 1969
 "Die frühgriechische Reliefkunst", *Archaiologike Ephemeris* 1969, pp. 215-236

Kopcke, G., 1992
 "What Role for Phoenicians?", in: Kopcke, G. - Tokumaru, I., eds., *Greece between East and West: 10th-8th Centuries BC*, (Papers of the Meeting at the Institute of Fine Arts, New York University, March 15-16th, 1990), Mainz, von Zabern, pp. 103-113

Kuftin, B.A., 1941
 Arkheologitcheskiye raskopki v Trialeti I, Opit periodizatsii pamyatnikov, Tbilisi, Akademii Nauk Gruzinskoy S.S.R.

Kukahn, E., 1936
 Der griechische Helm, Diss., Marburg-Lahn, H. Bauer

Kunze, E., 1931
 Kretische Bronzereliefs, Stuttgart

Kunze, E., 1938a
 "Helme", in: Kunze, E. - Schleif, H., *II. Bericht über die Ausgrabungen in Olympia*, Berlin, W. de Gruyter, pp. 93-96

Kunze, E., 1938b
 "Waffenfunde", in: Kunze, E. - Schleif, H., *II. Bericht über die Ausgrabungen in Olympia*, Berlin, W. de Gruyter, pp. 67-103

Kunze, E., 1941
 "Helme", in: Kunze, E. - Schleif, H., *III. Bericht über die Ausgrabungen in Olympia*, Berlin, W. de Gruyter, pp. 106-114

Kunze, E., 1944
 "Bronzestatuetten", in: Kunze, E. - Schleif, H., *IV. Bericht über die Ausgrabungen in Olympia*, Berlin, W. de Gruyter, pp. 105-142

Kunze, E., 1958
 "Der frühgriechische Kegelhelm", in: Kunze, E., *VI. Bericht über die Ausgrabungen in Olympia*, "Helme", Berlin, W. de Gruyter, pp. 118-151

Kunze, E., 1961a
 "Die Ausgrabungen in den frühjahren 1956 bis 1958", in: Kunze, E., *VII. Bericht über die Ausgrabungen in Olympia*, Berlin, W. de Gruyter, pp. 1-28

Kunze, E., 1961b
 "Korinthische Helme", in: Kunze, E., *VII. Bericht über die Ausgrabungen in Olympia*, Berlin, W. de Gruyter, pp. 56-128, pls. 13-55

Kunze, E., 1961c
 "Ein Bronzehelm aus der Perserbeute", in: Kunze, E., *VII. Bericht über die Ausgrabungen in Olympia*, Berlin, W. de Gruyter, pp. 129-137, pls. 56-57

Kunze, E., 1961-1962
 "Die Ausgrabungen in Olympia. Laufbahn und Nordwall des Stadions", *Arch.Delt.* 17, pp. 107-124

Kunze, E., 1967a
 "Helme. Der frühgriechische Kegelhelm", in: Kunze, E., *VIII. Bericht über die Ausgrabungen in Olympia*, Berlin, W. de Gruyter, pp. 111-116

Kunze, E., 1967b
 "Kleinplastik aus Bronze", in: Kunze, E., *VIII. Bericht über die Ausgrabungen in Olympia*, Berlin, W. de Gruyter, pp. 213-250, pls. 106-119

Kunze, E., 1967c
 "Waffenweihungen", in: Kunze, E., *VIII. Bricht über die Ausgrabungen in Olympia*, Berlin, W. de Gruyter, pp. 83-110, figs. 28-37, pls. 30-49

Lamb, W., 1929
 Greek and Roman Bronzes, London, Methuen

Lempesi, A.K., 1976
 Hoi steles tou Prinia, Athinai

Lempesi, A.K., 1985
To Hiero tou Herme kai tes Aphrodites ste Symi Biannou, vol. I, 1. Chalkina Cretica Toreumata, Athen

Lepore, L., 1984
"Un elmo bronzeo della collezione Ceccanti", in: *Studi di antichità in onore di Guglielmo Maetzke*, vol. II (Archaeologica 49), Roma, Bretschneider, pp. 329-332, pl. 1

Ligabue, G. - Salvatori, S., 1977
"Oriental Bronzes in Private Collections in Venice", *Rivista di Archeologia* 1, pp. 7-15, figs. 1-18

Lloyd, S., 1967
Early Highland Peoples of Anatolia, London, Thames and Hudson

Lorimer, H.L., 1950
Homer and the Monuments, London, Macmillan

Luckenbill, D.D., 1927
Ancient Records of Assyria and Babylonia II. Historical Records of Assyria from Sargon to the End, Chicago, U.P.

Lullies, R., 1962
"Neuerwerbungen der Antikensammlungen in München 1958-1961", *Arch.Anz.* 77, pp. 594-631

Lullies, R. - Hirmer, M., 1960
Greek Sculpture, London, Thames and Hudson

Maass, M., 1987
"Helme, Zubehör von Wagen und Pferdegeschirr aus Urartu", *Archäologische Mitteilungen aus Iran* 20, pp. 65-92, pls. 1-10

Maass, M., 1988
Badisches Landesmuseum. 150 Jahre Antikensammlungen Karlsruhe 1838-1988, Karlsruhe, Badisches Landesmuseum

Maass, M., 1989
"Badisches Landesmuseum, Neuerwerbungen 1988, Antike", *Jahrbuch der Staatlichen Kunstsammlungen in Baden-Württemberg* 26, pp. 194-197

Magou, E. - Pernot, M. - Rolley, C., 1991
"Bronzes orientaux et orientalisants analyses complémentaires", *BCH* 115, pp. 561-577

Maier, F.G. - Karageorghis, V., 1984
Paphos. History and Archaeology, Nicosia, Leventis Foundation

Mallowan, M.E.L., 1966
Nimrud and Its Remains, vols. I-II, London, Collins

Mallowan, M.E.L. - Davies, L.G., 1970
Ivories in Assyrian Style, (Ivories from Nimrud (1949-1963), vol. 2), London, British School of Archaeology in Iraq

Marfoe, E., et al., 1982
A Guide to The Oriental Institute Museum, Chicago, The Oriental Institute

Marinatos, Sp., 1936
"Le temple géométrique de Dréros", *BCH* 60, pp. 214-285

Markoe, G., 1985
Phoenician Bronze Bowls from Cyprus and the Mediterranean, (University of California Publications, Classical Studies 26), Berkeley - Los Angeles, University of California Press

Mastrokostas, E., 1961-1962
"Chronika: Achaia", *Arch.Delt.* 17, pp. 126-132

Maxwell-Hyslop, K.R., 1959
"An Urartian Archer on the Zinjirli Chariot Relief", *Bulletin of the Institute of Archaeology* 2, pp. 65-66, pl. 3

Maxwell-Hyslop, K.R., 1974
"Assyrian Sources of Iron", *Iraq* 36, pp. 139-154

Medvedskaya, I., 1988
"Who Destroyed Hasanlu IV?", *Iran* 26, pp. 1-15

Medvedskaya, I., 1991
"Once More on the Destruction of Hasanlu IV: Problems of Dating", *Iranica Antiqua* 26, pp. 149-161

Mellink, M.J., 1976
"Local, Phrygian and Greek Traits in Northern Lycia", *RA* 1976, pp. 21-34

Monloup, Th., 1984
Les figurines de terre cuite de tradition archaique, (Salamine de Chypre XII), Paris, de Boccard

Moorey, P.R.S., 1987
The Ancient Near East, (Ashmolean Museum Publications), Oxford, Ashmolean Museum

Müller-Karpe, H., 1962
"Zur spätbronzezeitlichen Bewaffnung in Mitteleuropa und Griechenland", *Germania* 40, pp. 255-287

Muscarella, O.W., 1980
The Catalogue of Ivories from Hasanlu, Iran, (University Museum Monograph 40, Hasanlu Special Studies 2), Philadelphia, The University Museum

Muscarella, O.W., 1988
Bronze and Iron. Ancient Near Eastern Artifacts in the Metropolitan Museum of Art, New York

Muscarella, O.W., 1989
"King Midas of Phrygia and the Greeks", in Emre, K., et al., *Anatolia and the Anient Near East: Studies in Honour of Tahsin Özgüç*, Ankara, 333-344

Muscarella, O.W., 1992
"Greek and Oriental Cauldron Attachments: A Review", in: Kopcke, G. - Tokumaru, I., eds., *Greece between East and West: 10th-8th Centuries BC*, (Papers of the Meeting at the Institute of Fine Arts, New York University, March 15-16th, 1990), Mainz, von Zabern, pp. 16-45

Myres, J.L., 1914
Handbook of the Cesnola Collection of Antiquities from Cyprus, New York, The Metropolitan Museum of Art

Neeft, C.W., 1977
"Two Corinthian Helmets in the Allard Pierson Musuem, Amsterdam", in: Boersma, J.S., et al., eds., *Festoen. Opgedragen aan A.N. Zadoks-Josephus Jitta bij haar zeventigste verjaardag*, (Scripta Archaeologica Groningana 6), Groningen, H.D. Tjeenk Willink, pp. 443-449

Neugebauer, K.A., 1922
"Neuerwerbungen der Antikensammlungen in Deutschland, Berlin", *Arch.Anz.* 37, pp. 59-119

Nunn, A., 1988
Die Wandmalerei und der glasierte Wandschmuck in Alten Orient, (Handbuch der Orientalistik I/2/B/6), Leiden, Brill

Oded, B., 1974
"The Phoenician Cities and the Assyrian Empire in the Time of Tiglath-Pileser III", *ZDPV* 90, pp. 38-49

Orthmann, W., 1971
Untersuchungen zur Späthethitischen Kunst, (Saarbrücker Beiträge zur Altertumskunde, Band 8), Bonn, R. Habelt

Overlaet, B.J., 1979
"Pointed Helmets of the Iron Age from Iran", *Iranica Antiqua* 14, pp. 51-63, pls. 1-4

Özgen, E., 1982
The Urartian Bronze Collection at the University Museum: The Urartian Armor, Ph. D. Diss. University of Pennsylvania, Ann Arbor, University Microfilms

Papathanasopoulos, G.A., 1969
"Archaiotetes kai mnemeia Eleias: 1. Mouseion Olympias", *Arch.Delt.* 24, pp. 146-150

Parrot, A., 1961
Ninieveh and Babylon, London

Paterson, A., 1912
Assyrian Sculptures, Palace of Sinacherib, Hague, M. Nijhoff

Payne, H.G.G., 1927-1928
"Early Greek Vases from Knossos", *BSA* 29, pp. 224-298

Perdrizet, P., 1908
Monuments figurés. Petits bronzes, terres-cuites, antiquités diverses, (Fouilles de Delphes V), Paris, A. Fontemoing

Pernice, E., 1892

"Geometrische Vase aus Athen", *AM* 17, pp.

Pflug, H., 1988a
"Griechische Helme Geometrischer Zeit", in: A. Bottini, et al., *Antike Helme. Sammlung Lipperheide und andere Bestände des Antikenmuseums Berlin*, (Römisch-Germanisches Zentralmuseum, Monographien 14), Mainz, Verlag des Römisch-Germanisches Zentralmuseums, pp. 11-26

Pflug, H., 1988b
"Kyprische Helme", in: A. Bottini, et al., *Antike Helme. Sammlung Lipperheide und andere Bestände des Antikenmuseums Berlin*, (Römisch-Germanisches Zentralmuseum, Monographien 14), Mainz, Verlag des Römisch-Germanisches Zentralmuseums, pp. 27-41

Pflug, H., 1988c
"Korinthische Helme", in: A. Bottini, et al., *Antike Helme. Sammlung Lipperheide und andere Bestände des Antikenmuseums Berlin*, (Römisch-Germanisches Zentralmuseum, Monographien 14), Mainz (1988), Verlag des Römisch-Germanisches Zentralmuseums, pp. 65-106

Pflug, H., 1989
"Kyprische Helme", in: H. Pflug, *Schutz und Zier. Helme aus dem Antikenmuseum Berlin und Waffen anderer Sammlungen*, (Antikenmuseum Basel und Sammlung Ludwig), Basel, pp. 17-18, Kat. 1

Piotrovsky, B.B., 1955
Karmir Blur III, Rezultaty Raskopok 1950-1953, Erevan, Akademii Nauk Armyanskoy S.S.R.

Place, V., 1867-1870
Ninive et l'Assyrie, vol. I, Paris

Pleiner, R. - Bjorkman, J.K., 1974
"The Assyrian Iron Age: The History of Iron in Assyrian Civilization", *PAPS* 118, pp. 283-313

Protonotariou-Deilaki, E., 1971
"Chronika: Argos", *Arch.Delt.* 26, pp. 74-82

Protonotariou-Deilaki, E., 1973
"Chronika: Argos", *Arch.Delt.* 28, pp. 97-99

Protonotariou-Deilaki, E., 1982
"Apo to Argos tou 8ou kai 7ou AI II. Ch.", *Annuario della Scuola Archaeologia di Atene*, 60, pp. 33-48

Reade, J.E., 1972
"The Neo-Assyrian Court and Army: Evidence from the Sculptures", *Iraq* 34, pp. 87-112

Renfrew, C., 1983
Before Civilization: The Radiocarbon Revolution and Prehistoric Europe, Pelican Books

Richards, G.C., 1891
"Archaic Reliefs at Dhimitzana", *JHS* 12, pp. 41-45

Richter, G.M.A., 1934
"A Colossal Dipylon Vase", *Bulletin of the Metropolitan Museum of Art* 29, pp. 169-172

Röllig, W., 1992
"Asia Minor as a Bridge between East and West: the Role of the Phoenicians and Arameans in the Transfer of Culture", in: Kopcke, G. - Tokumaru, I., eds., *Greece between East and West: 10th-8th Centuries BC*, (Papers of the Meeting at the Institute of Fine Arts, New York University, March 15-16th, 1990), Mainz, von Zabern, pp. 93-102

Salvatori, S., 1975
"Un elmo assiro figurato proveniente dal Luristan", *Oriens Antiquus* 14, pp. 255-264, figs. 1-2, pls. 36-38

Schaaff, U., 1973
"Frühlatènezeitliche Grabfunde mit Helmen Typ Berru", *JRGZM* 20, pp. 81-106

Schauer, P., 1983
"Orient im Spätbronze- und Früheisenzeitlichen Occident. Kulturbeziehungen zwischen der Iberischen Halbinsel und dem Vorderen Orient während des späten 2. und des ersten Drittels des 1. Jahrtausends v. Chr.", *JRGZM* 30, pp. 175-194

Schauer, P., 1988
"Die Kegel- und Glockenförmigen Helme mit Gegossenem Scheitelknauf der Jüngeren Bronzezeit Alteuropas", in: A. Bottini, et al., *Antike Helme. Sammlung Lipperheide und andere Bes-

tände des Antikenmuseums Berlin, (Römisch-Germanisches Zentralmuseum, Monographien 14), Mainz, Verlag des Römisch-Germanisches Zentralmuseums, pp. 181-194

Schmidt, G., 1968
Kyprische Bildwerke aus dem Heraion von Samos, (Samos, Band VII), Bonn, R. Habelt

Schweitzer, B., 1971
Greek Geometric Art, London, Phaidon

Seeden, H., 1980
The Standing Armed Figurines in the Levant, (Prähistorische Bronzefunde, Abteilung I, Band 1), München, C.H. Beck

Shaw, J.W., 1980
"Excavations at Kommos (Crete) During 1979", *Hesperia* 49, pp. 207-250

Shaw, J.W., 1989
"Phoenicians in Southern Crete", *AJA* 93, pp. 165-183

Smith, S., 1938
Sculptures in the British Museum, from Shalmaneser III to Sennacherib, London, The Trustees of the British Museum

Snodgrass, A.M., 1964
Early Greek Armour and Weapons from the End of the Bronze Age to 600 B.C., Edinburgh, University Press

Steiner, P., 1906
"Bronze-Statuette aus Olympia", *AM* 31, pp. 219-227

Tadmor, H., 1975
"Assyria and the West. The Ninth Century and its Aftermath", in: Goedicke, H. - Roberts, J.J., eds., *Unity and Diversity*, Baltimore, pp. 36-48

Tatton-Brown, V., 1979
"A Terracotta "Geryon" in the British Museum", *RDAC* 1979, pp. 281-288

Terrace, E.L.B., 1962
The Art of the Ancient Near East in Boston, Museum of Fine Arts, Boston

Thureau-Dangin, F. - Barrois, A. - Dossin, G. - Dunand, M., 1931
Arslan-Tash, (Bibliothèque Archéologique et Historique XVI), Paris, Geuthner

Thureau-Dangin, F. - Dunand, M., 1936
Til Barsib, (Bibliothèque Archéologique et Historique XXIII), Paris, Geuthner

Tölle, R., 1963
"Figürliche bemalte Fragmente der Geometrischen Zeit vom Kerameikos", *Arch.Anz.* 78, pp. 642-665

Törnkvist, S., 1973
"Arms, Armour and Dress of the Terracotta Sculpture from Ajia Irini, Cyprus", *Medelhavsmuseet Bulletin* 6, pp. 7-55

Tufnell, O., et al., 1953
Lachish III. The Iron Age, Oxford, Oxford University Press

Ussishkin, D., 1969
"The Date of the Neo-Hittite Enclosure in Karatepe", *Anatolian Studies* 19, pp. 121-137

Ussishkin, D., 1982
The Conquest of Lachish by Sennacherib, Tel Aviv, Institute of Archaeology

Vanden Berghe, L., 1959
Archéologie de L'Iran Ancien, Leiden, Brill

Vanden Berghe, L. - De Meyer, L., 1982
Urartu een vergeten cultuur uit het bergland Armenië, Sint-Pietersabdij - Gent, 9 oktober 1982 - 30 januari 1983

van Loon, M.N., 1966
Urartian Art. Its distinctive Traits in the Light of New Excavations, (Uitgaven van het Nederlands Historisch-Archaeologisch Instituut te Istanbul 20), Istanbul, Nederlands Historisch-Archaeologisch Instituut

Verdelis, N.M., 1963
"Neue geometrische Gräber in Tiryns", *AM* 78 (1963), pp. 1-62

von Gaertringen, H. - Wilski, P., 1904

> *Stadtgeschichte von Thera*, (Thera III), Berlin, Reimer

von Lipperheide, F., 1896
> *Antike Helme*, Munich

von Luschan, F., et al., 1902
> *Ausgrabungen in Sendschirli*, vol. III, (Mitteilungen aus den Orientalischen Sammlungen, Heft XIII), Berlin

von Luschan, F. - Andrae, W., 1943
> *Die Kleinfunde von Sendschirli. Ausgrabungen in Sendschirli*, vol. V, (Mitteilungen aus den Orientalischen Sammlungen, Heft XV), Berlin, Walter de Gruyter

Waldbaum, J.C., 1989
> "B. Metalwork from Idalion, 1971-1980", in: L.E. Stager - A.M. Walker, eds., *American Expedition to Idalion, Cyprus 1973-1980*, (Oriental Institute Communications no. 24), Chicago, The Oriental Institute of the University of Chicago, pp. 328-351, pls. 1-4

Waldstein, Ch., 1905
> *The Argive Heraeum, vol. II*, Boston and New York, Houghton, Mifflin and Co.

Walters, H.B., 1899
> *Catalogue of the Bronzes, Greek, Roman, and Etruscan, in the Department of Greek and Roman Antiquities, British Museum*, London

Wartke, R.-B., 1991
> "Production of Iron Artifacts", in: R. Merhav, ed., *Urartu. A Metalworking Center in the First Millennium B.C.E.*, Jerusalem, Israel Museum, pp. 322-331

Weiss, C., 1977
> "An Unusual Corinthian Helmet", *California Studies in Classical Antiquity* 10, pp. 195-207

Wide, S., 1899
> "Geometrische Vasen aus Griechenland", *AM* 14, pp. 78-86

Winter, I., 1988
> "North Syria as a Bronzeworking Centre in the Early First Millennium BC: Luxury Commodities at Home and Abroad", in: Curtis, J.E., ed., *Bronzeworking Centres of Western Asia c. 1000-539 BC*, London, Keegan and Paul, pp. 193-225

Woolley, C.L., 1921
> *Charchemish II, The Town Defences*, London

Woolley, C.L. - Barnett, R.D., 1952
> *Charchemish III*, London

Wright, G.E., 1958
> *Biblische Archäologie*, Göttingen, Vandenhoeck & Ruprecht

Yalouri, A., 1971
> "A Hero's Departure", *AJA* 75, pp. 269-275

Yalouris, N., 1960
> "Mykenische Bronzeschutzwaffen", *AM* 75, pp. 42-67

Yesaian, S.A., 1976
> *Drevnyaya Kultura Plemen Severo-Vostotshnoy Armenii (III-I Tis. do N.E.)*, Erevan, Izdatyelstvo Akademii Nauk Armyanskoy S.S.R.

Yesaian, S.A., 1986
> *Dospeh Drevney Armenii*, Erevan, Izdatelstvo Erevanskogo Universiteta

Young, J.H. - Young, S.H., 1955
> *Terracotta Figurines from Kourion in Cyprus*, (Museum Monographs), Philadelphia, University Museum

Zaccagnini, C., 1983
> "Pattern of Mobility among Ancient Near Eastern Craftsmen", *JNES* 42, pp. 245ff.

Zervos, Ch., 1946
> *L'Art en Grèce du troisieme millénaire au IV^{e}siècle avant notre ère*, Paris, Cahiers d'Art

ILLUSTRATIONS

Ill. 1 *The Evolution of Assyrian, Syro-Assyrian and orientalizing Eastern Mediterranean helmet types of the 9th-7th centuries B.C. The finds.*

Ill. 1 The evolution of Assyrian, Syro-Assyrian and orientalizing Eastern Mediterranean helmet types of the 9th-7th centuries B.C. The finds.

1. Venice, Maria & Giancarlo Ligabue Collection
2. Venice, private collection (reconstructed from a fragment)
3. Teheran, private collection (reconstructed from a fragment)
4. Schaffhausen, Museum Aller Heiligen (galvano copy: Munich, Prähistorische Staatssammlung, neg. no. 26-27)
5. Manchseter, University of Manchester Museum, inv. no. 1618
6. London, British Museum, WA 22496
7. Munich, Prähistorische Staatssammlung, inv. no. 1980/6227-6228
8. Karlsruhe, Badisches Landesmuseum, inv. no. 89/12
9. Munich, Prähistorische Staatssammlung, inv. no. 1979/1181
10. London, British Museum, 48-11-4, 115 (reconstructed from fragments)
11. London, British Museum, 48-11-4, 115 (reconstructed from fragments)
12. Zinçirli, S.3965 (Berlin?)
13. London, British Museum, WA 134611
14. Zinçirli, S.3964 (Berlin?) (reconstructed from fragments)
15. Private collection
16. British Museum, 2841 (Richard Payne Knight Bequest)
17. Nicosia, Cyprus Museum, inv. no. 1965/XI-29/62
18. Nicosia, Cyprus Museum, inv. no. Alassa T16/1
19. Argos, Archaeological Museum (Argos, Odos Perseous 41)
20. Argos, Archaeological Museum (Argos, Odos Diomidous)
21. Budapest, Museum of Fine Arts, inv. no. 8442)
22. Argos, Archaeological Museum (Argos, Tomb 45)
23. Olympia Museum (Olympia, from the Alpheios)
24. Olympia Museum, inv. no. B. 51
25. Olympia Museum, old inv. no. Br. 10533
26. Florence, Collection A. Ceccanti, inv. no. prov. CC 436 (Ordona)
27. Ordona, South Italy
28. Venice, private collection
29. Hamburg, Museum für Kunst und Gewerbe, inv. no. 1970.26c
30. Istanbul, Archaeological Museum, inv. no. 16
31. Nicosia, Cyprus Museum, inv. no. 98/1971
32. Berlin, Antikenmuseum, inv. misc. 8142,620

I.
ORIENTAL

700

Ayia Irini M.2.1
Ayia Irini M.2.2
Ayia Irini M.2.3
Ayia Irini M.2.4

II.
ORIENTALIZING / TRANSITIONAL

680
670

Ayia Irini M.2.7
"Cyprus" M.2.5
"Cyprus" M.2.6

III.
DEVELOPED CYPRIOTE

650

Tamassos type

Idalion M.2.18
Tamassos (Istanbul)
Tamassos (Nicosia)
Samos M.2.19
Samos M.2.20
Tamassos (Berlin)

Geryon type

Pyrgia M.2.8
Tamassos M.2.9
"Cyprus" M.2.10

600

Salamis M.2.11
Salamis M.2.12
Salamis M.2.13
Salamis M.2.14
"Cyprus" M.2.15

Salamis M.4.23

Ill. 2 *The evolution of Cypriote conical/pointed helmets*

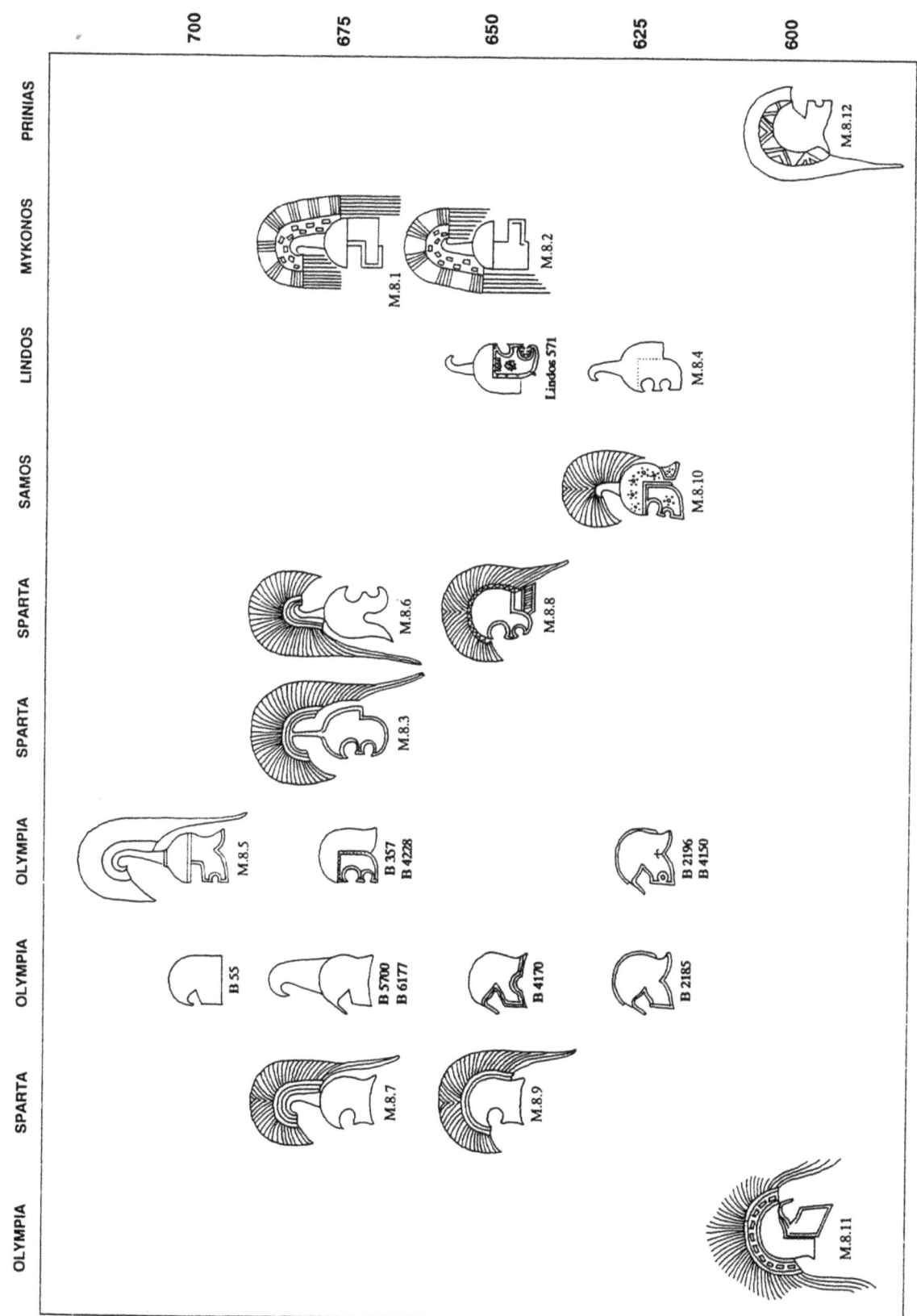

Ill. 3 *The evolution of Corinthian and 'pseudo-Corinthian' types of helmets*

Ill. 4 *The evolution of Assyrian, Syro-Assyrian and Eastern Mediterranean conical/pointed helmets*

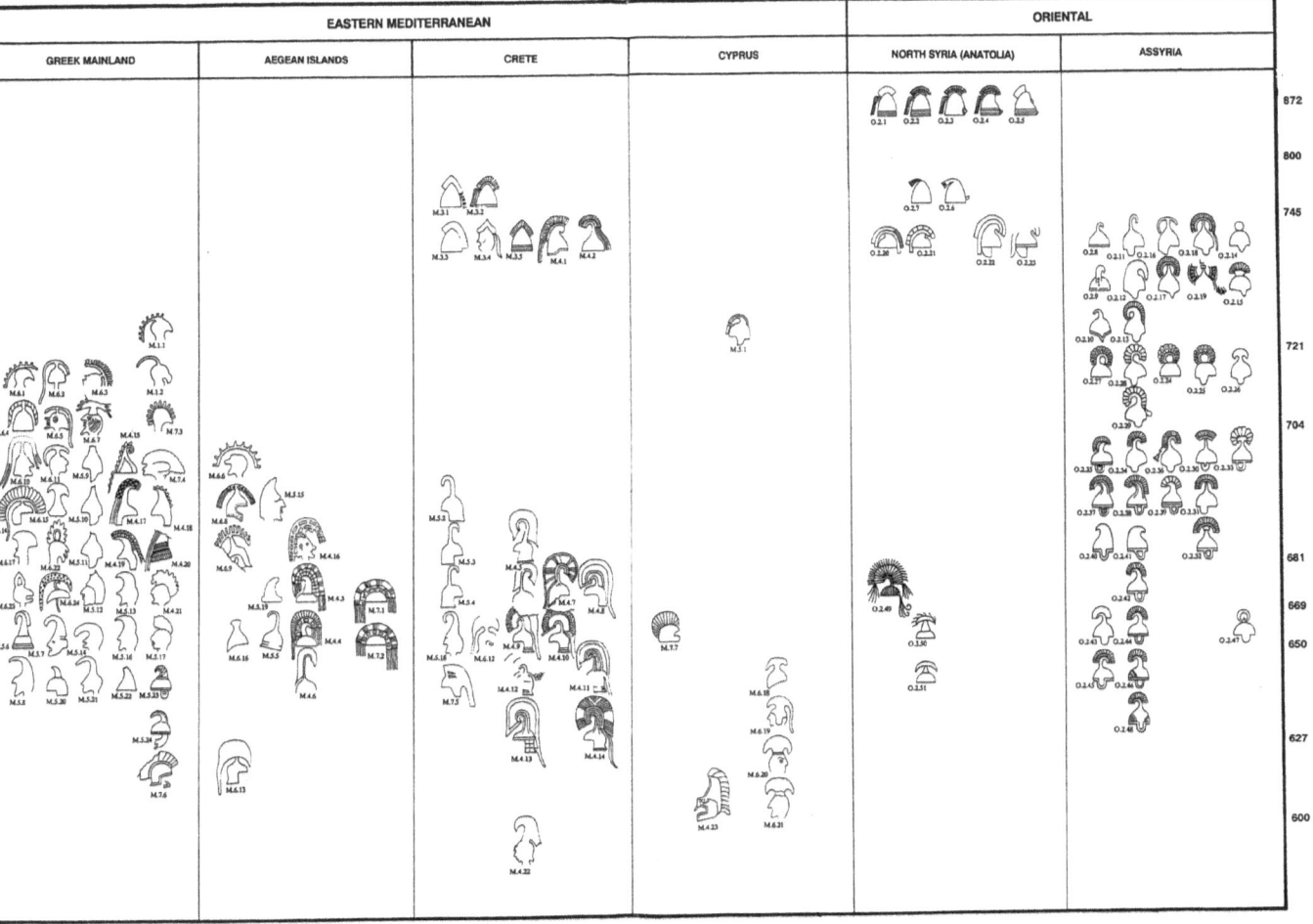

Ill. 5 *The Evolution of Assyrian, North Syrian and Eastern Mediterranean crested helmets*

Ill. 6 *Conical bronze helmet. Palaepaphos, Kouklia, Mavrommatis Tomb (Nicosia, Cyprus Museum, inv. no. 1965/XI-29/62)*

Ill. 7 *Fragment of a conical bronze helmet. Alassa, "Pano-Mandilaris", Tomb 16 (Nicosia, Cyprus Museum, inv. no. T.16/1)*

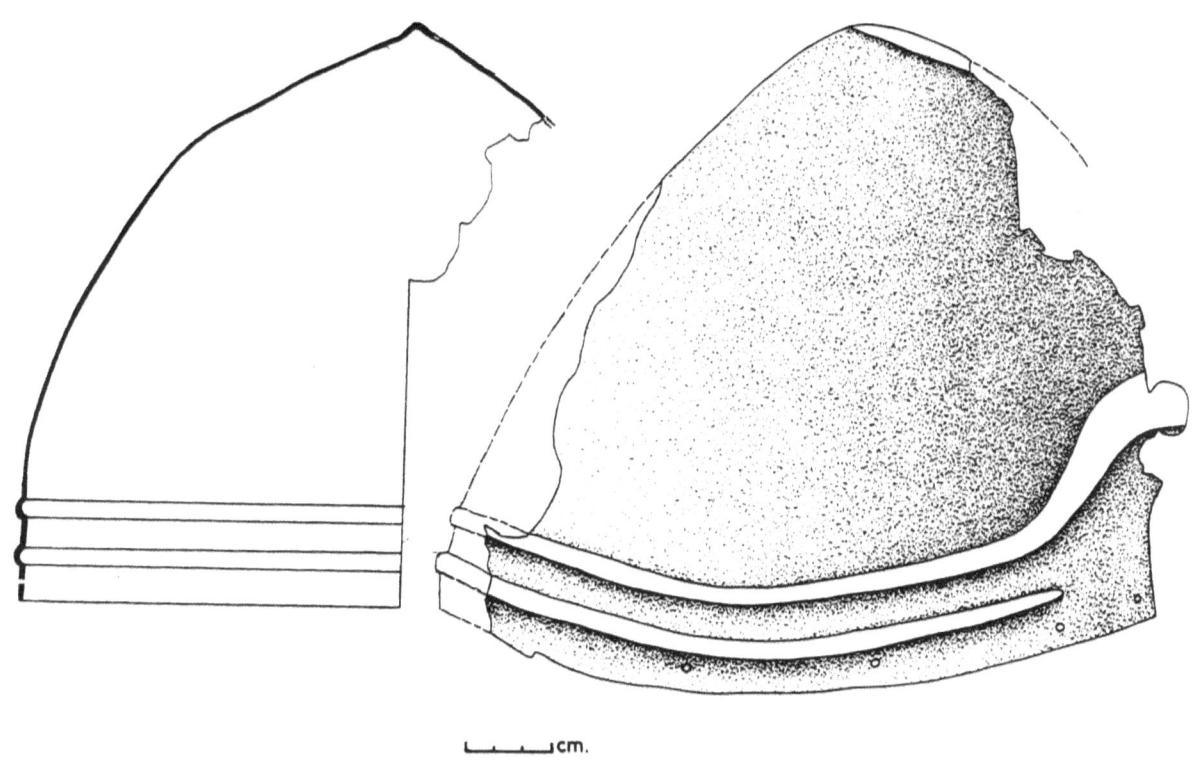

Ill. 8 *Drawing of the Alassa fragment*

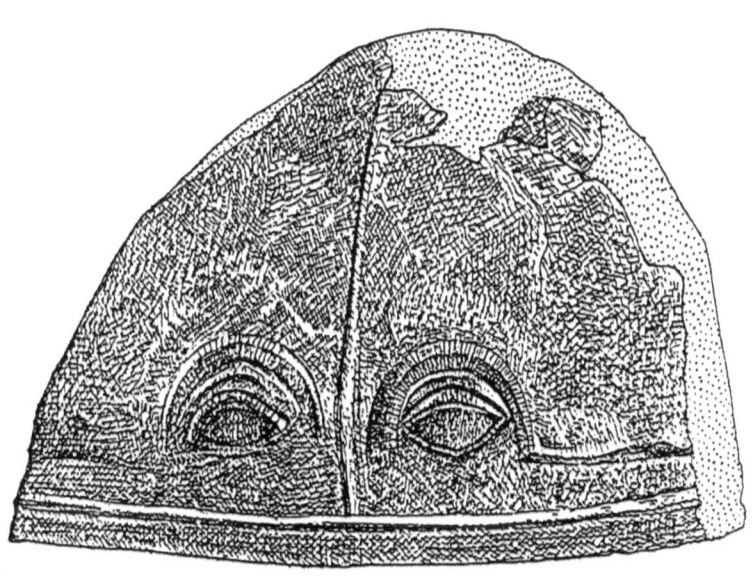

Ill. 9 *Drawing of a conical bronze helmet. Argos, Odos Perseous 41 (Argos, Archaeological Museum), (Gröschel 1986, p. 72, fig. 4)*

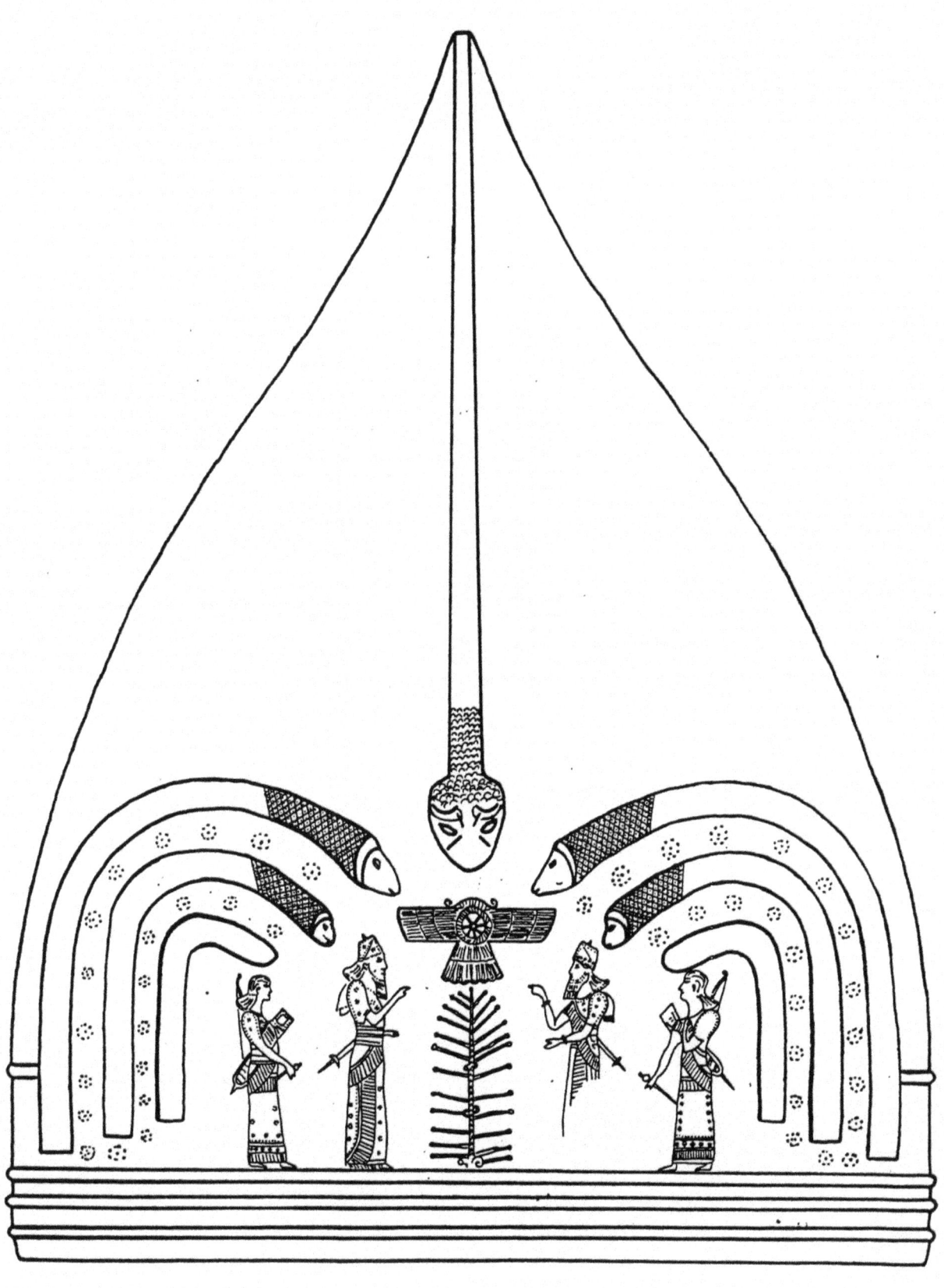

Ill. 10 *Drawing of an Assyrian conical bronze helmet (Venice, Maria & Giancarlo Ligabue Collection)*

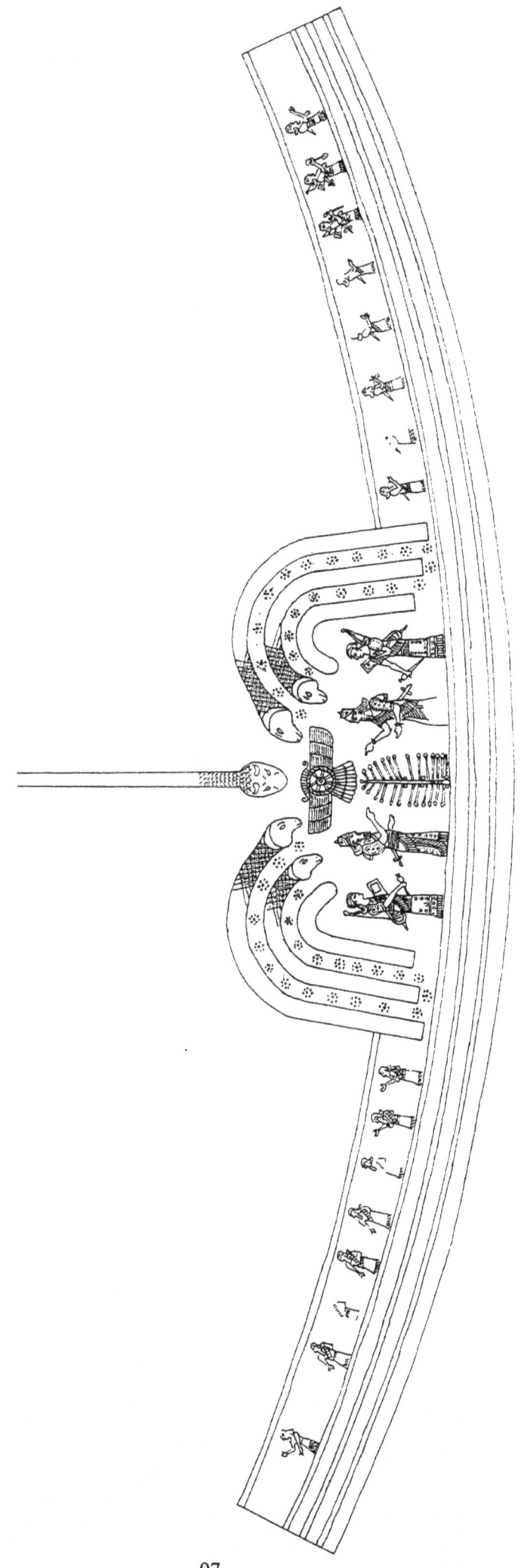

Ill. 11 *Drawing of decoration of the Ligabue helmet*

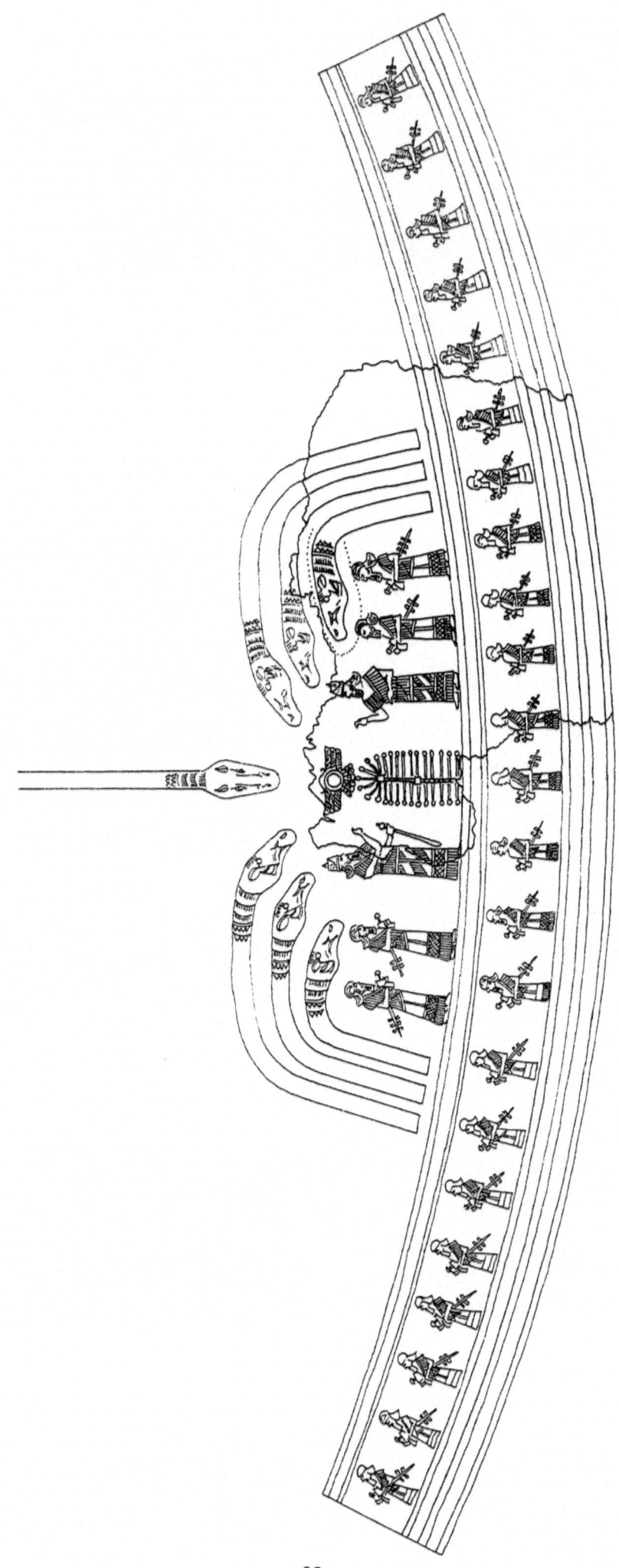

Ill. 12 Drawing of reconstruction of the decorative system of a fragmentary Assyrian conical bronze helmet (Venice, private collection)

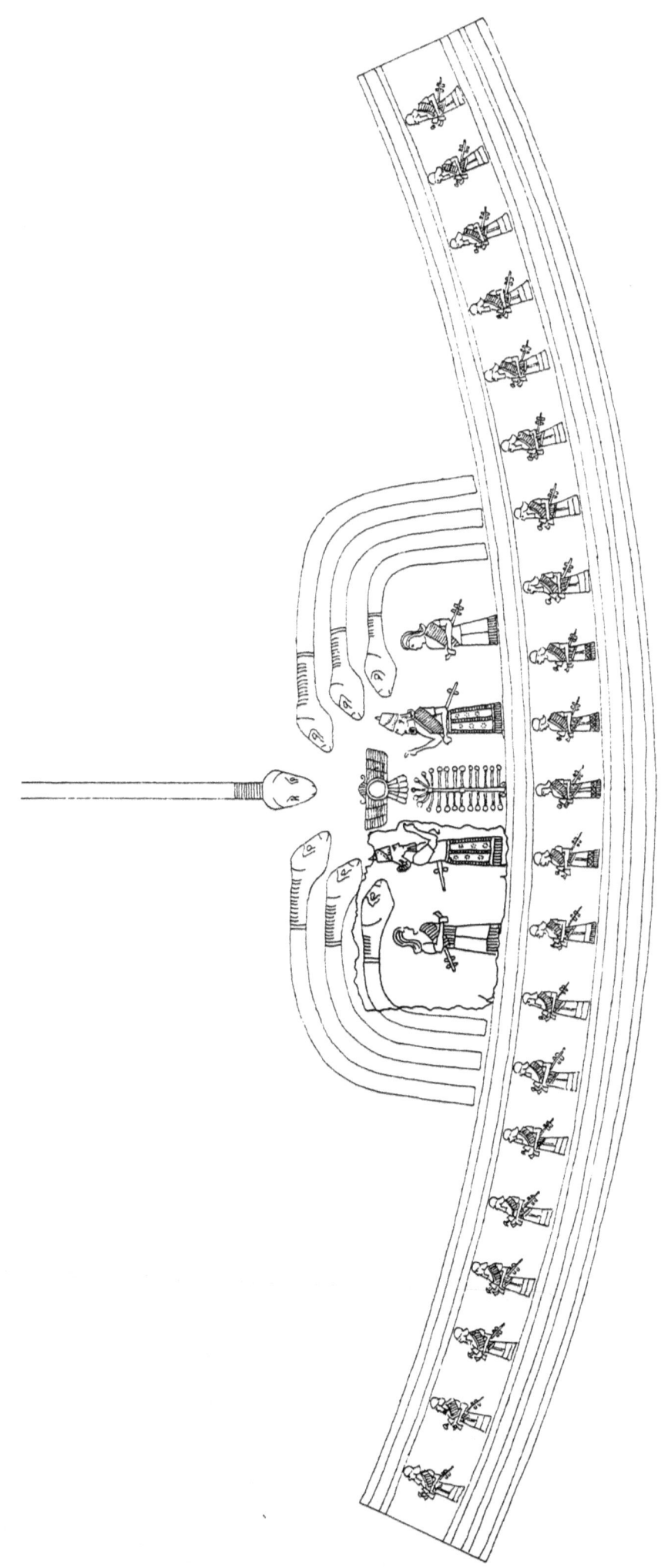

Ill. 13 *Drawing of reconstruction of the decorative system of a fragmentary Assyrian conical bronze helmet (Teheran, private collection)*

Ill. 14 *Pointed bronze helmet. Tamassos, Dromos of Royal Tomb IV (Nicosia, Cyprus Museum, inv. no. 98/1971)*

Ill. 15 *Pointed bronze helmet. Tamassos, Dromos of Royal Tomb IV (Nicosia, Cyprus Museum, inv. no. 98/1971)*

Ill. 16 *Pointed bronze helmet (Budapest, Museum of Fine Arts, inv. no. 8442), (side view)*

Ill. 17 *Pointed bronze helmet (Budapest, Museum of Fine Arts, inv. no. 8442), (front view)*

Ill. 19 *Crested bronze helmet. Argos, Tomb 45 (Argos, Archaeological Museum)*

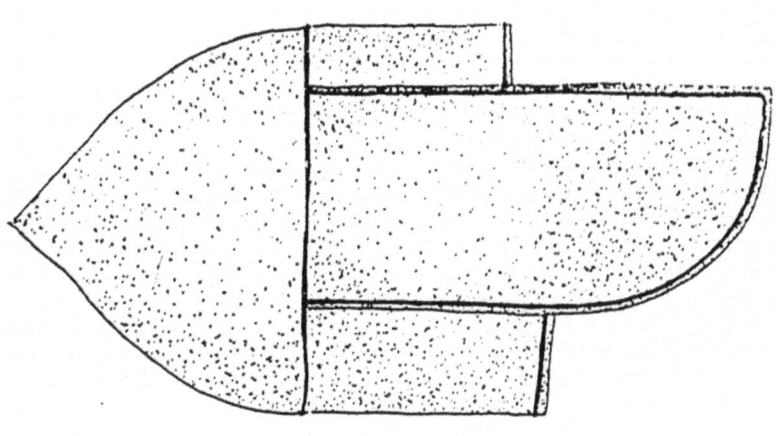

Ill. 18 *Pointed bronze helmet. Argos, Odos Diomidous (Argos, Archaeological Museum). (Pflug 1988a, p. 15, fig. 4)*

Ill. 20 *Fragmentary crested bronze helmet. Olympia, South of the Heraion (Olympia Museum, old inv. no. Br. 10533)*

Ill. 21 *Fragmentary crested bronze helmet. Olympia, probably from the Alpheios (Olympia Museum)*

Ill. 22 *Fragmentary crested bronze helmet. Olympia, from the North Wall of the Stadion (Olympia Museum, inv. no. B 51)*

Ill. 23 *Fragmentary crested bronze helmet. Olympia, "Brunnen 23 im Stadion-Nordwall" (Olympia Museum, inv. no. B 4714)*

Ill. 24 *Syro-Assyrian crested bronze helmet. Without provenance (British Museum, inv. no. 2841, Richard Payne Knight Bequest)*

Ill. 25 *Urartian crested bronze helmet. "Urartu" (Mainz, Römisch-Germanisches Zentralmuseum, inv. no. O.39702)*

Ill. 26 *Assyrian crested bronze helmet. Without provenance (Munich, Prähistorisches Staatssammlung, inv. no. P.S. 1979/1181)*

Ill. 27 *Assyrian crested bronze helmet. Without provenance (Karlsruhe, Badisches Landesmuseum, inv. no. 89/12)*

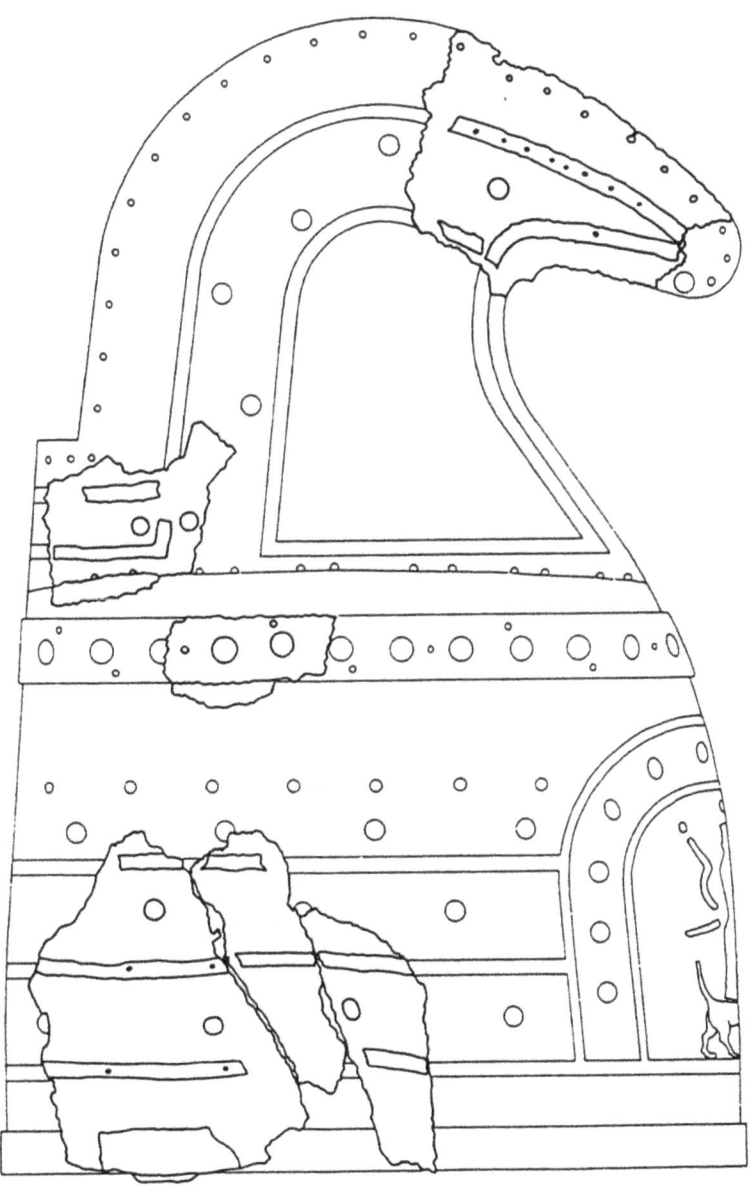

Ill. 28 *Drawing of an Assyrian crested iron helmet reconstructed from fragments. Nimrud, NW-Palace, Chamebr I (London, British Museum, 48-11-4, 115)*

Ill. 29 *Fragmentary bronze and iron composite helmet. Sardis, Colossal Lydian Structure*

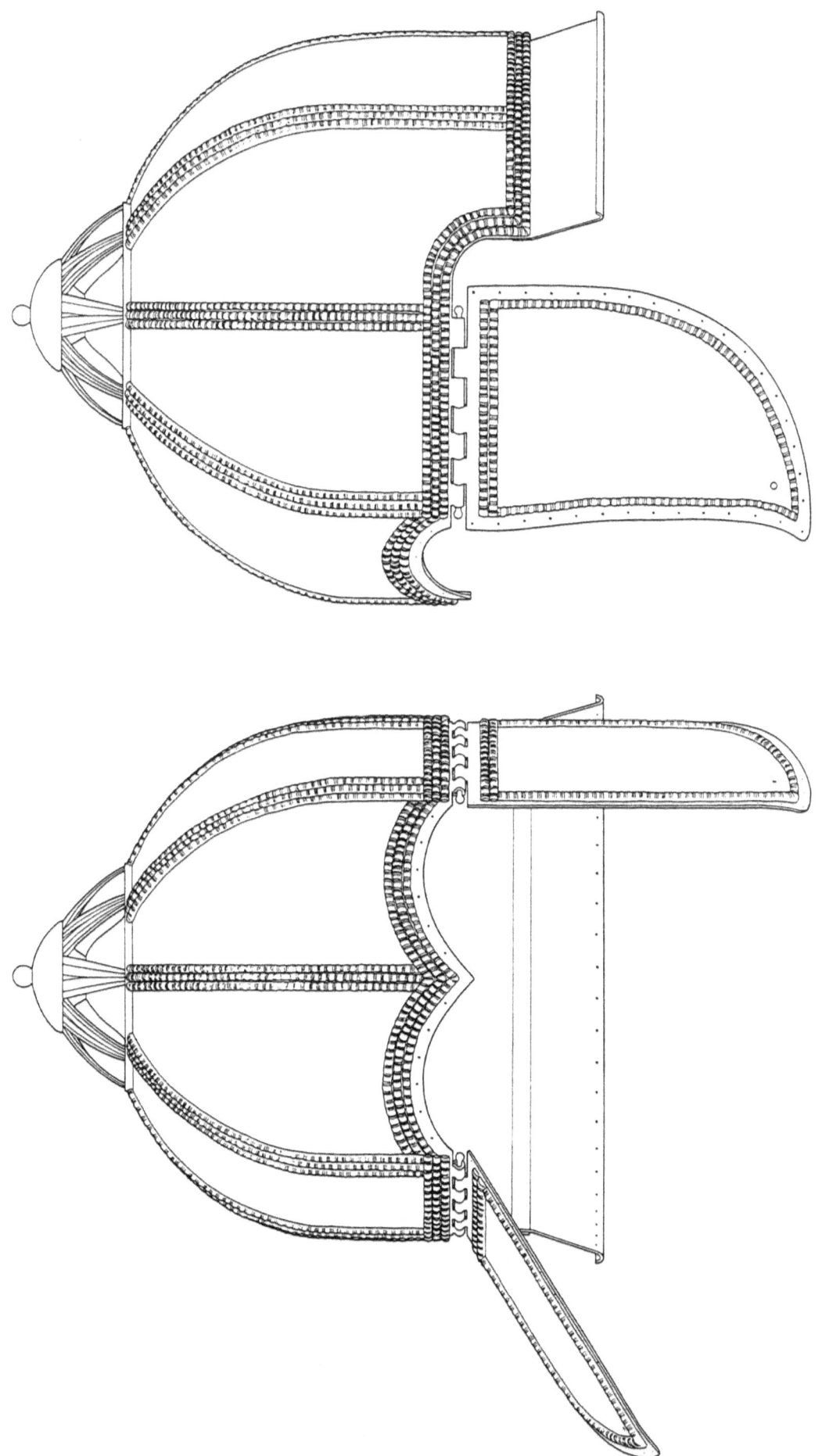

Ill. 30 *Reconstructional drawings of the Sardis helmet*

www.ingramcontent.com/pod-product-compliance
Lightning Source LLC
Chambersburg PA
CBHW061543010526
44113CB00023B/2781